Academic Vocabulary in Use

Vocabulary reference and practice

Self-study and classroom use

Second Edition

Michael McCarthy
Felicity O'Dell

CAMBRIDGE
UNIVERSITY PRESS

University Printing House, Cambridge CB2 8BS, United Kingdom

One Liberty Plaza, 20th Floor, New York, NY 10006, USA

477 Williamstown Road, Port Melbourne, VIC 3207, Australia

4843/24, 2nd Floor, Ansari Road, Daryaganj, Delhi – 110002, India

79 Anson Road, #06–04/06, Singapore 079906

Cambridge University Press is part of the University of Cambridge.

It furthers the University's mission by disseminating knowledge in the pursuit of education, learning and research at the highest international levels of excellence.

www.cambridge.org
Information on this title: www.cambridge.org/9781107591660

First published 2008
Second edition 2016
20 19 18 17 16 15 14 13 12 11 10 9 8 7 6

Printed in Malaysia by Vivar Printing

A catalogue record for this publication is available from the British Library

ISBN 978-1-107-59166-0 Paperback

Contents

Reading and vocabulary

Reference

Acknowledgements

The authors wish to thank Helen Freeman, Chris Capper and Sheila Dignen for their invaluable intellectual and editorial support during the course of the preparation of this new edition.

We must also thank the lexicography and computational team at Cambridge University Press whose work with the Cambridge International Corpus, the Cambridge Learner Corpus and the CANCODE corpus of spoken English (developed at the University of Nottingham in association with Cambridge University Press), enabled us to make a fully corpus-informed selection of the academic vocabulary we focus on in these materials.

We acknowledge with gratitude the pioneering work on academic word lists done by Averil Coxhead. In planning this book we made considerable use of her lists at http://www.victoria.ac.nz/lals/resources/academicwordlist/

We also acknowledge the work of Annette Capel and the English Vocabulary Profile. The EVP enabled us to select vocabulary appropriate to the level.

Michael McCarthy and Felicity O'Dell

Development of this publication has made use of the Cambridge English Corpus, a multi-billion word collection of spoken and written English. It includes the Cambridge Learner Corpus, a unique collection of candidate exam answers. Cambridge University Press has built up the Cambridge English Corpus to provide evidence about language use that helps to produce better language teaching materials.

The authors and publishers acknowledge the following sources of copyright material and are grateful for the permissions granted. While every effort has been made, it has not always been possible to identify the sources of all the material used, or to trace all copyright holders. If any omissions are brought to our notice, we will be happy to include the appropriate acknowledgements on reprinting and in the next update to the digital edition, as applicable.

New Scientist for the text on p. 25 adapted from 'Simulator could predict where epidemics will strike next', *New Scientist*, 30.03.2006. Copyright © 2006 Reed Business Information UK. All rights reserved. Distributed by Tribune Media Services; Scientific American for the text on p. 27 adapted from 'Shutting Down Alzheimers' by Michael S. Wolfe, *Scientific American*. Reproduced with permission. Copyright © (2006) Scientific American, Inc. All rights reserved; Nature Publishing Group for the text on p. 39 adapted from 'Abridged Extract timing is life and death', *Nature*, Vol 441, no. 7089, 04.05.2006. Copyright © 2006 Nature Publishing Group. Reproduced with permission; Text on p. 110 adapted from J. Anderson, Colorado State University Extension foods and nutrition specialist and professor; S. Perryman, CSU Extension foods and nutrition specialist; L. Young, former foods and nutrition graduate student; and S. Prior, former graduate intern, food science and human nutrition. Reviewed and revised, July, 2015 by Colorado State University Jessica Clifford, Research Associate and Extension Specialist and K. Maloney, graduate student in the Dept. of Food Science Human Nutrition; Dunedin Academic Press Ltd for the text on p. 111 adapted from 'Introducing the planets and their moons' by Peter Cattermole. Reproduced with permission from Cattermole Introducing the Planets and their Moons (Dunedin, Edinburgh, 2014); Text on p. 112 adapted from David Crystal, *The Cambridge Encyclopedia of Language 2nd Edition*, 1997, © David Crystal 1997, published by Cambridge University Press, adapted and reproduced with permission of the author and publisher; Scientific American for the text on p. 113 adapted from 'A Chronicle of timekeeping' by William J. H. Andrews, *Scientific American*, Vol 23. Reproduced with permission. Copyright © (2014) Scientific American, Inc. All rights reserved; Text on p. 114 adapted from Patricia A. Baker, *The Archaeology of Medicine in the Greco-Roman World*, 2013, © Patricia A. Baker 2013, published by Cambridge University Press, adapted and reproduced with permission of the author and publisher; Text on p. 115 adapted from 'Seeing Things Differently' by Shaaron Ainsworth, *RSA Journal*, Issue 2. Copyright © 2014 *RSA Journal*. Reproduced with permission of Shaaron Ainsworth.

Photographs

p. 20: © Lars Wallin/Etsa Images/Corbis; p. 21: Plume Creative/Getty Images; p. 35: kikujungboy/Shutterstock; p. 36: © Radius Images/Corbis; p. 54 (photo 1): picamaniac/Shutterstock; p. 54 (photo 2): payaercan/Getty Images; p. 54 (photo 3): © YAY Media AS/Alamy; p. 64: © Ken Welsh/Alamy; p. 70: © Radius Images/Alamy; p. 71: © Michael Ochs/Corbis; p. 80: © Wavebreak Media Ltd/Alamy; p. 108: © moodboard/Corbis.

Illustrations

Kamae Design pp. 40, 41, 46, 52, 76, 77, 78, 79.

To the student and the teacher

Who is this book for?

This book is for anyone who wants or needs to learn the kind of English which is used in academic contexts. It deals with the language used in written works such as textbooks and journal articles as well as with the spoken language of lectures and seminars. It also presents vocabulary relating to being a student at a university or college in that it covers topics relating to university life. It will be particularly useful for students preparing for IELTS, the Pearson Academic English Test or any other examination aimed at assessing whether candidates' English is at a high enough level to study in an institution where English is the medium of instruction. It will be helpful for people who need to attend – or indeed give – lectures or presentations in English or to participate in international conferences. It will enable students who have to prepare assignments or write up a dissertation in English to do so in a much more natural and appropriate way.

What kind of vocabulary does the book deal with?

The book presents and practises the kind of vocabulary that is used in academic contexts regardless of which discipline you are specialising in. So it considers words and expressions like *concept, put forward a theory* and *come to a conclusion*. It does not deal with the specialist vocabulary of any particular subject such as anatomy or physics. Specialist terms are often relatively easy to master – they will be explained and taught as you study the subject and indeed these words may sometimes be similar in English and your own language. However, it is the more general vocabulary used for discussing ideas and research and for talking and writing about academic work that you need to be familiar with in order to feel comfortable in an academic environment. Despite the fact that such vocabulary items are much more frequent than specialist vocabulary, they are often felt to be more difficult to learn. It is, therefore, useful to approach them in the systematic way suggested by this book.

One positive aspect of academic vocabulary is that there are relatively few differences, depending on whether you are studying in London or New York, Delhi or Sydney, Johannesburg, Dublin, Wellington, Toronto or Singapore or indeed any other place where you may be using English for academic purposes. Academic English tends to be a truly international language and the units of the book focus on vocabulary that will be essential for you regardless of where you are studying now or where you may be likely to study in the future. There are some differences between words used to describe people and places and these are highlighted in Unit 19. Reference sections 3 and 4 also focus on some vocabulary and spelling variations. In the units of the book we use British English spelling conventions, except when quoting texts which originally used American spellings.

Much of the vocabulary used in the book is neutral in that it is equally appropriate in both written and spoken contexts. We indicate those instances where a word is too formal to be used in speech or too informal to use in academic writing.

How was the vocabulary for the book selected?

The academic vocabulary focused on in this book was all selected from language identified as significant by the Cambridge International Corpus of written and spoken English and also the CANCODE corpus of spoken English developed at the University of Nottingham in association with Cambridge University Press. These enormous corpora include large collections of written and spoken academic text and so it was possible to identify language that is distinctive for academic contexts. We also made considerable use of the Cambridge Learner Corpus, a corpus of more than 60 million words of text taken from hundreds of thousands of learner scripts from students taking Cambridge English exams all over the world. From this corpus we were able to learn what kinds of errors students taking, for example, IELTS, were typically making.

In planning this book we made considerable use of Averil Coxhead's work on developing academic wordlists. Her lists can be found at, for example, http://www.uefap.com/vocab/select/awl.htm

How is the book organised?

Each unit consists of two pages. The left-hand page presents the academic vocabulary to be focused on in the unit. You will usually find words and expressions presented in context with, where appropriate, any special notes about their meaning and usage. The right-hand page checks that you have understood the information on the presentation page by giving you a series of exercises to complete.

The units are organised into different sections: The book begins with a Unit Zero called *Before you start*. The first section then includes nine units which look at basic aspects of academic vocabulary such as what is special about academic vocabulary, key verbs and key quantifying expressions. The second section devotes eight units to how words typically combine with one another in academic English. The third section has six units focusing on aspects of life in academic institutions. The fourth section provides four units considering aspects of planning and starting a piece of work and the fifth consists of five units relating to thinking and interacting. The sixth section has six units dealing with ways of talking about different concepts such as numbers, time and cause and effect. The seventh section includes twelve units covering aspects of the organisation and presentation of ideas.

Towards the end of the book you will find six reading texts relating to different academic disciplines with exercises based on the vocabulary in those texts. We hope you will find these useful examples of how to use texts to expand your knowledge of academic vocabulary in English and would recommend that you read these texts and do the exercises on them even if they relate to an academic subject that is very different from your own.

There are five reference sections dealing with some key areas where we felt it would be useful for you to have lists of items that could not be presented as fully in the main body of the book, i.e. Formal and informal academic words and expressions, Numbers, units of measurement and common symbols, British and North American academic vocabulary, Spelling variations and Word formation. Where appropriate, these reference sections provide space for you to add further examples of your own.

At the end of the book there is a Key with answers to all the exercises and an Index of all the key words and expressions, indicating the units where they can be found. The pronunciation is provided for standard British English.

Do Unit Zero first followed by Unit 1 *What is special about academic English?* Then work through the remaining units in any order that suits you.

So, good luck with your work on academic English. We hope that the materials in this book will help you to enjoy and to benefit fully from your studies. We hope that you will be able to share ideas in a creative, exciting way with scholars from all over the world and we wish you the very best for a successful and rewarding academic life.

0 Before you start

A What do I need

- a notebook or file – to write down the vocabulary that you study in this book as well as words and expressions that you come across elsewhere
- some good dictionaries

We strongly recommend the *Cambridge Advanced Learner's Dictionary* as this contains exactly the kind of information you need in order to be able to understand and use English vocabulary. Through its example sentences it shows you how the word is used and which other words it typically combines with. The dictionary also helps you with difficult items such as phrasal verbs indicating, for example, whether the object can come before the particle (set up the apparatus, set the apparatus up, go through a set of calculations but not ~~go a set of calculations through~~). The dictionary is available in both paper and electronic versions and can be accessed online at http://dictionary.cambridge.org.

You will need a specialist dictionary relating to your own subject area as well. Your teacher may also be able to recommend other dictionaries for your specific needs.

B What should I note about new vocabulary?

Here are some things to note – though it won't be appropriate to note them all for all words you come across.

- examples of the word or expression in use
- typical word combinations - you might, for example, note down adjectives or verbs typically associated with a noun that you want to learn or nouns, adverbs or prepositions associated with a verb
- any special features of the word (e.g. is there anything special about its grammar or pronunciation or is it particularly characteristic of either written or spoken English?)
- any other information that might help you to learn the word (e.g. is it similar to any word in your own language or does it share a root with a word you already know?)
- any additional vocabulary that learning this word may help with (e.g. does a verb have a related noun or what is the opposite of an adjective?)
- any other uses of the word (e.g. can it be used metaphorically or does it have any other meanings in the way that so many English words do?)

Diagrams can be useful, for example, word bubbles:

inconclusive
preliminary
to interpret
results
suggest
to analyse
demonstrate

or word forks:

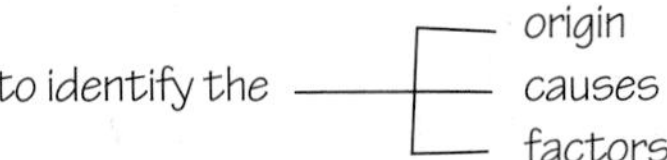

a common
an isolated
a universal
phenomenon

C What else can I do to improve my vocabulary?

As well as working through the units in this book, read as much English as you can in the subject areas that are most relevant to you. If you are new to studying in English, you could start by reading a textbook aimed at students who are at a slightly lower level than you are as far as the subject area is concerned; or you might prefer to read the latest articles in your field from a journal on the internet.

There is an enormous wealth of material available online for you to study and learn from. Try the websites of universities and other academic institutions which have extensive websites, for example, or blogs written by specialists in your field. Don't forget that, as well as written texts, you can find plenty of lectures and other listening materials online too.

Exercises

0.1 Answer the questions about what you will use to help you learn new words.

1 Where do you plan to note down vocabulary – a notebook, a folder, an electronic file…?
2 What dictionaries (printed or online) are there relating to your own special subject?
3 What other good dictionaries are there that will be useful for you, e.g. a good bilingual dictionary?

0.2 Look up the following words in a good dictionary and note them down with any of the relevant types of information listed in B opposite.

1 university 2 academic 3 degree

I hope to go to university next year. (example of the word in use)

0.3 Look up the following phrasal verbs. Note down where the object *an interesting expression* can go.

1 look up 2 note down 3 come across

look up an interesting expression, look an interesting expression up

0.4 Complete the word forks. Use a dictionary if necessary.

1 (verbs)
to carry out ....
.... an experiment
....
....

2 (adjectives)
higher ....
.... education
....
....

0.5 Complete the word bubbles. Use a dictionary to help you.

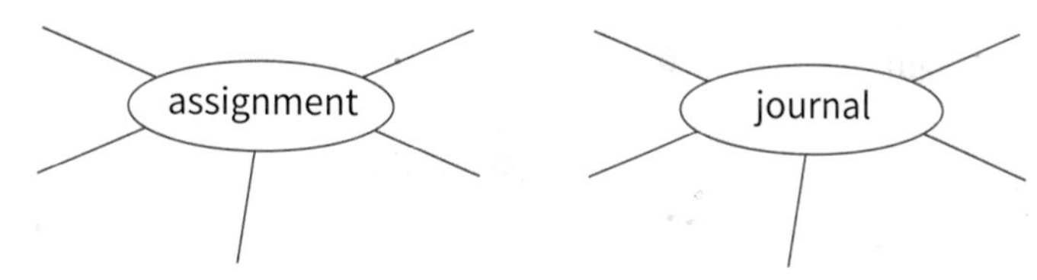

0.6 Do the following tasks to help you explore academic vocabulary on the internet.

1 Check out a university website e.g.
the University of Cambridge at http://www.cam.ac.uk
Massachusetts Institute of Technology at http://web.mit.edu
the University of Sydney at http://sydney.edu.au
the University of Cape Town at http://www.uct.ac.za

Note down the different kinds of information you can find there.

2 Put *lecture* and the name of your subject e.g. *lecture psychology* into a search engine. Make a note of any interesting links it takes you to.
3 Put *blog* and the name of your subject e.g. *blog law* into a search engine. Check out some of the links it suggests. Make a note of any that look as if they may be worth reading regularly.

1 What is special about academic English?

A Everyday words and academic uses

Many words in academic English are the same as everyday vocabulary, but they are often used with a slightly different meaning, which may be specialised.

everyday use	meaning	academic use	meaning
Standards of **discipline** in schools have declined.	ability to control yourself or other people	Nanotechnology is a relatively new **discipline**.	area of study
Underline your family name on the form.	draw a line under it	The research **underlines** the value of case studies.	gives emphasis to
The lake was frozen **solid**.	not liquid or gas	We have no **solid** evidence that radiation has caused the problem.	certain or safe; of a good standard

B Vocabulary and academic style

In writing, academics use many neutral expressions. They also use rather formal expressions which are not common in everyday language. Knowing whether an expression is formal or just neutral is important.

neutral	more formal	neutral	more formal
in short, briefly, basically	in sum, to sum up, fundamentally	try	attempt
only	sole(ly)	mainly, mostly	primarily
almost, more or less	virtually	typical of	characteristic of

However, very informal vocabulary may be used in *spoken* academic styles in classes and lectures. Learn to understand informal language when you hear it but be careful not to use it in essays and written assignments. Here are some examples of teachers using informal language.

'OK. **Have a shot at** doing task number 3.' [more formal: *Try/Attempt to do* ...]

'There's no way schools can be held responsible for failures of government policy.' [more formal: *Schools cannot in any way be held* ...]

Academic language tries to be clear and precise, so it is important to keep a vocabulary notebook (see page 8) and learn the differences between similar words, as well as typical word combinations (underlined here).

The building is a **prime** example of 1920s architecture. [excellent in quality or value]

The group's **primary** concern is to protect human rights. [main; most important]

C Noun phrases

Academic language often uses complex noun phrases. For example, instead of saying *Radiation was accidentally released over a 24-hour period, damaging a wide area for a long time,* an academic might say *The accidental release of radiation over a 24-hour period caused widespread long-term damage.* It is therefore important to learn the different forms of a word, for example:

noun	verb	adjective(s)	adverb(s)
accident		accidental	accidentally
quantity/quantification	quantify	quantitative/quantifiable	quantitatively/quantifiably

Finally, be aware of 'chunks' or phrases which occur frequently, and learn them as whole units. Examples: *in terms of, in addition to, for the most part, in the case of,* etc. (See Unit 16).

Language help

Using complex noun phrases improves your writing style and can contribute to higher grades in essays and assignments.

Exercises

1.1 **The words in the box each have an everyday use and an academic use. Complete each pair of sentences using the same word in the correct form.**

generate turn solid confirm identify underline character ~~pose~~ nature focus

1 She loves to ....*pose*.... for photographs in front of her fabulous house.
The events ....*pose*.... a threat to stability in the region.
2 The photograph was useless. It was blurred and out of ....
Child poverty should be the .... of our attention in the coming years.
3 I went online and .... my flight reservation.
The data .... the hypothesis that animal-lovers enjoy better health.
4 The power plant .... electricity for the whole region.
This issue always .... a great deal of debate among academics.
5 The murderer was .... from fingerprints discovered at the scene.
In this theory of history, progress is closely .... with technology.
6 I saw her .... to her husband and whisper something in his ear.
Let us now .... to the subject of social networking.
7 He always .... every new word when he's reading.
The study .... the fact that very little research exists.
8 The liquid became .... as the temperature was lowered.
The study lacks .... evidence and its conclusions are questionable.

1.2 **Rewrite the underlined words using more formal words and phrases from B opposite.**

1 The book is mainly concerned with the problem of policing the internet.
2 Almost every school in the county had reported problems with the new system.
3 The work of the Institute is not only devoted to cancer research.
4 Basically, we believe we have demonstrated a significant link between the two events.
5 Several research teams have had a shot at solving the problem, without success.
6 The reaction is typical of the way large corporations keep control of their markets.

1.3 **Read the text and answer the questions.**

1 Underline two verbs followed by adverbs which it would be useful to learn as pairs.
2 Underline two adverbs next to each other which it would be useful to learn together.
3 What are the noun forms of the verbs *produce*, *rely*, *discover* and *claim*?
4 A novel is a kind of book, but what does the adjective *novel* mean here?

The production of plastics depends heavily on petroleum, but a novel way of making plastics out of sugar could reduce our reliance on oil.
The discovery that a chemical in sugar can be converted relatively easily into a substance similar in structure to the material obtained from petroleum has led to the claim that plastics could soon be produced cheaply by the new method.

1.4 **Complete the second sentence using a noun phrase. Use a dictionary if necessary.**

1 People who investigated the problem biologically came to no firm conclusions.
....*Biological investigations*.... of the problem came to no firm conclusions.
2 When they developed antibiotics, it revolutionised medicine.
The .... antibiotics caused a .... in medicine.
3 They solved the problem by altering the deck of the bridge.
The .... to the problem was an .... to the deck of the bridge.
4 Exploring Antarctica has always been especially challenging.
The .... of Antarctica has always presented special ....

Over to you

Look at an academic text you have read recently and underline pairs of words which you think it would be useful to learn and remember together.

2 Key nouns

This unit focuses on some important nouns in academic English. See also Units 10, 11 and 15.

A General nouns referring to ideas

She wrote an article on the **subject** of class. [thing which is being discussed, considered or studied]

The **theme** of the poem is emigration. [main subject of a talk, book, etc.]

The students were given a list of essay **topics**. [specific subjects that someone discusses or writes about]

There was a lively debate on the **issue** of globalisation. [important subject or problem]

Political **theory** is a popular undergraduate subject. Einstein's **theory** of gravitation has been questioned recently. [statement of the rules on which a subject of study is based or, more generally, an opinion or explanation]

The **model** of climate change presented in the Stern Review seems to be becoming a reality. [description of a system or process which explains how it works]

The book is called 'The **Nature** of Intelligence'. [basic character of something]

Human behaviour is based on the **principle** of least effort. [basic idea or rule that explains how something happens or works]

B More specific nouns connected with ideas and phenomena

Repetition is an important **aspect** of speech development in children. [one individual part of a situation, problem, subject, etc.]

Automatic backup is a **feature** of the new software. [a typical quality that something has]

The political motives for the government's actions are beyond the **scope** of this essay. [range of a subject covered by a book, discussion, class, etc.]

The study revealed a **pattern** of results. [a regularly repeated arrangement]

During 2005, the **number** of violent attacks increased to an alarming degree. [amount or level]

C Nouns referring to ways of thinking, processes and activities

Read these titles of academic books and articles. Note the key nouns and their prepositions.

Micro-organisms in water: their **significance**[1] and **identification**[2]

Renewable energy: a critical **assessment**[3] of recent **research**

Citizens' **Views** on Healthcare Systems in the European Union

The **Case**[4] for Change: Rethinking Teacher Education. Towards a New **Approach**[5]

Perspectives[6] on Ecological Management: A study of public **awareness**[7] of river pollution

Epidemiological research into asthma and allergic disease: establishing a standardised **methodology**[8]

[1] importance [2] ability to establish the identity of something [3] judgement of the amount, quality or importance of something [4] arguments and facts in support of or against something [5] way of considering something [6] particular ways of considering something [7] understanding based on experience or information [8] set of methods used when studying something

Common Mistake

Research *is uncountable. Don't say: They carried out some useful ~~researches~~. To make it plural, say research studies or pieces of research.* ***Research*** *is followed by on or into not ~~of~~. Say, for example, do research on/into memory loss.*

Exercises

2.1 Look at the nouns in A and B opposite and note the prepositions that are associated with them. Answer the questions.

1 Which preposition often follows the nouns in both A and B?
2 Which preposition is often used before the nouns in A?
3 Which preposition would fill this gap – The postwar period is .... the scope of this paper and will be dealt with in a later study.

2.2 Choose the best noun to complete each sentence.

1 Environmental *topics / issues / principles* should be at the top of today's political agenda.
2 In the exam students had to choose three from a choice of ten essay *subjects / theories / topics*.
3 There are still people who are reluctant to accept Darwin's *nature / topic / theory* of evolution.
4 The professor decided to take moral courage as the *issue / theme / model* for his inaugural lecture.
5 Economists used a *model / principle / topic* of human behaviour to help them forecast likely inflation trends.
6 The Peter *Issue / Principle / Theme* states that members of a hierarchical group will usually end up being promoted to the point at which they become incompetent.

2.3 Match the beginnings and endings of the sentences.

1 The study revealed a regular
2 The research focuses on one particular
3 The writer makes a powerful
4 The writers take an original
5 Until recently there was little
6 I think you should broaden the
7 To date, there has been little research
8 There are many important

a scope of your research.
b awareness of the problem.
c issues facing the world today.
d into the environmental effects of nanoparticles.
e approach to their theme.
f aspect of modern society.
g pattern of changes in temperature.
h case for restructuring parliament.

2.4 Correct the mistakes in the underlined phrases.

[1]Recent researches that were carried out for a report by a government agency showed that local police can play an important role in crime prevention. The report makes [2]a strong case of boosting the numbers of community police officers although it warns against increasing police presence on the streets to an alarming degree. [3]Its methodological was based on a range of interviews asking members of the public for [4]their views in how best to prevent crime. Unfortunately, how to implement this recommendation was [5]out of the scope of the study but at least it serves a useful purpose in [6]raising awareness to the issue.

2.5 These book titles have been rephrased to sound more academic. Complete them using words from the box.

assessment	features	identification	nature	patterns	perspectives	principles	significance

1 What democracy is really like – The .... of Democracy
2 Why dreams are important – The .... of Dreams
3 What do we see in glaciated landscapes? – The .... of Glaciated Landscapes
4 How to evaluate language skills – The .... of Language Skills
5 Ways in which human behaviour repeats itself – .... of Human Behaviour
6 How to recognise different species of bees – The .... of Bees
7 Thinking about taxation from different angle – .... on Modern Taxation
8 How to make sure that a business is successful – The .... of Successful Business

3 Key verbs

A Key verbs for structuring academic assignments

Look at these tasks which students have been given.

Discuss some of the problems **involved**[1] in **investigating** attitudes to diet and health. Write a critical review of an investigation you have read about, or describe an investigation you yourself could **conduct**[2]. **Consider** the advantages and disadvantages of different methods.

Starting from rest, an aircraft accelerates to its take-off speed of 60 ms^{-1} in a distance of 900 metres. **Illustrate**[3] this with a velocity-time graph. **Assuming**[4] constant acceleration, **find**[5] how long the take-off run lasts. Hence **calculate**[6] the acceleration.

'The fact that nations agree to follow international law **demonstrates**[7] that we can **identify**[8] ideals that are trans-national and trans-cultural.' How far is this statement true? Critically **analyse** any recent event which **supports** or **challenges**[9] the statement.

Examine[10] how industrial growth has **affected** any two developing countries. **Provide**[11] statistical evidence where necessary and **include** a discussion of likely future trends.

[1] which are part of/included in [2] organise and do [3] draw something in order to explain something [4] accepting something to be true [5] discover by calculating (see 6) [6] judge the number or amount of something by adding, multiplying, subtracting or dividing numbers [7] shows, makes clear [8] recognise someone or something and say or prove who or what they are [9] questions whether something is true [10] look at or consider carefully and in detail [11] give

B More key verbs

These extracts from academic books contain more key verbs.

In **developing** methods to explain the significance of health status measures, one can **classify**[1] ways of **establishing**[2] quality of life into two main types.

The length of time spent on the tasks may **account for**[3] the decrease in motivation which **was seen**[4] in many of the participants.

The data **presented**[5] in Chapter 3 **showed**[6] that the age of the subjects was not the main factor.

Political theory **attempts**[7] to build bridges between different schools of political thought.

[1] divide things into groups according to their type [2] discovering or getting proof of [3] explain [4] see is often used in the passive in academic style [5] given [6] proved [7] tries

C Noun forms of key verbs

In academic style, noun forms of key verbs are often used instead of the verbs.

key verb	verb + noun form of key verb	example
explain	give/provide/offer an **explanation** (of/for)	The model **provides an explanation for** the differences between the two sets of data.
explore	undertake / carry out an **exploration** (of)	Kumar **undertook an exploration of** music genius.
emphasise	place/put **emphasis** (on)	The hospital **puts a lot of emphasis on** training.
describe	give/provide a **description** (of)	The book **gives a description of** modern Europe.
affect	have an **effect** on	Climate change **has an effect on** sea levels.
prove	offer/provide **proof** (that)	This research **offers proof** that bees are on the decline.

Common Mistake

Notice the difference in spelling between the verb *affect* and the noun *effect*. Don't confuse them. The verb ***to effect*** means to make something happen. *The invention of the world wide web* ***effected*** *a transformation in global communications.*

Exercises

3.1 Match the verbs from A in the box on the left with their synonyms in the box on the right.

affect attempt calculate challenge demonstrate identify include investigate provide

compute distinguish give influence involve question show study try

3.2 Complete the sentences with the correct form of verbs from B opposite.

1. As can .... from Table II, participation figures have been steadily falling since 1970.
2. Different authors have .... for the President's actions in different ways.
3. Mendel attempted to devise a system for .... the many different types of pea plant that he grew.
4. It is often most effective to .... your data in a chart or table.
5. The data we have collected .... that there has been a downward trend with regard to job satisfaction over the last 50 years.
6. The aim of the research is to .... a new software application which will help aviation engineers design more sophisticated aircraft.
7. The archaeologists should be able to use carbon dating techniques to .... exactly how old the bones are.
8. Charles Darwin .... to explain the existence of different species in terms of evolution.

3.3 Explain the difference in meaning between each pair of sentences.

1. A Greig's article supports Park's theory. B Greig's article challenges Park's theory.
2. A Describe the new tax regulations. B Discuss the new tax regulations.
3. A Lodhi provides new data. B Lodhi considers new data.
4. A Titova conducted four sets of experiments. B Titova examined four sets of experiments.
5. A Lee established why such changes occur. B Lee investigated why such changes occur.
6. A Okaz assumed that the data were reliable. B Okaz proved that the data were reliable.
7. A Illustrate the magnitude of the deceleration. B Find the magnitude of the deceleration.
8. A The events effected economic development. B The events affected economic development.

3.4 Rewrite the underlined verbs using nouns from the box.

description emphasis explanation exploration

Erikson's (2005) book [1]<u>explains</u> the changing patterns of educational achievement in children of poorer families. She [2]<u>explores</u> the relationship between income, family background and achievement at school and in further education. The book [3]<u>describes</u> a study carried out in 12 inner-city neighbourhoods. Erikson's research [4]<u>emphasises</u> the importance of support within the home.

3.5 Complete the phrases with the correct noun forms of the verbs. Use a dictionary if necessary.

1. investigate = conduct, carry out an .... into/of
2. illustrate = provide an .... of
3. analyse = provide, carry out an .... of
4. affect = have an .... on
5. attempt = make an .... to/at
6. classify = make, provide a .... of

Over to you

Using the tasks in A as a model, prepare some assignment topics for students studying any subject that you are familiar with.

4 Key adjectives

For any key adjective it is useful to note (a) whether it is typically followed by a specific preposition, (b) what nouns it typically collocates with, (c) whether it has any antonyms (adjectives of opposite meaning) and (d) whether it has any related nouns.

A Adjectives and prepositions

Here are some extracts from academic texts, with adjectives followed by *to* or *of.*

Language development is conceived as **relative**[1] **to** one's own past performance, or relative to that of others.

Some of the responses to the questionnaire were **specific**[4] **to** young male respondents. Others were **common to** all the respondents.

How can we make science **relevant**[2] **to** environmental policy? Poor communication between scientists and politicians is **characteristic**[3] **of** the situation today.

We need to plan technologies which are **appropriate**[5] **to** the needs of small farmers. It was **typical of** the farmers in the study that they had a negative attitude to technology.

[1] true to a particular degree when it is being compared with other things connected with what is happening or being discussed [2] connected with what is happening or being discussed [3] typical of [4] only found in [5] suitable or right for a particular situation or occasion

B Some key adjectives and their typical noun collocates

There was an **apparent**[1] discrepancy between the two sets of results.

We noted a **potential**[2] problem with the experimental design which we had to deal with first.

The **principal**[3] cause of the failure was a sudden temperature change.

The research used a **rigorous**[4] methodology which had been tested on many occasions.

[1] seeming to exist or be true [2] possible when the necessary conditions exist [3] first in order of importance [4] careful to look at or consider every part of something to make certain it is correct

C Adjectives and their opposites

Each sentence in this text on drug abuse contains a pair of adjectives which are opposites.

We cannot discuss drug abuse as an **abstract**[1] problem without considering **concrete**[2] examples of abuse and their social consequences. Abuse is rarely a **simple** issue; it usually results from a **complex** set of circumstances. Both **quantitative**[3] and **qualitative**[4] research is necessary to gain a full picture of the situation. By combining research methods, we may obtain an **accurate** picture of the causes and results of abuse, in contrast with the **inaccurate** assessments which often result from purely quantitative studies. A **significant**[5] amount of fear and prejudice surrounds the notion of abuse, and the media have a role which is also not **insignificant** in promoting such fears. The dissertation concludes that **rough**[6] estimates of the number of drug addicts need to be made more **precise** by properly defining addiction.

[1] existing only as an idea, not as a material object [2] existing in a form that can be seen or felt [3] using or based on numbers and statistics [4] using non-number-based methods such as interviews, focus groups, etc. [5] important or noticeable [6] fairly correct but not exact or detailed

D Nouns related to adjectives

Often in academic style, a noun form of the key adjective is used.

I admire her **simple** style.	I admire the **simplicity** of her style.
These statistics are less **relevant**.	These statistics have less **relevance**.

Exercises

4.1 Use the information in A opposite to correct the mistakes with prepositions in the sentences.

1 A lengthy discussion of the advantages of solar power is not relevant with this essay topic.
2 It is typical to the disease for it to start with an itchy rash.
3 This methodology is not appropriate about the kind of research you are planning.
4 The use of original metaphors is characteristic from the writer's style.
5 Relative with previous explanations, this theory is quite persuasive.
6 Dark hair and eyes are common for all people from the region.

4.2 Complete the sentences with adjective and noun collocates from B opposite.

1 There is an .... in your figures.
2 Management's refusal to listen to the workers' demands was the .... of the riots.
3 Lamaque devised a .... for doing research in the field.
4 We spotted a .... with our procedure and so we changed it in two areas.

4.3 Replace the underlined adjectives with their opposites.

1 Karlsson checked the figures and agreed with me that they were <u>accurate</u>.
2 The solution to the problem is a <u>simple</u> one.
3 Make <u>rough</u> calculations before you begin to write up your results.
4 The army played <u>a significant</u> role in events.
5 Hernandez prefers to discuss ideas in <u>abstract</u> terms.
6 Volkova's article reports on a fascinating piece of <u>quantitative</u> research.

4.4 Complete the sentences with adjectives from the box.

complex	potential	rigorous	specific	rough	qualitative

1 The plant is difficult to grow and needs very .... conditions to survive.
2 His tutor was critical of his work for not being .... enough.
3 In the past the northern tribes looked on the tribes of the south as .... enemies.
4 We chose a .... approach to our research and interviewed individuals personally.
5 A .... set of circumstances led to a civil war in 1897.
6 The .... estimates that we made turned out to be surprisingly accurate.

4.5 Complete the table with nouns formed from the adjectives. Use a dictionary if necessary.

adjective	noun	adjective	noun
appropriate		complex	
significant		accurate	
precise		rigorous	

4.6 Rewrite the underlined words using nouns formed from the adjectives.

1 The professor praised Carla for <u>her rigorous work</u>. *The professor praised Carla for the rigour of her work.*
2 The slight discrepancy in the two sets of figures <u>is not significant</u>.
3 <u>The complex language used by the poet</u> makes his work difficult to interpret.
4 <u>You must be precise</u> when taking measurements.
5 The later part of the book <u>will be more relevant</u> for next year's course.
6 The tutor was pleased with <u>how simple and appropriate our research proposal was</u>.

Over to you

When you come across a key adjective from this unit in your reading, note it down in a phrase so you build up a set of useful phrases using the adjective.

5 Key adverbs

A Adverbs that compare

adverb	meaning	example
comparatively/relatively	in comparison with something else	Our sample was **relatively/comparatively** small.
especially/particularly	more than usual	The process was not **especially/particularly** difficult.
specially	for a specific purpose	We used **specially** designed equipment.
somewhat (opposite: **considerably**)	(slightly formal) rather, to some degree	The second experiment involved a **somewhat/considerably** larger sample.
primarily	mainly	The article is **primarily** concerned with the effects of pesticides.
mostly/largely	almost completely (but not totally so)	The project was **largely/mostly** successful.
directly (opposite: **indirectly**)	without anything else being involved	The illness is **(in)directly** linked to poor housing.

B Adverbs that relate to numbers or time

There are **approximately** 20,000 pairs of birds on the island. [around, about]

The figure of 17% is **roughly** equivalent to the decline in population in the north of the country from 1980 to 2010. [more or less]

The phenomenon occurs relatively **frequently/infrequently**. [often/not often]

We **eventually** obtained the figures we were hoping for, which were **precisely** the same as those found by Rosenberg (2008). [in the end, after some time; completely and accurately]

Ultimately, we plan to repeat the study using **exactly** the same number of informants. [finally, after other things have been completed. *Exactly* is similar to *precisely*, but is more often used to refer to numbers]

The team **initially** failed to establish the cause of the death of the whales. [in the early stages]

Common Mistake

Eventually means 'after some time'. Use *finally* or *lastly* when beginning the last point in a discussion. *Finally/Lastly, let us consider the impact of tourism on local cultures.*

C Adverbs that relate to how things are stated

Hall's 1968 book **essentially**[1] differs from his earlier work in that it is **explicitly**[2] critical of the government of the time. **Generally**[3] his disapproval of government was only conveyed **implicitly**[4] in his previous works, but here he **specifically**[5] condemns their handling of a number of issues. The 1968 work is more **broadly**[6] in line with other political commentaries of the period.

1 referring to its main characteristics; also **basically** 2 openly 3 usually, also **on the whole**
4 not directly, suggested or implied rather than stated; opposite of **explicitly**
5 in particular; opposite of **generally** 6 in general, without considering minor details

D Adverbs that restrict or limit

merely The medication will **merely** make the symptoms bearable; it will not cure the disease. [exactly and nothing more]

simply Note that **simply** can have different meanings. To **put it simply**, the risks of this approach would seem to outweigh its advantages. [plainly] The book presents difficult ideas **simply**, in a way appropriate for the non-expert. [easily] The exam results were **simply** dreadful. [without doubt]

solely Certain events are **solely** confined to our planet. [only, involving nothing else]

Exercises

5.1 Use the information in A and B opposite to explain the difference in meaning between each pair of sentences.

1 A Heinrich's experiments were mostly criticised on ethical grounds.
  B Heinrich's experiments were particularly criticised on ethical grounds.
2 A The results were somewhat surprising given the circumstances.
  B The results were especially surprising given the circumstances.
3 A First-year students are directly affected by the new rules relating to tuition fees.
  B First-year students are particularly affected by the new rules relating to tuition fees.
4 A The study was primarily concerned with urban alienation.
  B The study was ultimately concerned with urban alienation.
5 A The team eventually obtained unpredicted results.
  B The team frequently obtained unpredicted results.

5.2 Use the information in C and D opposite to choose the best adverbs to complete the text.

What you are saying is [1]*essentially / merely* true. To put it [2]*basically / simply*, there is [3]*implicitly / basically* no significant difference between the two writers' theories. However, one of them writes in a [4]*simply / solely* dreadful style while the other has a style that is [5]*eventually / generally* very impressive.

5.3 Replace the underlined adverbs with their opposites from the box. Use each adverb in the box only once.

roughly generally exactly indirectly implicitly eventually infrequently precisely

1 There were roughly 350 people living in the village in 1958.
2 Floods happen frequently in this part of the country.
3 We investigated the problem and initially found some small errors in the calculations.
4 The temperature was exactly half a degree lower than the average.
5 Singh (1998) explicitly criticises existing theories of economic growth.
6 Soil erosion is specifically caused by water or wind.
7 The new results were broadly the same as the previous ones.
8 The disease is directly linked to environmental factors.

5.4 Underline the adverbs in the texts. Then answer the questions.

Marine conservationists are currently attempting to save the world's coral reefs. One plan is to literally glue the damaged reefs back together, using coral artificially raised in underwater laboratories. Reefs are increasingly under attack from human activity as well as from events which occur naturally, such as hurricanes and tsunamis. A recent UN report warns that 30% of the world's coral reefs have been completely destroyed or are severely damaged.

Scientists have recently discovered that ants can remember how many steps they have taken. By carefully shortening or lengthening the legs of ants, the team observed that short-legged ants apparently became lost and could not easily find their way home to the nest. Similarly, ants with longer legs typically travelled 50% further than they needed to and were also temporarily unable to find the nest. It seems ants can definitely count their steps.

1 Which adverb means 'in the same way'?
2 Find two pairs of adverbs that mean the opposite of each other.
3 Which adverb means 'a short time ago'?
4 Which adverb means 'more and more'?
5 Which adverb could be substituted by *seriously*?
6 Which adverb means 'for a limited time'?

Over to you

Find an interesting article in your discipline and underline all the key adverbs. Then check that you understand their meaning.

6 Phrasal verbs in academic English

Although phrasal verbs occur most frequently in more informal spoken and written English, they are also not uncommon in an academic context. You will hear them used in lectures and will read them in serious journals. Of the phrasal verbs in this unit, only *go/look back over* and *work out* are not appropriate for a formal written assignment.

A Phrasal verbs and one-word synonyms

Phrasal verbs often have one-word synonyms. These sound more formal than their phrasal verb equivalent but both are appropriate when writing or talking about academic subjects. Vary your language by using both.

phrasal verb	synonym	example
put forward (an idea/view/opinion/theory/plan)	present	In her latest article Kaufmann **puts forward** a theory which is likely to prove controversial.
carry out (an experiment / research)	conduct	I intend to **carry out** a series of experiments.
make up	constitute	Children under the age of 15 **make up** nearly half of the country's population.
be made up of	consist of	Parliament **is made up of** two houses.
point out	observe	Grenne **points out** that the increase in life expectancy has led to some economic problems.
point up	highlight	The study **points up** the weaknesses in the current school system.
set out (to do something)	aim	In his article Losanov **sets out** to prove that …
set out	describe	The document **sets out** the terms of the treaty.
go into	discuss	In this book Sergeant **goes into** the causes of the Civil War in some depth.
go/look back over	revise, review *	Please **go/look back over** this term's notes.
go through	check	**Go through** your calculations carefully.

**Revise* is the BrE synonym and *review* the AmE synonym. (*Revise* in AmE only means to edit or change something to make it better; *review* is not used in BrE in the context of preparing for a test as focused on here.)

B Carrying out research

After completing her first degree in zoology Meena **went on to**[1] apply to graduate school. She wanted to **work on**[2] animal behaviour at a well-known institute in New Zealand. She **set up**[3] a series of experiments investigating how bees communicate. She has noticed some curious behaviour patterns but has not yet **worked out**[4] why her bees behave as they do. What she has observed seems to **go against**[5] current theories of bee behaviour. When she has completed all her research she will have to **write** it all **up**[6].

[1] do something after doing something else [2] study, work in the field of [3] prepared, arranged [4] come to a conclusion about [5] not be in agreement with [6] (of an important document) write in a final form

Language help

Consult a good dictionary when you use phrasal verbs in your writing. For example, a good dictionary tells you when the object can be used before the particle (e.g. ***write** your results **up***) and when it cannot (e.g. *this **goes against** current theories*).

Exercises

6.1 Rewrite the underlined words using phrasal verbs from A opposite.

1 We <u>conducted</u> a series of experiments to test out our hypothesis.
2 Before the test you should <u>revise</u> Chapters 7 and 8 of your textbooks.
3 In his article on the American Civil War Kingston <u>discusses</u> the reasons why the situation developed in the way it did.
4 Cole <u>presents</u> some fascinating theories on the development of language in his latest book.
5 The psychologist <u>observed</u> that it was very unusual for a young child to behave in this way.
6 Please <u>check</u> your work carefully before handing it in.
7 Simpson's book <u>aims</u> to prove that the Chinese reached America long before the Vikings.
8 Women now <u>constitute</u> over half the student population in universities in this country.

6.2 Complete the paragraph with the missing words.

As part of my MA I've been researching language acquisition. I've been working [1] .... how young children learn their mother tongue. I've been carrying [2] .... experiments to see how much reading to young children affects their language development. I've had a great supervisor who has helped me set [3] .... my experiments and she's also pointed [4] .... lots of interesting things in my data that I hadn't noticed myself. I'm busy writing my work [5] .... now and I think I should be able to put [6] .... some useful ideas. It's been really fascinating and I hope I may be able to go [7] .... to do a doctorate in the same field although I certainly never set [8] .... to do a PhD.

6.3 Match the beginnings and endings of the sentences.

1 Feudal society was made
2 Carlson was the first to put
3 Her results appear to go
4 The investigation pointed
5 It took him a long time to work
6 The geography book sets

a forward a convincing theory with regard to this question.
b up the flaws in the school's testing methods.
c out the solution to the algebra problem.
d out a lot of basic information about all the world's countries.
e against what she had found in her earlier studies.
f up of clearly defined classes of people.

6.4 Complete the collocations for the phrasal verbs. Choose nouns relevant in an academic context. Use a dictionary if necessary.

1 to carry out *research*
2 to write up ....
3 to put forward ....
4 to point up ....
5 to go through ....
6 to set up ....

Over to you

Look through an article on an academic subject that interests you. Copy out any sentences that you find using phrasal verbs. If there is a one-word synonym for the phrasal verb, make a note of it too.

7 Key quantifying expressions

Quantifying expressions are important in academic English as it is often necessary to comment on figures or trends. There is more useful language for talking about numbers in Units 33 and 34.

A Expressing numbers and amounts

We use **amount** with uncountable nouns: *a large amount of money/interest/influence.*

We use **number** with plural countable nouns: *a small number of articles/books/words.*

The words *number* and *amount* can be used with adjectives such as **small**, **considerable**, **substantial**, **significant**, **huge**, **enormous**, **vast**, **total**, **surprising**, **excessive** [too much/many], **fair** [quite a lot] and **reasonable** [acceptable].

We can also use the phrase **a great deal of** [a large amount of] with uncountable nouns: a great deal of *time/money/effort*.

B Other ways of expressing quantity

The size of our survey was relatively **small-scale**[1]. We sent out 2,500 questionnaires **in total**[2]. Although a **handful**[3] of people did not respond, the **bulk**[4] (95%) of those sent questionnaires completed them. The survey shows that, **for the most part**[5], the population is becoming more aware of the importance of recycling. **All of** the people said that they recycled at least some of their rubbish, and **none of** them felt that recycling was a waste of time. Only **one of** the respondents said that he recycled less than he used to.

[1] only involving a small number [2] in all [3] a relatively very small number
[4] the majority [5] as regards the greatest number

Common Mistake

Notice how *respondents* is in the plural. We use a plural noun after *one of*: *one of our surveys.* But we use a singular verb: *One of our surveys* **was** *reported on local radio.*

C Comparing numbers and quantities

expression	example	comment
exceeding	Results **exceeding** 5 cm were eliminated from the survey.	more than
in excess of	The team has secured research grants **in excess of** €20m.	more than, used mainly in official or legal writing
fewer and fewer / less and less	**Fewer and fewer** people are staying in the same job throughout their lives. Young people are becoming **less and less** interested in politics.	a steadily declining/decreasing number of, decreasingly
more and more	There is **more and more** interest in the topic. People are becoming **more and more** aware of the need to conserve energy.	a steadily increasing amount of, increasingly
more or less	The events happened **more or less** simultaneously.	(slightly informal) approximately
no fewer than	**No fewer than** 200 people responded.	used to suggest the number was unexpectedly large

Exercises

7.1 Complete the sentences using the correct form of the word in brackets.

1 In a .... number of cases, there was no reaction at all to the drug. (SURPRISE)
2 The analysis demanded an .... amount of computer time. (EXCEED)
3 .... numbers of birds inhabit the lake during the winter. (CONSIDER)
4 The course requires a .... amount of prior knowledge. (REASON)
5 The survey took a .... amount of research time and costs were high. (SUBSTANCE)
6 The two dams can hold in .... of two cubic kilometres of water. (EXCEED)
7 In .... , 12 areas of the Southern Indian Ocean are now closed to deep-sea fishing. (TOTALITY)
8 Only a .... of students chose the course, so it was cancelled. (HAND)
9 No .... than 2,000 new computer viruses are created every year. (FEW)
10 In a .... number of cases, surface damage was noticed. (SIGNIFY)

7.2 Choose the correct words to complete the paragraph.

[1]*A vast amount of / A huge number of* money was spent on the project. From the outset, [2]*a huge amount of / a substantial number of* time was wasted waiting for laboratory facilities to be provided by the university. Meanwhile, [3]*a small number of / a huge number of* dedicated employees (just five) struggled with trying to get the project off the ground. [4]*A significant number of / An enormous amount of* information had to be gathered and processed before the first experiments could be designed. One of the [5]*result / results* of the delays [6]*has been / have been* a decline in the number of applicants for research posts on the project.

7.3 Replace the underlined words with their opposites. Make any other necessary changes.

There have been a [1]small number of studies investigating the impact of email on interpersonal communications. [2]None of the studies has been [3]large-scale but they suggest some interesting trends in patterns of email use. From one of the studies it seems that [4]fewer and fewer people send over 50 emails daily. Moreover, it appears that a [5]substantial number of senior citizens use email a lot more frequently than younger people do.

7.4 Read the text and answer the questions. Use a dictionary if necessary.

For some years now, scientists have been using a powerful new machine to recreate the conditions that existed at the birth of the universe. The machine generates a massive number of hot, dense, bursts of matter and energy, simulating what happened in the first few microseconds of the beginning of the universe. After no more than ten microseconds, the particles of matter joined together, like water freezing, forming the origin of more or less everything we see in the universe today.

1 Which expression explains how long scientists have been using this machine?
2 Which expression tells us how many bursts of matter and energy the machine generates?
3 Which time period does the machine simulate?
4 Which expression states how long it was before the particles of matter joined together?
5 Which expression in the last sentence means *approximately?*

Over to you

Find five quantifying expressions from one of your textbooks and use them to write your own sentences.

8 Words with several meanings

A Set

Many words in English have more than one meaning. *Set*, for example, has a large number of different meanings. Here are some examples which are relevant to academic English.

a) (verb) adjust something to a particular level: ***Set** the instruments to zero.*

b) (verb) establish: *I would like to **set** some ground rules for the course.*

c) (verb) cause to be in a stated condition: *The decision **set** a number of changes in motion.*

d) (verb) arrange: *We must **set** a time for our next meeting.*

e) (verb) become solid: *Concrete **sets** as it cools.*

f) (noun) group: *The condition is associated with a particular **set** of symptoms.*

g) (adjective) that must be studied: *We have a number of **set** texts to read for our course.*

B Academic uses for familiar words

These words have a distinct academic meaning as well as more familiar meanings.

word	academic meaning	example
accommodate (verb)	change to allow something to fit in	He had to adapt his theory to **accommodate** new information.
charge (verb)	refresh the supply of electricity	You need to **charge** the batteries every day.
contract (verb)	become smaller, shorten	As the metal cools, it **contracts**.
occur (verb)	exist	Some valuable minerals **occur** in these rocks.
reference (noun)	details of author or book mentioned in a piece of writing, to show where information was found	You must provide a list of **references** at the end of your assignment.
revolution (noun)	complete turn (e.g. of a wheel)	Time is measured by the **revolution** of the earth around the sun.
structure (noun)	way in which parts of a system or object are organised or arranged	The **structure** of this element is particularly complex.

C Words with several different academic uses

Many academic words have distinct meanings in different disciplines. **Channel**, for example, has specific meanings in electronics, linguistics, biology, physics, social sciences and geography [e.g. *channels of communication*, *irrigation channels*, *government channels*, *to channel something*]. So you will, of course, need a specific dictionary for your own subject.

Other words have several distinct meanings that are important in general academic English.

The writer **takes issue with** Kwame's interpretation. [raises arguments against]

In your essay you need to address a number of key **issues**. [topics]

Have you seen the latest **issue** of the Malaysian Medical Journal? [edition]

Jackson raises some important **points** in his article. [opinions, ideas, information]

The writer takes a long time to get to the **point**. [most significant part]

Only 10.2 [ten **point** two] per cent of the people who received questionnaires responded.

Draw a straight line between **points** A and B on the map. [mark showing the position of something on a plan or diagram]

Language help

If you come across a word that you know but it does not seem to make sense in that context, check to see whether it has another distinct meaning. If it does, write it down with both (or all) its meanings in your vocabulary notebook.

Exercises

8.1 Match the uses of *set* in the sentences with the meanings a–g in A opposite.

1 Before we start you must all set your watches to precisely the same time.
2 Professors will set a date for the submission of assignments relating to their own courses.
3 We expected the mixture to set quickly but it had not hardened by the morning.
4 Before leaving the area, the retreating army set the farm buildings on fire.
5 The engine's performance has set a new fuel consumption record.
6 During the first semester, music students have to study a number of set pieces.
7 There are a whole set of issues that you should address in your essays.

8.2 Complete the sentences with the correct form of words from B opposite.

1 When you are doing research, you must keep good records of your .... as it can be difficult to locate sources later.
2 This medical condition is most likely to .... in fair-skinned people.
3 Engine speed can be measured in .... per minute.
4 Hope, the theme of the anthology, is general enough to .... a variety of approaches.
5 The .... of society in Ancient Rome has parallels with that of the modern USA.
6 The experiment was designed to discover whether gold .... or expanded under different conditions.

8.3 Complete each set of phrases with the same word.

1 discuss the following .... / underline the key .... / make some insightful ....
2 to .... a precedent / a .... book / a .... of exercises
3 take .... with / the current .... of the New Scientist / a controversial ....
4 to .... your energies into / a .... of communication / an irrigation ....
5 the French .... / the .... of the earth around the sun / a .... in science

8.4 The text contains some more words that have distinct academic meanings. Use a dictionary to check the meaning of the underlined words. What other meanings can each word have?

A simulator showing how outbreaks of infection might spread around the world would be of great assistance in the struggle to <u>contain</u> such diseases. Researchers <u>maintain</u> that to effectively <u>check</u> emerging infectious diseases, they need a significant amount of computing power. A global epidemic simulator would mimic climate simulators which <u>monitor</u> the movement of weather systems. It would <u>record</u> when disease outbreaks occur, where they are heading and, crucially, would <u>allow</u> scientists to test out virtual mitigation <u>measures</u> to assess which might <u>perform</u> best on the ground.

8.5 Jokes are often based on words having several meanings. Explain this joke.

A neutron goes into a bar, orders a drink and asks how much it will be. The barman replies: 'For you, sir, no charge.'

9 Metaphors and idioms

A metaphor is an expression which describes something by comparing it to something else with similar characteristics. For example, you might say an academic 'attacks' or 'demolishes' someone's theory or argument, just as an army can attack an enemy or workers can demolish a building.

If a metaphor is used so often that the original comparison becomes forgotten, then it may be called an idiom. For example, people often say, 'I'm snowed under with work at the moment.' Originally this was a metaphor comparing a great deal of work to deep snow (overwhelming everything and making movement difficult). However, this expression has been used so frequently that it no longer usually makes people think of snow. Academic English uses various metaphors and idioms.

A Metaphors and idioms referring to light and darkness

Data from the comet may **shed (new) light on** / **shine a (new) light on**[1] how life on earth began.

Views on depression have changed **in (the) light of**[2] recent studies of the brain.

Novelists, poets and essayists often refer to historical events to **illuminate**[3] their understanding of human behaviour.

The book provides an **illuminating** discussion of how languages change.

The report revealed the **glaring**[4] discrepancy between patients' needs and what the health service can offer them, and **highlighted**[5] the need for a new approach.

Researchers **remain in the dark**[6] about what can ensure successful recovery from drug addiction.

The book dealt with economic policy **in the shadow of**[7] the Civil War of 1994–1999.

[1] provide a clearer explanation for it [2] because of [3] show more clearly something that is difficult to understand [4] something bad that is very obvious (to *glare* means to shine too brightly) [5] emphasised something important [6] continue in a state of not knowing something [7] in a situation where something bad has happened or is happening

B Metaphors and idioms referring to war and conflict

Look at these extracts from lectures and note the metaphors and idioms.

Critics **opposed to** D. H. Lawrence **attacked** his novels on various grounds. But despite the apparent diversity of opinion, Lawrence's critics were **united** on what they saw as several serious problems.

In the 19th century, travellers in the region were especially vulnerable to **the onslaught of**[3] tropical diseases.

It's useful at the present time to look at Japan's experience in **the battle against** air pollution, and it's **a battle** no nation can afford to lose.

Children have been **bombarded with**[4] increasing amounts of violence in the media. But campaigners have recently **scored a victory**[5] with tighter regulations now going through Parliament.

Following **a barrage**[1] of hostile criticism, in his later works we see the artist becoming increasingly detached from the material world, **retreating**[2] more into his own mind than before.

Parents and teachers need to **maintain a united front**[6] on the question of bad conduct at school.

[1] action of firing large guns continuously, here meaning a great many criticisms all at once [2] going back to escape from attacks [3] a very powerful attack [4] forced to experience, subjected to [5] won a battle [6] remain united in their opinions and agree on how to act

Language help

Make notes of metaphors and idioms in your vocabulary notebook and group them together into themes such as 'war', 'light', 'temperature and weather', and so on.

Exercises

9.1 Complete the sentences with the correct form of the words in the box.

remain glare illuminating shadow highlight shed illuminate shine light

1 The results of the investigation have .... a light on the pressures of the global economy on farmers in developing countries.
2 Until recently, scientists have .... in the dark as to the causes of the disease, but a recent breakthrough promises to .... new light on the problem.
3 Our whole notion of time and space has changed in the .... of recent developments in physics.
4 Professor Delrio gave a very .... talk on one of Shakespeare's later plays .
5 These communities have lived for decades in the .... of poverty and social deprivation.
6 The team carried out a series of experiments in an attempt to .... the mysterious processes at work in the organism.
7 The collapse of the bridge in 1998 .... the need for a more rigorous analysis of the effects of constant traffic movements.
8 The professor found some .... errors in one student's calculations.

9.2 Rewrite the underlined phrases using metaphors of conflict from B opposite.

1 Scientists <u>who don't agree with</u> this theory have recently attacked its basic assumptions.
2 Governments need to <u>remain in complete agreement</u> on the issue of economic migrants.
3 Nowadays, we are <u>forced to see</u> advertisements every time we watch TV or visit our favourite websites.
4 In the face of counter-arguments, several economists have recently <u>moved away</u> from the view that economic processes cannot be altered.
5 The <u>efforts</u> against crime will fail without police and community cooperation.
6 Many traditional rural societies and cultures have been destroyed by the <u>sudden powerful impact</u> of urbanisation.
7 Following <u>a great number all at once</u> of hostile questions from reporters, the Minister suddenly ended the press conference and left the room.
8 Parents recently <u>won a battle</u> by forcing the city council to reduce speed limits near schools.

9.3 Read the text and underline key words and phrases which construct the main metaphor: 'the human brain is a computer'.

Shutting down Alzheimer's

The human brain is a remarkably complex organic computer, taking in a wide variety of sensory experiences, <u>processing and storing this information,</u> and recalling and integrating selected bits at the right moments. The destruction caused by Alzheimer's disease has been likened to the erasure of a hard drive, beginning with the most recent files and working backward. As the illness progresses, old as well as new memories gradually disappear until even loved ones are no longer recognized. Unfortunately, the computer analogy breaks down: one cannot simply reboot the human brain and reload the files and programs. The problem is that Alzheimer's does not only erase information; it destroys the very hardware of the brain, which is composed of more than 100 billion nerve cells (neurons), with 100 trillion connections among them.

Over to you

Look at some of the textbooks you use. Can you find any examples of metaphors or idioms there relating to light and darkness or war and conflict? What other types of metaphors or idioms have you noticed in your subject area?

10 Nouns and the words they combine with

Nouns often combine with specific adjectives, for example *medical research*, *undivided attention* or with specific verbs, for example *carry out research*, *pay attention*.

A Nouns and the adjectives they combine with

adjective + noun combinations	example
useful, valuable, personal, constant, close, frequent, intermittent[1] **contact**	I made some **useful contacts** at the conference.
considerable, heated[2], intense, public, animated[3] **debate**	After the lecture there was a **heated debate**.
crucial, decisive, fundamental **element** [=factor]	Timing is a **crucial element** of the experiment.
conflicting, contrasting, constituent[4] **elements** [=parts]	There are **conflicting elements** in the artist's work.
excess, sufficient, nuclear **energy**	Wind turbines create **sufficient energy** for the town's needs.
common, isolated, natural, recent, universal **phenomenon**	Such anti-social behaviour is a **recent phenomenon**.
conflicting, (in)conclusive, unforeseen[5], preliminary[6], encouraging, interim[7] **results**	Our **preliminary results** were **encouraging**.
decisive, challenging, conflicting, influential, key, pivotal[8] **role**	Student activists played a **pivotal role** in the riot.
random, representative **sample**	A **representative sample** of the population was surveyed.
alternative, efficient, fair, practical, convenient, proper, acceptable **way**	It is important to treat your research subjects in a **fair way**.
in absolute, broad, relative, general, practical, economic **terms**	People are better off **in economic terms**.

[1] from time to time [2] strong, often angry [3] lively [4] that combine to make something
[5] not expected [6] first [7] temporary [8] important

B Nouns and the verbs they combine with

Most of the nouns in the table above are also strongly associated with specific verbs.

You can **come into contact with** someone or something or you can **establish**, **maintain**, **break off** or **lose contact**.

Academics may **engage in debate** or **contribute to a debate**. You talk about **the debate surrounding** an issue.

You can **combine**, **differentiate** or **discern** [recognise] **the elements** of, for example, a chemical compound.

You **consume** [use], **conserve**, **generate** [create], **save** or **waste energy**.

Phenomena emerge or **occur** and students will try to **observe**, **investigate** and then **explain** those **phenomena**.

Academics **collect**, **collate** [organise] and **publish** their **results**. Sometimes **results are questioned** or **invalidated** [shown to be wrong]. Occasionally they are even **falsified**!

Roles may be **defined** or **strengthened**. People or factors can **play a role** or **take on a role**.

You can **take**, **provide** or **analyse a sample**.

You can **discover**, **devise** [think up], **work out** or **develop a way** to do something.

Language help

Whenever you notice a noun that seems to be key as far as your own studies are concerned, write it down with the adjectives and verbs it is typically associated with.

Exercises

10.1 Look at the adjective and noun combinations in A opposite. Answer the questions.

1 Put these types of contact in order of frequency – *frequent*, *constant*, *intermittent*.
2 If two of the four *constituent elements* of most language exams are reading and speaking, what are the other two?
3 Which adjective suggests more energy than the other – *excess* or *sufficient energy*?
4 Which adjective describes the opposite of a *common phenomenon*?
5 Would you be pleased if you did some research and got *inconclusive results*?
6 What adjective other than *key* can be used with *role* to give a similar meaning?
7 Can you name three people who play an *influential role* in a child's development?
8 Which of these is a *representative sample* and which is a *random sample*: a sample chosen by chance, a sample chosen as typical of the population as a whole?

10.2 Complete the sentences with the correct form of verbs from B opposite.

1 I first .... into contact with Abdul when I started my doctoral research in 2007.
2 The country .... so much energy that we don't .... enough to meet all our needs.
3 The space race .... an important role in post-war politics.
4 In her research project Diana .... the phenomenon of extra-sensory perception but she was not able to come to any significant conclusions.
5 Although Hans's rivals attempted to .... his results, they met with no success.
6 Green's poetry successfully .... elements from a number of different traditions.

10.3 Match the beginnings and endings of the sentences.

1 It took the team a long time to devise
2 During the war we had to break
3 There has been a lot of heated debate
4 Ian Hartmann was invited to take on
5 Part of my role was to collate
6 The doctor wanted me to provide
7 Scientists all over the world contributed
8 A new and unexpected phenomenon
9 Using shading helps to differentiate

☐ a surrounding the issue of global warming.
☐ b a blood sample for analysis.
☐ c the role of project leader.
☐ d to the debate on cloning.
☐ e off contact with colleagues abroad.
☐ f seems to be emerging.
☐ g the key elements in a graph.
☐ h a way to solve their problem.
☐ i the results of our experiments.

10.4 Complete the sentences using words from the box.

conflicting heated publish crucial interim random define maintaining natural discern occurs engaging acceptable taking practical

1 She obtained her results by .... a .... sample of the population.
2 Before we go any further we must .... each of our roles more precisely.
3 We must decide what is an .... way to proceed, in .... terms.
4 The group succeeded in .... contact long after they had all left college.
5 My trip to Africa was the .... element in my decision to work in conservation.
6 Specialists in the field of bio-engineering have been .... in .... debate on this issue for some time.
7 I am told that Smythe is about to .... some .... results. The final results won't be available until next year.
8 Professor Powell was able to .... some .... elements in different accounts of the incident.
9 Lightning is a .... phenomenon which .... most frequently in the tropics.

11 Adjective and noun combinations

Noun phrases are an important feature of academic style. This unit focuses on a number of adjective + noun combinations which are particularly frequent in academic English.

A Adjectives suggesting importance

adjective	comment	frequently combines with ...
important	**significant** can convey the same meaning and both adjectives often go with these nouns	aspect, contribution, difference(s), implications, point, question, reason, element
major	the opposite, **minor**, also often goes with these nouns	role, changes, problem, factor, issue, concern, difference, theme, contribution, point
central	means main or most important	role, theme, issue, question, concern, feature, focus, element, problem, argument
particular	means special	interest, attention, significance, importance, concern

B Adjectives suggesting amount/extent

adjective	comment	frequently combines with ...
significant	large in size	increase, effect, reduction, number, proportion
enormous / considerable	**enormous** can mean very large or very important; **considerable** means large or of noticeable importance (i.e. slightly less strong than enormous)	amount, expansion, number, range, diversity, difference, variation, extent, degree, impact, power, influence, significance, interest
vast	means extremely big	majority, array, amount, range, quantity/ quantities, sums, scale, improvement
widespread	means that something happens in many places or among many people	belief, acceptance, support, opposition, assumption, use
common*	means that something is normal or frequent and found on many occasions	experience, practice, use, concern, problem, view

Common** can also mean 'shared' and as such it combines with *knowledge*, *ground* [areas of interest], *feature*, *interest*, e.g. *There is much* ***common ground *between the two writers.*

C Other useful adjective and noun combinations

Specific means relating to one thing and not to things in general. It often combines with *context*, *information*, *case*, *type*, *form*, *purpose*, *characteristics*, *conditions*, *example*. For example, *The reaction occurs only under* specific conditions.

Inevitable is often used with words relating to results or changes such as *consequence*, *outcome*, *collapse*, *decline*, *conflict*, *effect*, *developments*. [unavoidable]

Explicit combines with words relating to how things are presented, e.g. *reference*, *statement*, *comparison*, *account*, *mention*. [clear and exact, communicated directly]

Relevant combines with words relating to evidence of different types, e.g. *data*, *documents*, *information*, *details*, *factors*. [connected with what is being discussed]

D Adjectives and prepositional phrases

A feature of academic writing is that it often uses the noun form of an adjective in a prepositional phrase beginning with *of*, instead of just using an adjective.

Sagan's contribution is **of particular significance**. (= particularly significant)

Helvena's work is **of great interest** to researchers. (= very interesting)

This is a work **of considerable importance**. (= very important)

Exercises

11.1 Choose the best adjective to complete each statement about an academic.

1 Davison did *a considerable / an important* amount of research into earthquake prediction.
2 Rawlinson drew *significant / particular* attention to the problem of energy consumption.
3 The *central / major* argument of Parry's book is that work can be organised in a variety of ways, some more efficient than others.
4 Werner's work had *a widespread / an enormous* impact on the way we design bridges today.
5 *An important / A significant* proportion of Thomaz's work was devoted to international law. Three of her five books were on the subject.
6 Prestyn made only a *minor / particular* contribution to modern psychology, but it was an interesting one, nonetheless.
7 Baklov's work has some extremely *important / central* implications for our work today.
8 Mortensen's work has played a *central / vast* role in changing attitudes to parenthood.

11.2 Rewrite the underlined words and phrases using adjective and noun combinations.

1 There is opposition among students in many places to the idea of longer semesters.
There is widespread opposition among students to the idea of longer semesters.
2 Destruction of the riverbank will cause a decline which is bound to happen in the numbers of small mammals.
3 School standards are a concern which occurs frequently among parents nowadays.
4 Nowhere in the article does the author make mention in a direct, clear and exact way of the 20 cases which were never resolved.
5 There is very little ground which is shared between the two ways of addressing the problem.
6 The paper is too general and lacks examples which relate only to individual things.
7 The work covers an extremely big array of themes from Asian political history.

11.3 Complete the table with the noun forms of the adjectives. Use a dictionary if necessary.

adjective	noun	adjective	noun
significant		important	
relevant		valuable	
interesting		useful	
frequent		broad	

11.4 Look at the examples of prepositional phrases in D opposite. Rewrite the underlined words using prepositional phrases. Use adjectives from the box and appropriate nouns.

huge high enormous great considerable

1 Johnson's work is very relevant for any student of medical engineering.
Johnson's work is of great relevance for any student of medical engineering.
2 The research will be very valuable to anyone interested in economic planning.
3 It was an event which was terribly important in the history of Latin American politics.
4 Partich's book is an extremely broad work.
5 Sorlan's book was a very significant work in the development of political theory.
6 This software will be quite useful in the analysis of large amounts of numerical data.
7 The method outlined is very interesting to anyone investigating sleeplessness.
8 'You know' is an expression which is very frequent in informal spoken English.
9 DNA evidence is centrally important.

12 Verbs and the words they combine with

A How verbs combine with other words

When you learn verbs in an academic context, it is useful to note a number of things about them.

Do they combine with any nouns, and does the noun go before or after the verb, for example, **the research / theory is based on, to pose a problem / question / threat**?

Do they combine with any adverbs, for example, **mainly / partly / loosely based on**?

Are they followed by any prepositions, for example, to **base** something **on** something else?

Are they often used in the passive, for example, **be based on**, **be associated with**?

verb	nouns	adverbs	examples
base (on)	research, theory, story, hypothesis	mainly, partly loosely	The story **was loosely based on** a true event which occurred in 1892. The **theory is mainly based on** the writer's initial study.
associate (with)	word, idea, theory, term	generally, commonly, invariably	A decrease in consumer spending **is generally associated with** fears of instability. The **word is commonly associated with** youth culture.
discuss	idea, problem, issue, question, topic, theme	at length, briefly, thoroughly	Wilson and Crick (1965) **discuss the problem at length**. Sim's article **discusses the issue thoroughly**.
establish	relationship, connection	firmly, clearly, conclusively	Geologists have been unable to **firmly establish a connection between** the two types of fossils. Lopez **conclusively establishes a relationship between** the two phenomena.
examine	facts, evidence, effects, aspects	briefly, critically, thoroughly	We shall now **briefly examine the evidence** for the existence of dark matter. Our aim is to **thoroughly examine the effects of** stress.
demonstrate	existence, need, effects, importance	clearly, convincingly	The study clearly **demonstrates the importance of** support for dementia sufferers. Harvey's work **convincingly demonstrates the need** for a new approach to the problem.
identify (with) (often used in passive)	causes, factors, issues, properties, needs, approach, origin	correctly, clearly, closely	This **approach is closely identified with** the work **of** H. Crowley during the 1950s. The article **clearly identifies the factors** influencing the decision to go to war.

B More verbs in combination with nouns, adverbs and prepositions

pose: This **inevitably poses a question** concerning the stability of society. Parks **poses a challenge** to Kahn's theory.

suggest: The most recent results **strongly suggest a different interpretation** of the situation. The article **suggests a new approach** to the problem.

list: Here I **simply list** the main **hypotheses** / **causes** / **features** / **characteristics**; they will be examined in detail below.

refer: The book **refers frequently** / **specifically** / **in passing** to the 1956 economic crisis.

observe: This is due to the **changes** / **trends** / **differences** we **observed** earlier.

Common Mistake

Remember we say *based on* NOT ~~based in~~.
We say *discuss a problem / an issue* NOT ~~discuss about a problem~~

Exercises

12.1 **Choose the most appropriate adverb for each underlined verb, and add it to the sentence in the correct place.**

1. Paulson's research demonstrated the need for a new approach to the study of stress. (invariably convincingly closely)
2. As was observed, there is a strong correlation between house prices and inflation. (closely critically earlier)
3. In the study of languages, 'tense' refers to the coding of time in form of the verb. (specifically strongly briefly)
4. Classical liberal economics is identified with the theories of Milton Friedman. (thoroughly closely conclusively)
5. Chapter 1 discusses the main issues, but they are dealt with in detail in Chapter 2. (closely simply briefly)
6. To date, no research exists that establishes a connection between behaviour, personality traits, and leadership traits. (firmly thoroughly critically)
7. SENTA is a computer programming language based on Logo. (strongly slightly loosely)
8. Social research techniques were applied to examine the effects of the policy on the poor. (strongly mainly critically)

12.2 **Complete the sentences with suitable nouns. There may be more than one possible answer.**

1. Here we list again the main .... of the present study and show which have been proven and which have been rejected.
2. The graph enables us to observe recent broad .... in mortality rates.
3. The researchers concluded that it is still difficult to identify the .... of the time-related changes in human beings that we call ageing.
4. A seminar was held to discuss the .... of children's rights in the light of the Convention on the Rights of the Child.
5. Wu demonstrated the .... for a comprehensive plan in preparation for a pandemic.

12.3 **Cross out the one noun which does not fit in each sentence. Use a dictionary if necessary.**

1. These figures lead me to suggest an alternative *theory / solution / importance / interpretation*.
2. It is clear that these developments pose a new *question / challenge / threat / factor*.
3. Before we reach any conclusion, it is important to examine the *matters / evidence / facts / issues*.

12.4 **The following text contains eight more useful verb + adverb combinations. Read the text and underline them.**

The world is facing a looming water crisis. Disputes over allocation have steadily increased in the last decade, and demand has grown rapidly. Water is likely to generate the same degree of controversy in the 21st century as oil did in the 20th. If we take no action now, new conflicts are likely to occur periodically around the world. At the moment, instead of seeking solutions which directly address multiple needs, countries focus a little too narrowly on local issues and typically opt for expensive and inferior solutions. What is needed are decisions which can be quickly implemented and a debate which will seriously consider more than the short-term needs of individual states.

12.5 **Complete the sentences using verb + adverb combinations from 12.4.**

1. Various measures were introduced last year to .... the issue of identity theft.
2. The justice system needs to .... the impact of a prison sentence on offenders.
3. The number of university applications has been .... over the last 50 years.
4. The article .... on one aspect of the problem rather than taking a broad view.
5. The suggested measures should be .... to avoid further problems.

13 Prepositional phrases

Notice the prepositional phrases in bold in the texts below.

A A book review

★★★★

The *Guide to the Semi-Colon in English* was written by Keith Pedant **in conjunction with**[1] a team of researchers at Boredham University. **In comparison with** previous works on the semi-colon, this is a very substantial volume. **In addition to** the main text there are a number of appendices. These are **to some extent**[2] the most useful parts of the book as, **in line with**[3] modern linguistic practice, they provide a wealth of real data. **In spite of** its potentially dry topic, the book contains many fascinating examples, in the sections dealing with the history of the semi-colon **in particular. With the exception of**[4] the final chapter, this book may be of some interest to the general reader as well as the specialist but **on the whole**[5] is mainly for those who have a professional interest in punctuation marks. If it fails **in any respect**[6], it is **in relation to**[7] recent changes in the punctuation of e-communication, **in terms of**[8] the conventions of text-messaging, tweets and similar media.

[1] working together with [2] notice also **to a greater** / **lesser** / **certain extent** [3] following; also **in accordance with** [4] not including [5] generally [6] or **in any way** [7] in connection with [8] describes which particular area of a subject is being discussed

B A talk to a genealogy club

Chairperson: Now, **at this stage**[1] in the proceedings it's my pleasure to introduce our speaker tonight, Dr Anna Klein, the country's leading family history specialist. Anna, I'd like to welcome you **on behalf of**[2] all our members. Ladies and gentlemen, **in view of**[3] the fact that we only have 45 minutes, I would ask you to keep any questions till the end of Dr Klein's talk. Thank you.

Anna Klein: Thank you. Er … I should confess **from the outset**[4] that my own interest in genealogy came about **as a result of** discovering some old letters in the attic at home. You know, I found them purely **by chance**[5]. They'd been written by some relatives who'd emigrated to Canada a hundred years or so before … and for me, as a ten-year-old then, they were **by far**[6] the most exciting things I'd ever read. They were, **for the most part**[7], extremely well-written and, **from then on**[8], I was determined to learn as much as I could about my family. **In other words**[9], I had started out on my genealogical journey. **In some ways** I was very lucky. I was able, **so to speak**[10], to get to know my family **on the basis of** the old letters and this enabled me to track down some relations living in Montreal. They, **in turn**, provided some contacts with Australian cousins and so it continued. **In the process**[11], I've learnt a great deal, not only about my own family, but also **as regards** how to approach tracing one's family. **In most respects**[12] it's been a thoroughly enjoyable adventure though there have been some difficult moments …

[1] now, also **at this point** [2] representing [3] because of [4] from the beginning [5] accidentally [6] very much [7] generally [8] since that moment [9] to express something differently [10] what I am saying is not to be understood exactly as stated [11] while doing this [12] considering most aspects of the experience

Common Mistake

On the one hand and *on the other hand* are used to compare and contrast two different ways of looking at an issue. Do not confuse *on the other hand* with *on the contrary. On the contrary* means that the previous statement is not true or not correct. *Stoneworkers use a variety of names for types of stone. Geologists,* ***on the other hand****, use names that are too technical or specialised for ordinary use.* (Not: ~~Geologists, on the contrary, use names …~~)

Exercises

13.1 Look at the press announcements and complete the prepositional phrases with the missing words.

1 Professor Soltero said that, ... line .... government guidelines, the team would consult the local community as .... the best solution to the siting of the drilling platform. She promised that the community would be fully involved .... outset and that her team, ... turn, would inform the public at every stage.

2 A spokesperson for the company said that, ... stage, there is no proof of the side-effects of the drug, but in .... of the public concern, the company was withdrawing it. .... spite .... this necessary measure, she was sure that the drug would soon return to the market.

3 Dr Leiman said that while .... the .... hand the government wanted to encourage research, ... the .... hand they were reducing funding for universities; in .... words, research would inevitably suffer.

4 .... addition .... a new building on the campus, the team will receive a very generous grant to conduct their research. In .... to the university's plan, this represents an exciting and much-awaited development. .... particular, the new facility would attract outside investment.

5 .... the exception .... one study in 1986, no major research has been carried out into the problem, Dr Peters stated. The greatest need by .... at the moment was a concerted effort to kick-start a research programme.

6 Professor Karpal said that, ... the basis .... her studies so far, she was optimistic that a cure for the disease would be found. To .... extent, there was already cause for optimism, but, for the most ...., hopes had to rest on the possibility of a breakthrough in the near future.

7 Lauren Charles said that, ... whole, social conditions had improved since the report, especially .... terms .... jobs and housing for the poorer sectors. If economic and social policy had failed .... respect, it was in child care for the less well-off.

8 The professor said that he was delighted to accept the award .... behalf .... the whole university. He said that, in some ...., he had been the lucky one, ... speak, in that he had been able to work in .... with such a wonderful team.

13.2 Choose the correct prepositional phrases to complete the paragraph.

A bone discovered [1]*by chance / to some extent in the* 17th century was the beginning of the search for dinosaurs.[2]*By far / From then on*, scientists and the public have been fascinated by these creatures. [3]*In accordance with / In addition to* beliefs at that time, the initial discovery was thought to be the bone of a human giant. However, in 1824, a scientist, William Buckland, calculated that the bone belonged to a12-metre flesh-eating reptile and named it *Megalosaurus*, [4]*in comparison / in the process* giving us the first of the wonderful list of exotic names for dinosaurs. The 17th century discovery had, [5]*in turn / in other words*, led to a series of further finds around that time. All these [6]*to a greater or lesser extent / in any respect* confirmed Buckland's theories. [7]*By far / In turn* the biggest dinosaur discovered to date was probably over 40 metres long. [8]*For the most part / In comparison*, dinosaurs ranged from the size of a chicken to that of a giraffe. [9]*In most respects / In other words*, what we know about their habits is still very limited. What we do know is at least [10]*by chance / to some extent* based on pure speculation. [11]*On the contrary / On the other hand*, recent progress in the study of DNA is offering new possibilities for a better understanding of these creatures.

Over to you

Use a dictionary or search websites related to your studies to find an example sentence using each of these phrases: *on the one hand, on the other hand, on behalf of, as a result of, with the exception of, except*. Write them out and then add one more sentence for each one relating to your own studies.

14 Verbs and prepositions

A Verbs with *on* – sentences from academic articles

Chapter 1 of Huang's book **focuses on** violent human behaviour.
Sura's article **draws on** data gathered over a period of ten years. [uses in support of his/her case]

The introduction to the book **comments** briefly **on** a case study carried out in Brazil.

In this section I **concentrate on** the economic aspects of immigration.

The book **is based on** a number of studies carried out during the 1990s. [often used in passive]
The method used by Scanlon **relies on** / **rests on*** two basic principles. [*(formal) is based on]

B Verbs with *to* – teachers talk to students

We **assigned**[1] the tasks randomly **to** the experimental group and the control group to see how the subjects would **react to** the different problems.

Malaria poses a major health risk to people who **are exposed to** infection where malaria is common. Last year 13% of deaths among children **were attributed to**[2] malaria in one area of Zaire.

OK, let's **turn to** the more difficult cases that I mentioned earlier. How should a doctor **respond to** a patient who doesn't **consent to** treatment when it seems to be essential?

We can't really say that an increase in inflation of two per cent **amounts to**[4] an economic crisis, and I **refer** here **to** some recent stories in the media which are highly exaggerated and which can **be traced to**[5] a deep misunderstanding of how inflation operates.

When you're planning a questionnaire, you should always **attend to**[3] design issues such as the number of questions and how clear they are.

[1] give a particular job or piece of work to someone [2] say or think that something is the result of something (often used in passive) [3] deal with something, give your attention to something [4] be the same as something, or have the same effect as something [5] discover the origin of something by examining how it has developed (often used in passive)

C Other verb + preposition combinations

verbs + prepositions	examples
associate, provide, couple, equip + **with**	We try to **equip** our laboratories **with** the latest technology. Heart disease is often **associated with** unhealthy lifestyles. Note: In the active voice, as in the first example, this group of verbs follows the pattern verb + object + preposition + complement. Note also that these verbs are often used in the passive, as in the second example.
depart, benefit, emerge, exclude + **from**	In this book, Herne **departs from** his earlier theory. [takes a different view] Some of the data **were excluded from** the final analysis.
write, speak, convince, dispose + **of**	Abuka **writes / speaks of** the early years of industrial development. [both are rather formal] We must **convince** people **of** the need for water conservation.
account, search, call, argue + **for**	Lung cancer **accounted for** 20% of deaths in men. [formed a total of] Hopper (1987) **argues for** a new approach to English grammar. [opposite: **argue against**]

Common Mistake

The verbs *emphasise* and *stress* are used without any preposition (NOT ~~on~~). *The study* ***emphasises / stresses*** *the need for more controlled experiments to back up the conclusions.*
Divide is followed by *into* (NOT divide ~~in~~). *The subjects* ***were divided into*** *three groups.*

Exercises

14.1 **Choose the correct prepositions.**

1 The article focuses *in / on* economic changes.
2 The origins of the festival have been traced *on / to* a medieval celebration.
3 The professor commented *in / on* the students' essays in some detail.
4 It took the politicians some time to convince others *in / of* the need for change.
5 The theory is based *in / on* a series of hypotheses.
6 Jackson departed *from / off* his usual style in his final novel.
7 The research relies *in / on* some unusual experiments.
8 You must concentrate *in / on* your studies if you are to do well in your exams.
9 The author has drawn *in / on* some interesting primary sources.
10 Clark never spoke *of / at* his life during the 1930s.

14.2 **Complete the phrases with the correct prepositions.**

1 account .... a discrepancy in the figures
2 argue .... equality
3 assign something .... group A
4 be associated .... technological change
5 attribute a quotation .... someone
6 benefit .... government reforms
7 call .... an improvement in working conditions
8 consent .... medical treatment
9 convince someone .... your point of view
10 dispose .... waste paper
11 equip a lecture hall .... an interactive whiteboard
12 exclude someone .... society
13 provide students .... a reading list
14 react .... change
15 refer .... a source
16 search .... proof

14.3 **Complete the sentences with the correct form of verb + preposition combinations from 14.2.**

1 The lecturer .... us .... a number of very good writers on the subject.
2 Traffic accidents .... most hospital admissions at the weekend.
3 The poets John Keats and Lord Byron are closely .... the English Romantic Movement.
4 Remember to carefully .... all waste material.
5 Most people believe that they would .... enormously .... having more job security.
6 My parents tried to .... me .... the advantages of studying abroad.
7 I have been .... an article on this topic for ages.
8 Our experiments .... us .... the data we needed to prove our hypothesis.
9 The head of department .... the lecturer's request for leave of absence.
10 The professor .... positively .... the ideas I raised in my assignment.

14.4 **Correct the mistakes with prepositions in the sentences.**

1 The course leader divided her students in groups.
2 They had to trace everyone who had been exposed for the infection.
3 At the moment we have too few nurses attending at too many patients.
4 Excellent teaching coupled for first-class research have made this a successful college.
5 The country emerged off the crisis as a much stronger power.
6 Joe acquired an interest in politics from his uncle who often spoke over his days as a senator.
7 The government called to an investigation into the explosion at the nuclear reactor.
8 In your speech don't forget to emphasise on the advantages of studying here.

15 Nouns and prepositions

A Groups of related nouns sharing prepositions

Sometimes groups of nouns with related meanings share the same prepositions.

nouns	preposition	example
book, article, paper, essay, lecture, talk, seminar, presentation, dissertation, thesis, project, assignment	about, on	In 1978, Da Silva published a **book about**[1] the history of emigration. She wrote a **dissertation on**[2] teenage slang in New York and gave a **presentation on** it to the whole class.
research (see also B), investigation, inquiry	into	Kelly (1969) conducted an **investigation into** the origins of international terrorism.
analysis, examination, exploration (see also B), study	of	The article offers an **analysis of** the potential impact of the HSN I Avian Flu virus.
problem, difficulty, issue	of, with	He gave a lecture on the **problem of** global warming. One **difficulty with** this approach is that a set of results may allow different interpretations.
motivation, rationale (see also B)	for	Economists have recently questioned the **rationale for** government spending.

[1] and [2] *about* tends to be used for more general subjects; *on* is frequently used for more specific, detailed works, although both may be found in both uses. See also the notes on prepositions after nouns in Unit 46.

B Nouns commonly associated with particular prepositions

You can also learn the nouns which most frequently come before a particular preposition. Some of these are in A above. The following examples are all titles of academic articles.

nouns	preposition	example
look, attempt, point, age, rate	at	An **attempt at** integration of economic and psychological theories of consumption The relationship between obesity and the **age at** which hip and knee replacement is undertaken
changes, differences, increase, decrease	in	Gender **differences in** risk-taking in financial decision making
insight, inquiry, research, investigation	into	An **investigation into** sleep characteristics of children with autism
work, research, influence, emphasis, effect	on	Genetic **influence on** smoking - a study of male twins
basis, idea, part, lack, exploration, means	of	A computerised clinical decision support system as a **means of** implementing depression guidelines.
need, basis, case, preference	for	Assessing organisational culture: the **case for** multiple methods
relation, approach, response, attention	to	Communicating with strangers: an **approach to** intercultural communication
attitude, tendency, move, progress	to/towards	**Progress towards** sustainable regional development
principle, rationale, assumptions, logic	behind	Questioning the **assumptions behind** art criticism
relationship, difference, distinction	between	The **relationship between** educational technology and student achievement in mathematics

Common Mistake

The noun *reason* is followed by *for*, not *of*: *The* ***reason for*** *this change may be found in the development of a service-based economy.* (Not ~~The reason of this change~~ ...)

Exercises

15.1 **Complete the sentences with the correct prepositions. There may be more than one possible answer.**

1 One difficulty .... the questionnaire was the small number of respondents. The reason .... this was that some students had already left the course and could not be contacted.
2 She wrote a dissertation .... wild conservation in Finland in the 1990s. It is now considered to be one of the best studies .... conservation of its kind.
3 The book is an exploration .... the origins of the economic crisis of 2008. It offers new insights .... the events that led up to the crash.
4 I went to an interesting presentation .... research .... aspects of the human brain. The speaker began by saying that the rationale .... his investigation was the need to better understand the ageing process.
5 Research .... spoken language has been assisted in recent years by the availability of computerised databases or 'corpora'. The basis .... such research is that it is difficult to be objective about how we speak without recorded evidence.
6 Prippen's (1984) book was an inquiry .... the foundations of nationalism. Her approach .... the problem, however, was somewhat Euro-centric.
7 Can you recommend a good book .... educational policy? I'm looking for something that has a proper look .... the relationship .... social deprivation and educational achievement.
8 He did a study .... the problem of side-impact automobile collisions. All the car manufacturers seem to be paying more attention these days .... safety.

15.2 **Correct the mistakes with prepositions in the sentences. There may more than one mistake in each sentence.**

1 Her dissertation produced some interesting insights to how young children develop a visual sense and the age in which development is most noticeable.
2 The reason of people being unwilling to be interviewed after the demonstration was that they were afraid of being arrested later.
3 As regards solar phenomena, Hierstat's approach at the analysis is different from that of Donewski. He questioned the assumptions under much of the previous research.
4 Changes of the temperature of the soil were measured over time.
5 A lack in funding led to the project being cancelled, and social scientists blamed the government's negative attitude on social science research.
6 Jawil's article puts great emphasis into the need of more research over the problem and argues the case of greater attention on the underlying causes.

15.3 **Match each noun with the preposition that usually follows it.**

attitude difference effect emphasis insight preference principle rationale reason relationship tendency	behind between for into on to/towards

15.4 **Underline some more noun + preposition combinations in the text.**

The possible ecological <u>effects of</u> climate change are often in the news, as is the matter of whether the potential impact can be predicted. New work on a migratory[1] bird, the pied flycatcher, takes things a stage further by showing how a climate-related population decline was actually caused. Timing is key. Over the past 17 years flycatchers declined strongly in areas where caterpillar[2] numbers (food for the nestlings[3]) peak early, but in areas with a late food peak there was no decline. The young birds arrive too late in places where the caterpillars have already responded to early warmth. Mistiming like this is probably a common consequence of climate change, and may be a major factor in the decline of many long-distance migratory bird species.

[1] which travels to a different place, usually when the season changes [2] small, long animal with many legs which turns into a butterfly [3] young birds

16 Chunks: useful phrases

If we look at a corpus of academic texts, we see that certain chunks of language occur very frequently in spoken and written contexts. This unit looks at some of the most useful ones.

A Chunks expressing number, quantity, degree

Look at these comments written by a college teacher on assignments handed in by her students.

A good paper. It's clear you've spent **a great deal of** time researching the subject and you quote **a wide range of** sources.

Grade: B

Some good points here but it's not clear **to what extent** you're aware of all the issues involved. Global trade affects trade **in a variety of ways**.

Grade: C

I think you've misunderstood the topic **to some extent**. You've written **in excess of**[1] 3,000 words on areas that are not entirely relevant. Let's talk.

Grade: F

[1] more than

B Chunks for generalising and specifying

In this class discussion, the students make fairly general statements, while the teacher tries to make the discussion more specific.

Marsha: Well, I think **on the whole** parents should take more responsibility for their kids.

Teacher: Yes, **with respect to**[1] home life, yes, but **in the case of** violence, surely the wider community is involved, isn't it? I mean, **for the purposes of** our discussions about social stability, everyone's involved, aren't they?

Marsha: Yes, but **in general** I don't think people want to get involved in violent incidents, **as a rule** at least. They get scared off.

Teacher: True. But **as far as** general discipline **is concerned**, don't you think it's a community-wide issue? I mean discipline **as regards**[2] everyday actions, **with the exception of** school discipline. What do you think, **in terms of** public life, Tariq?

Tariq: I think the community **as a whole** does care about crime and discipline and things, but **for the most part** they see violence as something that is outside of them, you know, not their direct responsibility.

Teacher: OK. So, let's consider the topic **in more detail**[3], I mean **from the point of view of** violence and aggression specifically in schools. Let's look at some extracts from the American Medical Association's 2012 report on bullying. They're on the handout.

[1] or **in respect of**, or (more neutral) **with regard to** [2] another neutral alternative to 1
[3] or (more formally) **in greater detail**

C Chunks for linking points and arguments

The increase in house sales is **due to the fact that** inflation fell in 2004. **At the same time**, tax rate reductions were beginning to have an effect.

Joslav used an eight-point scale in the questionnaire, **as opposed to**[1] a four-point one, **by means of which** he showed that attitudes covered a very wide range, **in the sense that** the results were spread very evenly over all eight points.

It's very difficult to interpret these data. **Be that as it may**[2], there is some evidence of a decline in frequency. **For this reason**, we decided to repeat the experiment.

In addition to surveying the literature on population movements, we also reviewed work carried out on family names in five regions.

[1] rather than [2] a typical academic way of saying 'although I accept that this is true'; more common in speech than in writing

Exercises

16.1 Read the feedback to a student from a teacher and complete it with the correct chunks from A opposite.

You have had a very good term [1] ....
You have done [2] .... work and have also taken part in [3] .... social activities.
Your sporting activities may have interfered with your studies [4] .... but you still managed to write [5] .... 5,000 words for your end-of-term assignment, which, I am pleased to report, was of a high standard.

16.2 Complete the chunks with the correct words.

1 .... a rule
2 .... the same time
3 be .... as it may
4 .... the most part
5 .... this reason
6 .... general
7 .... terms of
8 on .... whole

16.3 Rewrite the underlined words and phrases using chunks from 16.2.

My dissertation topic may be complicated but, despite that, I have absolutely no regrets about choosing it. I have always been interested in the Romantic movement in English literature and that's why I decided to compare Romantic poetry in different European countries. I've focused mainly on poets from Britain and Germany. Although usually essay-writing comes easily to me, I'm finding it difficult to get down to writing up my research because I'm supposed to be revising for a couple of exams at the moment too. But I shan't have any problems when it comes to finding enough to say on the subject.

16.4 Decide which chunk in each set has a different meaning. Explain why it is different.

1 in general, by means of which, as a rule, on the whole
2 as regards X, as far as X is concerned, with the exception of X, with respect to X
3 as a whole, in addition to, for the most part, in general

16.5 Choose the best chunk to complete each sentence.

1 .... our discussion I'd like to focus on the US context.
A For the purposes of B In the sense that C From the point of view of
2 There is some evidence of an improvement in the economy but, ..., there is unlikely to be much change before next year.
A for this reason B as a rule C be that as it may
3 I'd like to consider education .... industry.
A in the case of B from the point of view of C with the exception of
4 I'm not sure .... you agree with Qian's theory.
A by means of which B to what extent C as regards
5 We will now discuss the development of the Surrealist Movement ....
A on the whole B to some extent C in more detail

16.6 Complete the sentences with your own ideas.

1 I enjoy watching most sports with the exception of …
2 A poor relationship between parents and children is often due to the fact that …
3 I love reading novels as opposed to …
4 In your first year of graduate school you have to take an end-of-year exam in addition to …
5 It was a very useful course in the sense that …

Over to you

Choose six chunks from this unit that you would particularly like to learn. Write them down in sentences that relate to your own studies.

17 Abbreviations and affixes

A Common abbreviations used in academic contexts

abbreviation	stands for	example or comment
e.g.	for example (from Latin, *exempli gratia*)	Many large mammals, **e.g.** the African elephant, the black rhino and the white rhino …
i.e.	that is (from Latin, *id est*)	Higher earners, **i.e.** those earning over £100,000 a year …
etc.	and so on (from Latin, *et cetera*)	Smaller European countries (Slovenia, Slovakia, Estonia, **etc.**) had different interests.
NB	note carefully (from Latin, *nota bene*)	**NB** You must answer all the questions on this page.
et al	and others (from Latin, *et alii*)	used when giving bibliographical reference, e.g. as mentioned in Potts **et al** (1995)
ibid.	in the same place as the preceding footnote (from Latin, *ibidem*)	I Lee, D. S. (1987) *History of Tea-Drinking in Europe*. 2 **ibid**.
Cf	compare (from Latin, *confer*)	**cf** Löfstedt (2005) for a different approach.
op. cit.	see previously quoted work by author (from Latin, *opus citatum*)	Potts **op**. **cit**. 33–54
ed(s).	editor(s)	used when giving bibliographical references
vol.	volume	used when giving bibliographical references
p. / pp.	page / pages	See McKinley 2015 **pp**. 11–19.

B Affixes: common prefixes and suffixes

prefix	meaning	examples
anti-	against	anti-bacterial, anti-pollution
bi-	two, twice	bilingual, bi-monthly
co-, col-, com-, con-	with	co-author, cooperate, collaborate, combine
contra-, counter-	against, opposing	contradict, counter-claim
eco-	relating to the environment	eco-tourism, eco-friendly
hyper-	having too much	hyperactive, hyper-inflation
il-, im-, in-, ir-	not	illogical, impossible, indistinct, irregular
inter-	between, connected	interrelated, interact
mal-	badly	malfunction, malpractice
multi-	many	multilingual, multi-storey
over-	too much	overload, overworked
pre-	before	pre-industrial, pre-war
post-	after	post-war, post-colonial

suffix	meaning	examples
-able	can be	predictable, identifiable
-ant	having an effect	coolant, anti-depressant
-cy	state or quality	accuracy, urgency
-ee	person affected by something	employee, trainee
-hood	state, condition	childhood, adulthood
-ify	give something a quality	clarify, purify
-ism / -ist	belief / person with that belief	heroism, modernism, anarchist, optimist
-ise, -ize	bring about a state or condition	modernise/ize, colonise/ize
-less	without	meaningless, colourless, fearless
-ocracy / -ocrat	type of ruling body, person ruling	autocracy, autocrat
-proof	protected against, safe from	waterproof, soundproof

Exercises

17.1 Replace the underlined words with abbreviations from A opposite.

1 Timson <u>and co-authors</u> (2008) discuss this issue extensively (however, <u>compare</u> Donato 2010, who takes a different view).
2 The article was published in a special issue of the *Journal of Sports Technology* in 2012 (<u>volume</u> 10, <u>pages</u> 256–279).
3 Some nouns in English have irregular plural forms, <u>for example</u> *mouse*, *sheep* and *woman*. For further examples, see Mitchelson and Friel (<u>editors</u>) 1995.
4 <u>Please note:</u> this and all further references to population statistics are taken from Aspenall (<u>work already cited</u>).
5 Smart phones, tablets <u>and so on</u> have made mobile learning a reality for many students around the world (Dudeney <u>same reference as the previous one</u>).
6 Blended learning (<u>that is to say</u> integrating the use of technology into learning and teaching) is now the norm in many university programmes.

17.2 Complete the sentences with the correct prefixes and suffixes. Use a dictionary if necessary.

1 The war began in 1986 and ended in 1990. During the ....-war period (1980-86), the economy was stable, but in the ....-war years (1991-1997) there were severe economic problems. ....-inflation meant that prices increased by 200% in just one year. Economic .... operation with neighbouring countries had ceased during hostilities and only resumed in 1998. Attempts to un.......... the different currencies of the region at that time proved unsuccessful.
2 The research symposium takes place ....-annually; we have one every six months in a different university. However, we need to public.......... it more on our website to increase the numbers attending. It is aimed at teacher train.........., especially those who will commence teaching in the following academic year.
3 There was a .... function and the circuit became .... heated, so the equipment shut down. We need to mod.......... the procedure so that it does not happen again. A new type of cool.......... will be used to keep the temperature constant.
4 ....-pollution measures brought in by the city authorities included reducing on-street parking spaces to discourage motorists from driving into the city centre and the closure of three ....-storey car parks with the same aim in mind. Better ....-connections between the various transport systems (buses, trains and ferries) were also planned.
5 In order to function in extreme conditions, the generator had to be both water.......... and dust.......... . An ....-friendly version of the generator, powered by wind, is also being developed. It is port.........., so it can be easily carried to wherever it is needed.
6 Claims and ....-claims about the assassination of the president have been made in the media. What we need now is an objective investigation to clar.......... the motives of the killers. There is a strong likeli.......... that an extrem.......... religious movement was behind the attack.

17.3 Complete the table with the correct suffixes. Do not fill the shaded boxes. Use a dictionary if necessary.

noun(s)	verb	adjective
modernity	modern..........	modern
sad..........	sadden	sad
fear		fear..........
urgen..........		urgent
demo.........., demo..........	demo..........	democratic
beauty	beauti..........	beautiful
Marx..........		Marxist
accura..........		accurate

18 Applications and application forms

Here we look at applying for a place at a UK university. Institutions in other countries may have slightly different processes. These will be described on their web pages.

A Preparing to apply

Read this information about preparing an application for postgraduate study.

What should I do first?
Do all you can to learn about the **careers** that will be open to you after studying – and what **qualifications** you will need in order to get the job you want.

What qualifications do I need for postgraduate study?
A **first degree** is **required** to study at postgraduate level.
The specific **entry requirements** for each course of study are listed on the individual course pages.
If needed, **clarification**[1] may be **sought**[2] from the department you are applying to.
Your performance in previous schooling is very important to your application **profile**[3].

What are the requirements for international students?
In addition to the general admission requirements, international applicants must **submit**[4]:

- A **transcript**[5] of university courses and grades, translated into English, and
- Results of the International English Language Testing System (IELTS) or Test of English as a Foreign Language (TOEFL), unless you have received **English-medium**[6] education for at least one year.

Applicants must have a **minimum** IELTS **score** of 6.5 or a TOEFL score of 580.

Are any grants[7] **or scholarships**[8] **available for international students?**
Visit our International Office pages for details.

[1] making clearer by giving more details [2] past participle of seek: 'to look for' [3] overall character of the application [4] give something officially [5] official document listing courses completed and grades [6] where all the classes are taught in English [7] money given to enable a person to study [8] money given by a college or university to pay for the studies of a talented student

B The application process

Look at this email from Tania to Liam. Tania is applying to study at Wanstow University.

Hi Liam,

At last I've **filled in** my **application form** and sent it off. It took ages. As well as all my personal details they wanted the names of two **referees**[1] , **financial guarantees**[2], and I had to attach a **personal statement** saying why I wanted to go to Wanstow. Anyway, the **deadline**[3] is next Friday, then the website said they'd take about six weeks to **process**[4] the application after they **acknowledge**[5] it, then I might be **called for**[6] an interview. By that time the **references** have to be in. I'm just hoping that because I'm a **mature student**[7] I might have a good chance of being **offered a place** – Wanstow has a lot of mature students and they have a strong **equal opportunities policy**[8]. The **fees**[9] are pretty high, but I can get a **student loan**[10] if I **get in**[11].

Love, Tania

[1] person who knows you and who is willing to support your application [2] proof of ability to pay [3] final date by which something must be done [4] deal with documents officially [5] say that they have received it [6] asked to attend [7] a student who is older than the usual age [8] principle of treating all people the same, regardless of sex, race, religion, etc. [9] amount of money paid for a particular service [10] money which must be repaid when you have completed your studies [11] (informal) am accepted

Exercises

18.1 Read the text in A opposite and answer a potential student's questions about the university.

1 Is it possible to do a postgraduate degree without having been to university before?
2 Where can I get more information about what qualifications I need for a specific course?
3 Will they want to know about my university grades?
4 When is an IELTS or TOEFL score not needed?
5 What IELTS score should applicants have?

18.2 Match the two parts of the word combinations.

1 personal	4 student	7 application
2 financial	5 equal	8 first
3 seek	6 mature	9 minimum

a opportunities	d degree	g statement
b score	e form	h clarification
c student	f guarantee	i loan

18.3 Rewrite the underlined words and phrases using word combinations from 18.2.

1 To get a place on the course I need to get <u>at least 6.5 at IELTS</u>.
2 Most of the people on this master's course <u>graduated</u> in economics..
3 This college welcomes applications from <u>students who are applying later in life</u>.
4 If you don't understand anything in our prospectus, the best place to <u>look for answers to your questions</u> is our website.
5 Your <u>description of yourself and why you want to do this course</u> must be no more than 300 words.
6 The university requires <u>proof that you can pay your fees</u>.

18.4 Complete the stages of applying to university with the correct words. Then number them in the order in which they usually happen.

☐ wait for the application to be ....
☐ find an appropriate .... at a university
☐ decide on what .... you would like to do after your studies
☐ be .... a place
☐ be .... for an interview
☐ check that you fulfil the necessary ....
☐ fill in the ....

18.5 Complete the email with the missing words. The first letter of each word is given to help you.

Hi Miles,

I'd love a [1]c.................. as an international lawyer and am really hoping I can [2]g .... in to Wanstow University to do a postgraduate course in law there. I've [3]f .... in all the necessary forms and just hope that my academic [4]p .... will be good enough for them. I think I fulfil all their [5]e .... r.................. but who knows! It took me ages to get the [6]t .... of my college [7]g .... etc. translated but I managed to get everything in by the [8]d.................., and Professor Atkins has agreed to act as my [9]r.................., which is great. So now I just have to wait to see if they [10]c .... me for an interview or not. Fingers crossed!

Lucia

Over to you

Look at the website of any English-speaking university that interests you. What information do they provide about applying to that university? Make a note of any other useful vocabulary you find there.

19 The social and academic environment

A Places

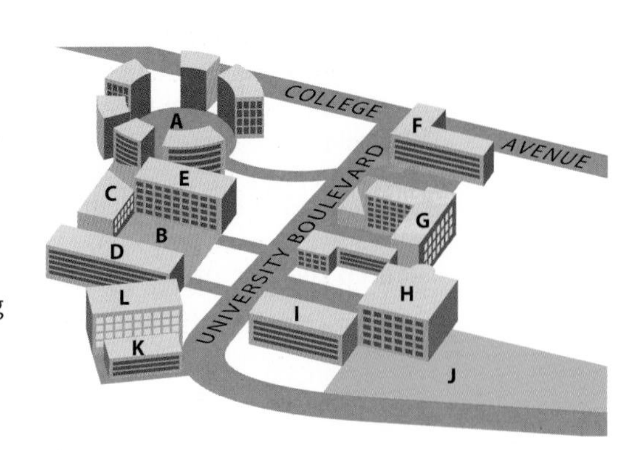

Key

A **Halls of residence**[1]
B Staff car park
C **Administration**[2] Building
D Arts **Faculty**[3] Building
E **Great Hall**[4]
F University **Health Centre**
G **Cafeteria**
H University **Library**
I **Student Union**[5]
J **Sports ground**
K **School**[6] of Engineering
L Arts **Lecture Theatre**[7]

[1] a building where students live [2] the main offices [3] a group of similar **departments** [4] a large hall where graduation ceremonies are held [5] a building where students meet socially [6] part of a university specialising in a particular subject; also **department** [7] a large hall where lectures are held

B People, structures and activities

person	meaning / example
professor	a senior university teacher: *The Head of Department is* Professor *Bradley.*
lecturer	a university teacher: *She's now a senior lecturer.*
staff	all the teachers in a university; also **faculty** AmE
head of department	the most senior person in a department
tutor	a teacher who looks after one student or a small group: *All students have a personal tutor.*
supervisor	a teacher with responsibility for a particular student's work; **adviser** AmE: *a dissertation supervisor*
postgraduate student	a student who has completed their first degree and is studying for a second degree; **graduate student** AmE
research student	a postgraduate student doing research
research assistant	someone who is paid to do research at the university
student counsellor	someone trained to give students advice about their problems
postgrad rep	someone who acts officially for postgraduate students; **postgraduate representative**

A **lecture** is a large formal class where students listen and take notes. A **seminar** is a smaller discussion group. A **tutorial** is a very small group where students discuss their work with a teacher.

A **semester** is a time when a university is open (also **term** BrE). A **vacation** is a time when it is closed (also **holiday** BrE). The **office hours** are the hours when the university offices are open.

C Ways of talking about academic life: American (AmE) and British English (BrE)

In the UK, **school** is your primary or secondary education. **University** is your undergraduate years. A **college** is a place that specialises in certain subjects, for example an art college. When you go to university, you start as a **fresher** in your first year, then you become a **second-year** student and, next, a **third-year** student, etc.

In the USA, **school** is often used to mean university. For example, you can say you go to Cornell **University**, or you go to school at Harvard. **College** refers to your undergraduate years. When you go to college, you start as a **freshman** in your first year. The following year you become a **sophomore**, then a **junior** and finally a **senior** in your fourth year.

Exercises

19.1 **Look at the map in A opposite. Which building must students go to if they want to:**

1 speak to a lecturer in the history department?
2 find information about student clubs?
3 visit a friend in the student accommodation?
4 listen to a talk about English literature?
5 attend a graduation ceremony?
6 enquire about payment of fees?
7 see a doctor?
8 borrow a book?

19.2 **Look at the information in B opposite and answer the questions.**

1 Are there likely to be more people in a seminar or a tutorial?
2 Who is the academic who guides a postgraduate student through their dissertation?
3 What word is used for the holiday period between university terms or semesters?
4 What is the difference between a personal tutor and a student counsellor?
5 What is the difference between a postgrad rep and a research assistant?

19.3 **Complete the email with the missing words.**

Hi Mum,

I've settled in well here at Wanstow. I like my room in this hall of [1].................................. . I went to my first [2].................................. this morning – it was on research methodology - and there were hundreds of students there. The [3].................................. was very good – it was Professor Jones, our head of [4].................................. . Tomorrow I'll have my first [5].................................. – that'll be just me and one other student. We'll be discussing what we have to get done by the end of the [6].................................. . I need to try to think some more about the topic for my [7].................................. . When that is finalised I'll be assigned a [8].................................. . I'll be expected to see him or her at least once a week during their office [9].................................. . I hope I'll like him or her. You hear some awful stories!

Daisy

19.4 **Write the words in the box under the correct headings.**

cafeteria counsellor sophomore lecture lecturer librarian library faculty (AmE) professor semester junior research assistant research student seminar faculty (BrE) sports centre sports grounds tutor tutorial lecture theatre

people	places	events or institutions

19.5 **Read the sentences and decide who is more likely to be speaking – a British person or an American. Explain why. Use a dictionary to help you if necessary.**

1 Only faculty can eat here.
2 All postgraduates must attend the research methods module.
3 I went to school at Millintown, where I got my masters and PhD.
4 I'm a junior. My brother's a freshman. He's just a year younger than me.
5 My dissertation adviser has been really helpful.
6 Did you go straight to college after high school?

Over to you

Are universities/colleges in your country roughly based on a similar system to the UK one or the US one, or are there important differences? Make sure you can describe the main features in English.

20 Academic courses

A Course descriptions

Look at this extract from a university's web pages.

Diploma/MA in English Language and Culture

- *Qualification*: **Diploma**[1] or **MA. Duration:** One year full-time or two years part-time.

  The course is a **180-credit**[2] course, consisting of 120 credits of **core**[3] and **elective** i.e. **optional**[4] **modules**[5] plus a 60-credit **dissertation** module. Core modules are **obligatory. Candidates** not wishing to **proceed** to the MA may **opt for**[6] the Diploma (120 credits without dissertation).
- *Course description*: The course covers all the major aspects of present-day English language and culture. Topics include grammar, vocabulary, language in society, literature in English (for a full list, see the list of modules). Elective modules only run if a minimum of ten students **enrol**[7]. The modules consist of a mixture of **lectures, seminars, workshops** and **tutorials**[8]**.**
- ***Assessment***[9]: A 3,000-word **assignment**[10] must be submitted for each core module. Elective modules are assessed through **essays, projects** and **portfolios**[11]**.** The **word limit** for the dissertation is 12,000 to 15,000 words. Candidates who achieve a grade average of 70% or more over all modules may be **eligible**[12] for a **distinction**[13].

[1] a qualification between a bachelor's degree and a master's degree [2] unit which represents a successfully completed part of a course [3] most important parts of a course of study, that all students must do [4] which are chosen [5] one of the units which together make a complete course taught especially at a college or university [6] choose [7] put your name on an official list of course members [8] see Unit 19 for the meaning of these [9] judgements of the quality of students' work [10] a piece of written work [11] a collection of documents that represent a person's work [12] having the necessary qualities or fulfilling the necessary conditions [13] a special mark given to students who produce work of an excellent standard

B Other aspects of courses

Dr Ward is holding a question-and-answer session for new MA students.

Reza: Can we **defer**[1] the dissertation if we can't stay here during the summer?

Dr Ward: Yes, you can defer for a year, but don't forget, if you do go home, you won't be able to have face-to-face **supervisions**[2].

Simon: Are the **in-sessional**[3] language courses compulsory?

Dr Ward: No. Most of you did the **pre-sessional**, which is the most important. But there are good in-sessional courses you can **sign up for**, especially the **EAP**[4] writing course.

Angela: If we get the MA, can we go on to do a **PhD** immediately?

Dr Ward: Not automatically. You have to show you can do PhD standard work first anyway, and then **upgrade**[5] to the PhD programme after a year or so.

[1] delay until a later time [2] individual meetings with the teacher who is responsible for the student's dissertation [3] courses held during the main teaching semesters; pre-sessional courses are held before the main teaching semesters begin [4] English for Academic Purposes [5] become officially registered for a higher level degree

Common Mistake

When addressing someone with a PhD, always use their family name, e.g. "Excuse me, Dr Lopez." Only medical doctors can be addressed simply as *Doctor*, without using their family name.

Exercises

20.1 Read the text in A opposite and answer the questions.

1 How many credits is a dissertation worth?
2 What is special about core modules?
3 How many students are required for an elective module to run?
4 On what types of assignment might students be assessed?
5 What is the maximum number of words allowed in a dissertation?
6 What do students have to do to get a distinction?

20.2 Complete the email from a student to a friend using words from the box.

Diploma dissertation in-sessional MA module PhD project sign

Hi Erika,

How are things going with you? I'm sorry not to have written to you sooner but I've been desperately busy with the linguistics [1].................... I have to do for the elective [2].................... I'm taking this term. It's really interesting and I think I might decide to do my final [3].................... on a similar topic. At first I was only planning to do the [4].................... but now I've decided to have a go at an [5].................... . I might even [6].................... up for a [7].................... if they'll have me! PhD students are usually offered some language teaching on the [8].................... EAP courses they run for foreign students, so it would be useful for my CV for the future.

Shoshana

20.3 Choose the correct word to complete each sentence.

1 I started out doing an MA but then decided to *upgrade / defer* to a PhD.
2 Students whose first language is not English usually have to attend a(n) *in-sessional / pre-sessional* language course before their main classes start.
3 Only six students have *enrolled / opted*, so the MEd programme will not run this year.
4 Most students decide to *sign / proceed* to the MA after completing their Diploma course.
5 Core modules are *obligatory / optional*.
6 When I was doing my PhD I had monthly one-to-one *seminars / supervisions*.
7 I won't be able to finish the dissertation this year, so I'll have to *opt / defer* till next year.
8 *Assessment / Assignment* consists of a three-hour end-of-module exam.

20.4 Complete the table. Do not fill the shaded boxes. Use a dictionary if necessary.

verb	noun	adjective
		obligatory
opt		optional
	supervision +	
	assessment +	
		eligible

20.5 Complete the sentences using words from 20.4.

1 It's important to meet your .... regularly when you're doing a PhD.
2 Our tutor has asked us to .... our own work before she gives us a grade.
3 Students taking the American history module have two .... : take an end-of-course test or write a 10,000 word essay.
4 The department secretary has some interesting information about .... for travel grants.
5 You're not .... to bind your final-year dissertation but many students choose to do so.
6 Which modules do you plan to .... for next year?

21 E-learning

A E-learning terminology

Look at this glossary of e-learning terminology.

Distance education: Education in which the instructor and the student are in different locations and may also be working at different times.

E-learning: Learning that occurs through the use of digitally delivered content and support.

Synchronous learning: Online learning in which instructors and participants are logged in at the same time and instructors and students communicate directly with each other in real time.

Asynchronous learning: Online learning in which students and instructors can participate **intermittently**[1] at times that suit them individually.

Learning environment: The physical or **virtual**[2] context for learning.

LMS (learning management system): Software that is used to organise the administration of learning. It allows instructors to register and **track**[3] learners, and can record data and provide feedback for all participants.

Online community: A meeting place on the internet for people who share common interests and needs, **facilitating**[4] contact and **collaboration**[5] between them.

Learning portal: Website offering **consolidated**[6] access to **multiple**[7] sources of educational resources.

[1] stopping and starting repeatedly, not continuously [2] that can be experienced via a computer, without the need to go to the physical location [3] follow the progress of [4] making easier [5] working together with the same goals [6] brought together in one place [7] very many

B E-learning environments

Blended learning combines work done in **conventional**[1] classrooms with **computer-mediated**[2] work. An important feature of blended learning is **the flipped classroom**[3], which enables teachers to choose the best combination of in-class and out-of-class work / homework. Online elements of blended learning include **blogs/vlogs**, **wikis**, **fora**[4] and **webinars**[5], as well as traditional tasks **monitored**[6] by an instructor. Students can usually work **at their own pace**[7]. **Peer assessment**[8] is also made easier and **plagiarism detection software**[9] can be used to check essays and assignments submitted online. Many universities now also have **virtual campuses** for distance learning and offer **MOOCs**[10] that can be accessed globally. **Mobile learning**[11] has also grown in popularity and developments in **adaptive learning**[12] technology are transforming the learning environment.

[1] traditional [2] which happens via a computer [3] where work usually done in class can become homework and vice-versa [4] a blog is a record of opinions and experiences on the internet; a blog with video is a vlog; a wiki allows users to add and edit content, a forum (plural fora) is a website where people can discuss subjects [5] seminars delivered over the internet [6] watched and checked [7] at their own speed [8] where students mark each other's work [9] software that checks whether someone has copied someone else's work [10] massive open online courses: courses delivered over the internet and free of charge [11] learning via smart phones, tablets, etc. [12] learning where the computer changes the feedback it gives according to the behaviour of the individual user

Exercises

21.1 Match the examples with e-learning phrases from A opposite.

1 a language course in which the teacher gives feedback to work that students deposited online earlier
2 a classroom
3 a student chat room online where students discuss their courses, problems, etc.
4 an engineering course where the teacher and students are in immediate contact, with each other
5 a college web page where students can find links to websites connected with their course
6 a social work course in which students study at home and correspond with their tutors by phone or email
7 software that lets a maths teachers see what work their students have done, how long they spent on it, etc.
8 studying geography via a computer rather than in a face-to-face classroom

21.2 Rewrite the underlined parts of the sentences using words and phrases from A opposite.

1 The LMS can follow the progress of courses and see how the students are using them.
2 The online course provides an environment experienced via the computer which makes learning easier for students.
3 Students can access material from very many sources via the learning portal. The portal gives them access all joined together to content, support and services.
4 In asynchronous learning, students only interact with their teachers at given times, not continuously. However, online learning encourages working together, sharing the same goals.

21.3 Read what Dr Phelan says about a blended learning programme and complete it with words from B opposite. The first letter of each word is given to help you.

Next semester we'll be going over to the blended learning programme. For the online elements you'll record your experience of the course and any thoughts you have on [1]b ...., or [2]v .... if you want to use video. And you can work together and edit stuff on [3]w .... and leave messages on the [4]f .... The good thing is that, for the tasks and exercises, you'll be able to work at your own [5]p .... I'll be [6]m .... your work but I won't be watching you all the time. You'll be assessed in the normal way for the assignments, just as you would in the [7]c .... classroom, but there'll also be [8]p .... assessment where you'll assess each other's work. One thing I would warn you about, though: the [9]p .... detection software is very good these days, so make sure everything you submit is your own work and not copied from the internet or from another student. And you won't have to panic to take notes at lectures and so on because there'll be [10]w .... you can watch at any time.

21.4 Complete the sentences using words from the box.

computer-mediated flipped classroom virtual campus
mobile learning MOOCs adaptive learning

1 Smart phones and tablets are useful .... resources.
2 .... improves as students input their essays to the system. The computer learns about each student's typical behaviour and can give individual feedback.
3 .... pedagogy only began on a large scale in the first decade of this century. Before that, most learning was done using books in face-to-face classrooms.
4 The .... alters the balance between what is done in class and what is done for homework.
5 When you enrol as a student in a ...., you do not even need to leave your home.
6 Popular .... can often attract hundreds of thousands of participants globally.

22 Study habits and skills

A Time management

West Preston University has a web-based self-assessment questionnaire on **time management**.

Time management: Rate your ability to organise your time.

	often	sometimes	never
1 Do you begin **end-of-semester** assignments early in the semester?	●	●	●
2 Do you **meet deadlines**[1] for submitting work?	●	●	●
3 Do you ever have to **request an extension**[2] for your work?	●	●	●
4 Do you spend hours **cramming**[3] just before an exam?	●	●	●
5 Do you **make a to-do list**[4] each week?	●	●	●
6 Do you include **extra-curricular**[5] **activities** in your study plan?	●	●	●

[1] complete your work by the official final day or time [2] ask for more time beyond the deadline [3] try to learn a lot very quickly before an exam [4] make a list of things you should do [5] activities outside of the subjects you are studying

B Study habits and problems studying

I try to **prioritise**[1] the most difficult or urgent task first, when I feel more motivated.

I'm a slow reader. I need to improve my **reading speed.** I find **revision** before exams really difficult. I can only **revise** for about two hours at a time. **My mind starts to wander**[2].

I always try to **review**[3] my **lecture notes** within 24 hours of the time I took them. I do need to improve my **note-taking**.

I use tricks to **memorise** things, like **mnemonics**[4] and **visualising**[5]. I try to **brainstorm**[6] the topic and draw **mind maps**[7] before I write a first **draft**[8] of an essay.

I know **rote learning**[9] isn't very fashionable nowadays, but I find it useful to **learn** some things **by heart** [10], especially lists of things.

I try to make a **study plan** each semester – but I never manage to keep to it!

I always try to get the books I need from the library on **long-term loan**. **Short-term loan** is never long enough, even though you can sometimes extend it for 24 hours.

In an exam I make **rough**[11] notes for each question, otherwise **my mind** just **goes blank**[12].

[1] decide which things are the most important so that you can deal with them first [2] I start thinking of things not connected to my studies [3] read or study again [4] a very short poem or a special word used to help you remember something [5] forming an image in your mind [6] think of a lot of ideas very quickly before considering some of them more carefully [7] diagram or drawing showing how different ideas on a topic are related [8] text containing all the main ideas but not in a fully developed form [9] (often used with a negative association) learning something so you can repeat it from memory, rather than understand it [10] learn something in such a way that you can say it from memory [11] not exact or detailed; approximate [12] I can't remember a particular thing, or I can't remember anything

Exercises

22.1 Complete the collocations.

1 to m _ _ _ a deadline
2 to make a t _- d _ list
3 to draw a m _ _ _ m _ _
4 to r _ _ _ _ _ _ an extension
5 extra-c _ _ _ _ _ _ _ _ _ activities
6 r _ _ _ learning
7 a first d _ _ _ _
8 time m _ _ _ _ _ _ _ _ _
9 on long-t _ _ _ loan
10 note-t _ _ _ _ _
11 l _ _ _ _ _ _ notes
12 a study p _ _ _

22.2 Complete the sentences with the correct form of collocations from 22.1.

1 My essay is due in on Friday. I always try to .... but this time I'm afraid I'm going to have to .... If only I could stick to the .... I make at the beginning of every semester!
2 You should show the .... of your essay to your tutor before you do any more work on it.
3 Helena missed the class but she borrowed the .... from a friend.
4 Some people find it more helpful to .... when they are studying than to take traditional notes.
5 This is an incredibly useful book. Fortunately, I've been able to take it out of the library ....
6 Students who are working part-time as well as studying have to be particularly good at ....
7 Some students get distracted from their studies by all the .... which most universities offer.
8 I always make a .... when I'm getting ready to go on a trip.
9 .... is considered a very old-fashioned way of learning nowadays.
10 .... is very important during lectures; you can't remember everything.

22.3 Answer the questions about study habits with your own ideas.

1 Do you ever use mnemonics to help you memorise things?
2 If you were brainstorming some good study habits, what would you write down?
3 In your opinion, what sorts of things are useful to learn by heart?
4 When do you start revising before an exam? Do you think cramming is effective?
5 Does your mind ever wander when you are studying? If so, what do you start thinking about?
6 Have you ever experienced your mind going blank during an exam?
7 Do you try to prioritise certain types of work? Which types?
8 Why is it a good idea to make rough notes before answering an exam question?
9 What kinds of information do you find it useful to visualise?
10 How often do you review your notes?

22.4 The notice below contains more useful words relating to study habits. Read it and explain the meaning of the bold words and expressions. Use a dictionary if necessary.

University Library: Notice to all undergraduates

Undergraduates are reminded that all books [1]**on loan** must be [2]**returned** by noon on June 30th. [3]**Overdue** items will incur a fine of 50 cents per day. Failure to [4]**clear** fines on overdue books may result in loss of [5]**borrowing rights**. Additional regulations apply to [6]**inter-library loans**.

Over to you

Ask some of your fellow students about their study habits using the questions from the questionnaire in A opposite.

23 Money and education

A Financing your studies

Read the texts and note in particular the collocations (word combinations).

Tuition fees[1]

It is important to know in advance what the fees will be, when they are payable and whether you will need to provide any financial guarantees. There are different ways in which you can **seek funding**[2] to **finance your studies**. In many countries, students can apply to **take out a student loan** to help **cover** their **living costs**[3] while studying. Student loans are often fixed at a low interest rate. Your **entitlement to**[4] a loan may have to be assessed. You may be eligible for a government grant or a **scholarship** or other **award**[5].

In many countries, **full-time** students from lower income households can apply for a non-repayable **maintenance grant**[6]. Grants may be payable as **a lump sum**[7] or **in instalments**[8].

Your personal finances

Student bank accounts are similar to normal current accounts but they often have additional benefits such as **interest-free overdrafts**[9] and the banks may **offer inducements**[10] to open an account. Students often find it difficult to **make ends meet**[11]. In the UK, for example, student debt has **soared**[12] and many UK students can now expect to **accumulate** considerable **debts**[13] which they will have to pay back over many years. It is a good idea to budget carefully and calculate your **monthly** or **annual expenditure**[14] and the total cost of your course. The **cost of living** in big cities is often very high, so plan carefully.

[1] what students pay for being taught [2] try to get money to pay for your studies [3] pay for their daily expenses [4] right to receive [5] money or a prize given following an official decision [6] money available for students to get (e.g. by doing well in an exam or by fulfilling certain requirements) [7] one large amount on one occasion [8] parts of the money paid at different times till the total is reached [9] money that can be borrowed from a bank without paying any interest charges [10] give things that are intended to persuade people [11] have just enough money to pay for the things you need [12] gone up very quickly [13] owe more and more money to someone [14] how much you spend each month or each year

B Spending money

We asked some students about their day-to-day expenditure. Here are some of the responses.

Books can be expensive, especially **hardbacks**[1], but you can get more and more stuff online now and you can get **second-hand**[2] books from people who've finished with them.

I'm doing business studies so I've taken out **subscriptions**[3] to a couple of online business magazines, which was an expense I didn't **anticipate**[4] really.

I share a house with three other students and we split the rent and **energy bills**[5] but it's still **a drain on my finances**[6].

Money was a bit **tight**[7] and I had to get **a part-time job** in a restaurant but it's **a low-paid job** and it means working pretty **unsocial hours**[8].

[1] book with a stiff cover [2] not new, used in the past by someone else [3] amounts of money paid regularly to receive a product or service [4] expect to happen [5] bills for gas, heating oil and/or electricity [6] an expense which causes my finances to reduce [7] there was only just enough of it [8] times when other people are not working

Exercises

23.1 Complete the text using words from the box.

awards seek grants entitlement cover take out
maintenance accumulate tuition meet scholarships

Not all students get [1].................... to help them study, so some students [2].................... a lot of debt or else they have to [3].................... a student loan to pay their [4].................... fees and to help make ends [5]..................... It is sometimes possible to [6].................... funding from other sources and some governments and official bodies give [7].................... and other types of prizes or [8].................... . If you intend to study abroad, you may have to provide financial guarantees to prove that you can pay your fees and [9].................... your living costs. Your [10].................... to funding may depend on your or your family's current financial situation. In addition to a grant to pay your fees, you may also be eligible for a [11].................... grant to cover your day-to-day expenses.

23.2 Rewrite the sentences using the words in brackets.

1 The bank gave me a loan where I don't have to pay anything extra when I pay it back. (INTEREST)
2 Most people seem to be finding it harder to find enough money for their everyday living costs. (ENDS)
3 Increasing numbers of students leave college owing a lot of money. (ACCUMULATE / CONSIDERABLE)
4 My grant was paid in one large amount on one occasion. (SUM)
5 The campus banks offer various things to persuade students to open a bank account. (INDUCEMENT)
6 I find it difficult to calculate how much money I spend each year. (ANNUAL)
7 The amount you have to pay to live in big cities can be very high. (COST)

23.3 Correct the two vocabulary mistakes in each sentence.

1 My month's expenditure is rather high, so I had to get a partly-timed job.
2 Why are hardbacked books so expensive? I can only afford second-handed ones.
3 My maintain grant is paid on instalments, so I get money every semester.
4 Our bills are very high so they're a big drone on our finances and I only have a low-earn job.
5 When you're a student, there are always expenses that you just don't antisimate, like high energetic bills for instance.
6 Even though money is tough for me, I don't want to get a job and work unsocial times.

23.4 Answer the questions about student finance with your own ideas.

1 What are the pros and cons of students having to pay tuition fees for higher education?
2 Should all students get a non-repayable maintenance grant to study? Why (not)?
3 What kinds of scholarships and other awards are available in your country?
4 Why might it be a bad idea to get a part-time job while doing a full-time course of study?

Over to you

Find a website relating to financial arrangements for students at a university you know or are interested in. Which of the words and expressions from this unit do you see there? Make a note of any other useful vocabulary you find there.

24 Identifying goals

A Talking about goals

word	in sentence or collocation	comment
goal	**have something as a goal, achieve your goal**	we don't usually say 'reach your goal'
intention	**with the intention of *-ing*, have no intention of *-ing***	verb = **intend** followed by the infinitive
motive	**motive for *-ing*** [reason]	verb = **motivate**; more general noun = **motivation**
objective	**meet**[1] **/ achieve objectives**	= what you plan to do or achieve
priority	**top priority, take priority over, give (top) priority to**	implies a list of important things
purpose	Our **purpose** was to test our theory.	**on purpose** means deliberately
strategy	Their **strategy** was to proceed slowly.	= detailed plan for success
target	**reach / achieve / attain a target**	= level or situation you hope to achieve
deliberate	We took the **deliberate** decision to keep our study small.	= intentional; is often used for something negative

[1]we also talk about meeting criteria

B An example of a mission statement

Look at this web page for the Centre of Research into Creation in the Performing Arts. Note how it uses the infinitive to express the aims, and note the formal language.

MISSION STATEMENT[1]

ResCen exists to **further**[2] the understanding of how artists research and develop new processes and forms, by working with professional artists and others.

AIMS

To **establish**[3] new **understandings**[4] of creative methods and their **application** in practice-as-research, extending **knowledge bases**[5] in these areas

To explore and **challenge**[6] traditional **hypothesis-based** and critical-analytical **research methodologies** established within the university

To establish a **critical mass**[7] of artist-researchers, meeting regularly, to **instigate**[8] and **inform**[9] new creative work across **disciplines**

To provide an **infrastructure**[10] for **practice-led** and artist-informed postgraduate study within the university

To further develop **criteria**[11] for the **definition** and **evaluation** of **creative practice-as-research**, as part of the wider **national debate**

To **contribute to** the development of a national infrastructure supporting practice-as-research, at the **interface**[12] between academic and other centres of art-making and its study.

[1] short written statement of the aims of an organisation [2] move forward, advance [3] encourage people to accept [4] understanding can be used as a countable noun in this context [5] the basic knowledge shared by everyone working in the areas [6] question [7] influential number [8] initiate, cause to start [9] provide knowledge that can influence [10] basic systems and support services [11] standards or principles that you use to judge something or make a decision; singular = **criterion** [12] place where two things come together and affect each other

Exercises

24.1 Answer the questions about the vocabulary in this unit.

1 What verbs are typically used with (a) *objective* and (b) *target*?
2 What word can we use to refer to the basic support services and systems of a country?
3 What phrase can we use if everyone in a country seems to be discussing an issue?
4 What is another word for academic subjects?
5 What are criteria and what is its singular form?
6 What is the opposite of theory-led research?

24.2 Choose the best word to complete each sentence.

1 Our hope was to *instigate / contribute / attain* a public discussion of the ethical issues involved.
2 Their target was to achieve a *deliberate / creative / critical* mass of support for their proposal.
3 The research *prioritises / challenges / achieves* existing theories in some exciting ways.
4 I hope my dissertation *meets / reaches / has* all the relevant academic criteria.
5 At the moment writing the assignment has to take *target / purpose / priority* over my social life.
6 What was your *goal / motive / intention* for choosing this particular university?

24.3 Complete the second sentence so it means the same as the first. Use the word in brackets.

1 Protecting the privacy of our subjects must take priority over absolutely everything else.
We must .... the privacy of our subjects. (PRIORITY)
2 Our intention in designing the questionnaire was to make it straightforward to answer.
We designed the questionnaire .... it straightforward to answer. (INTENTION)
3 We aimed to evaluate a new approach to urban planning.
We had .... a new approach to urban planning. (GOAL)
4 I did not intend to become a scientist when I began my studies.
I had .... a scientist when I began my studies. (INTENTION)
5 A methodology based on a hypothesis does not work in some cases.
A .... methodology does not work in some cases. (-BASED)
6 Our project is located in the area where sociology and psychology meet.
Our project is located .... sociology and psychology. (INTERFACE)

24.4 Complete the table. Use a dictionary if necessary.

verb	noun	verb	noun
	intention		hypothesis
	definition	establish	
achieve		base	..................., ...
	practice		application

24.5 Complete the sentences using words from 24.4.

1 Jack plans to .... his research on the unpublished letters of his favourite poet.
2 My tutor reminded us to .... all key terms at the beginning of our essays to make the meanings clear.
3 There are a number of practical ways in which industry can .... the results of our research.
4 I am conducting the experiment with the .... of publishing my results in the autumn.
5 1965 saw the .... of a centre for psychological research at the university.
6 There are a number of different .... about the origins of the legend.
7 I hope you will be able to .... your targets within the time frame you anticipate.

Over to you

Go to the website for a course or institution that you are interested in. What does it state on its Aims page? Note any interesting language there.

25 Planning a piece of work

A Reading for an assignment

Advice on reading for an essay or assignment

Don't **rush into**[1] your reading. When you are given your essay or assignment topic, write down your **initial thoughts**[2], or else make a **spider diagram**[3] or **mind map**[4] to help you organise your ideas.

You should **note briefly**[5] the following points. Ask yourself these questions:

- What do I *already* know about the topic? What do I know from general knowledge?
- What do I *not* know about the topic? What do I need to find out?
- What do I think my initial response might be? This may change later as you do your reading.

As you read, you should start to **formulate your argument**[6]. Doing this helps to **focus your reading**[7]; it enables you to **pinpoint**[8] what else you need to find out so that you can go directly to the most **relevant**[9] sources (particular articles, books, websites, etc.).

When you've done your reading – It's now time to **summarise** all your notes on a single page. This will be the overall plan for your essay/assignment. A spider diagram or mind map can help.

Next it's time to **bring together** the **key**[10] points from your reading and to **clarify**[11] what you have learnt. Your initial ideas may have changed **in light of**[12] the reading you've done. This is normal, and is a natural part of the planning process. The next step in the process is to **find a pathway through**[13] all the ideas you have **encountered**[14] in your reading.

Finally, don't forget to include brief details of authors and **page nos.**[15] for the most important information. Doing this provides you with a quick **at-a-glance**[16] guide for referring to the sources you will use to support your arguments.

[1] start too quickly [2] thoughts at the beginning [3] a plan with lines and circles for organising information [4] another name for a spider diagram [5] write in a few words [6] develop the details of why you support or oppose an idea [7] give attention to particular aspects of your reading [8] discover or describe the exact facts about something [9] important to the topic [10] most important [11] make clear [12] because of; also **in the light of** [13] identify a set of actions to take you through [14] found/experienced in your reading [15] short form of *page numbers* [16] which you can read quickly

B Other things to do when preparing work

Read these emails from postgraduate students to their tutors, asking for advice.

Dear Prof. Lewis,

I've just begun **collecting data**[1] for my project and I'm now wondering if the interviews I have **conducted**[2] will be sufficient to do an in-depth investigation of the topic, or should I **distribute**[3] some **questionnaires** too? If so, how many **informants**[4] should I **approach**[5] initially? Could I possibly come and see you about it?

Marissa

Hi Dr Nunan,

Thanks for the reading list you sent me. It will be very useful for the **review of literature**[6] in my dissertation. I've now **mapped out**[7] some **headings** and **sections** and have some notes in **bullet-point**[8] form. At this point should I start to **formulate** my **hypotheses**[9] or does that come later?

Thanks and best wishes,

Hideyuki

[1] information [2] done [3] give out to several people [4] people who give information that you need [5] speak to or write to [6] a report giving your opinion of the reading you have done [7] planned in detail [8] a small, black circle, used in text to separate things in a list [9] ideas which you have not yet proved

Exercises

25.1 **Look at A opposite, then read the comments by different students and answer the questions with the correct names.**

Rana

I'm making a list of the books I read on one page so I can refer to it quickly.

Thomas

I need to decide exactly which books I need to look at.

Joanna

I've put the main ideas in circles, now I'll draw lines connecting them.

Krishnan

I want to see how everything fits together so I can move from A to B.

Lisa

I always bring together the first ideas I have about the topic in note form.

Kevin

I've been developing some ideas for and against the essay topic.

1 Who wants to find a pathway through a number of different ideas?
2 Who writes down their initial thoughts?
3 Who is making an at-a-glance guide to something?
4 Who is formulating an argument?
5 Who is using a spider diagram or mind map?
6 Who wants to focus their reading?

25.2 **Complete the sentences with words from A opposite. The first letter of each word is given to help you.**

1 You should take your time and not r.................... into your reading.
2 I read the article but decided that it was not r.................... to my topic.
3 I'm a bit confused right now. I need to c.................... my thoughts.
4 Sometimes I find it hard to p.................... exactly what I should be reading.
5 It's hard to remember all the ideas you e.................... in your reading, so make sure you n.................... briefly the k.................... points and s.................... the most important arguments. And always make a note of p.................... nos.
6 Now it's time to b.................... together all the different notes I've made and start the essay. In l.................... of all the reading I've done, it should not be too difficult.

25.3 **Rewrite the underlined words and phrases using words and phrases from B opposite.**

1 I'm hoping to <u>write to</u> some care workers to ask them to complete my questionnaire.
2 My plan is to <u>give out</u> 40-50 questionnaires to carers in residential homes.
3 The <u>information</u> I <u>get</u> from these <u>people who have the information I need</u> will be very useful for my dissertation.
4 I intend also to <u>do</u> some interviews with social workers.
5 When I've done all that, I'll write my <u>report and judgement of the reading I've done</u>. I've already <u>planned</u> the various sections and made some notes. I use <u>little black circles</u> to help me list my ideas.
6 I will need to <u>make</u> some initial <u>explanations that I hope to prove later</u> about the psychological effects upon carers who work with terminally-ill patients.

Over to you

Many universities and colleges give advice on their websites about how to plan essays, assignments, projects, dissertations, etc. Find another advice page like the one at A opposite and compare the advice given. Make a note of any different or new vocabulary you encounter. What aspects of the advice given do you find most useful for your situation?

26 Describing methods

A Useful word combinations

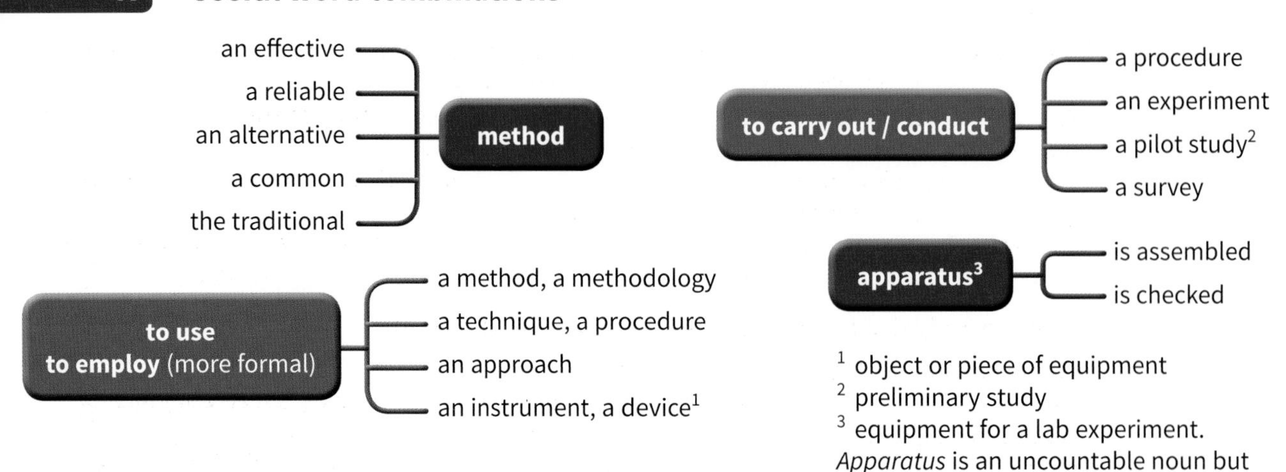

[1] object or piece of equipment
[2] preliminary study
[3] equipment for a lab experiment. *Apparatus* is an uncountable noun but you can talk about a *piece of apparatus*.

B Types of research method

method	what the researcher does	limitation of method
exploratory study	carries out a **preliminary** study of something not previously researched	often uses small samples so conclusions can only be **tentative**[1]
experimental study	**manipulates**[2] a **variable** [anything that can vary] under **controlled conditions** to see if this produces any changes in a **dependent variable**	done in the highly controlled conditions of the **laboratory** – these conditions are **artificial**[3] and may not **reflect** what happens in the more complex real world; other researchers often try to **replicate**[4] successful experiments
correlational study	attempts to **determine** the **relationship** between two or more variables, using **mathematical techniques** for summarising data	only shows that two variables are related **in a systematic way**, but does not **prove** or **disprove**[5] that the relationship is **a cause-and-effect relationship**
causal study	attempts to prove a cause-and-effect relationship	difficult to **eliminate** other variables in order to demonstrate a clear **causal relationship**
naturalistic (empirical) observation (also known as **field study)**	**observes** and **records** some behaviour or **phenomenon**[6], often over a prolonged period, in its **natural setting** without **interfering with**[7] the **subjects** or phenomena in any way	can be very **time-consuming** as researcher may have to wait for some time to observe the behaviour or phenomenon of interest; difficult to observe behaviour without **disrupting**[8] it
survey	**makes inferences from**[9] data collected via interviews or questionnaires	intentional deception, poor memory, or **misunderstanding** of the question can all contribute to **inaccuracies in the data**
case study	keeps **in-depth**[10] descriptive records, as an **outside observer**, of an individual or group	often focuses on a single individual and this person may not be **representative** of the general group or **population**
longitudinal study	follows the same **sample** [e.g. group of people] **over time** and makes repeated observations	takes a long time to **gather results**; maintaining the same sample can be difficult over time

[1] uncertain [2] makes changes to [3] not natural [4] do in exactly the same way [5] show something is not true [6] something that exists and can be seen, felt, tasted, etc. [7] altering [8] making it change [9] comes to conclusions on the basis of [10] detailed

Exercises

26.1 Complete the sentences using words from A opposite. There may be more than one possible answer.

1 It was a new .... of apparatus so we brought together all the things we needed and .... it first. We then .... it before using it.
2 The team carried out a .... before conducting the main .... to see if the .... they were using was reliable.
3 The team needed to employ a different .... for measuring the pressure, so they used a new .... which they manufactured in their own laboratory.
4 The researchers found the .... method of collecting data that was usually used did not work well for their purposes and so they had to find a more .... method.

26.2 Read the information in B opposite, then answer the questions.

1 Professor Patel would like to investigate the links between parental behaviour in their child's first year of life and later educational performance – is he more likely to carry out an experimental study or a longitudinal study?
2 Dr Antonova is interested in investigating the impact of a new technological device on social relationships – is she more likely to use a correlational study or an exploratory study?
3 Dr Lee wants to focus on how one particular business reacted to a radically new approach to management – is he more likely to use a causal study or a case study?
4 Professor Macdonald would like to observe the behaviour of a specific type of bird in the wild – will she use a field study or a survey?

26.3 Choose the correct words to complete the paragraphs.

Scientists disagree as to whether cold fusion, the controlled power of the hydrogen bomb in the laboratory, is possible. In the past, some believed it would be possible to conduct an [1]*experiment / experience* under laboratory [2]*circumstances / conditions* using palladium and platinum electrodes to cause heavy hydrogen atoms to fuse into helium and release energy, as the sun does. Using carefully controlled techniques, researchers believed they could [3]*manipulate / manouevre* the [4]*variations / variables* arising from the complexity of the electrodes and other equipment used. In such [5]*controlled / organised* conditions they argued, cold fusion was possible. However, attempts to [6]*reply / replicate* some of the experiments which claimed to be successful failed, and many now believe that cold fusion is in fact theoretically impossible.

Some linguists believe that we can best [7]*decide / determine* how language is processed by laboratory experiments. However, laboratory experiments are by definition [8]*artificial / superficial* and may not [9]*relate / reflect* what happens in the real world. Other linguists believe, therefore that [10]*empirical / imperial* observation is better, and prefer to carry out [11]*field / land* studies and [12]*casual / case* studies of individuals in natural [13]*settings / sets*. In this way, [14]*in-depth / inaccurate* data can be [15]*collected / completed* by observers without [16]*interrupting / interfering* with the process in any way, even though this may be a more [17]*time-consuming / time-wasting* method. However, individual studies in real situations may not be [18]*representative / relevant* of the general [19]*people / population* of second language learners. In short, both approaches have their advantages and disadvantages.

26.4 Match words and expressions in B opposite with the less academic synonyms below.

1 indefinite and not certain
2 show something is not true
3 rule out something as a possibility
4 at different points in time
5 be the same as
6 makes a note of
7 draws conclusions
8 failure to understand
9 initial
10 repeat
11 watches
12 typical

26.5 Correct the eight spelling and vocabulary mistakes in the sentences.

1 It was very difficult to make clear interferences from the data as we had so little.
2 A correlational study is a good way of seeing if one phenomena is related to another in a system way.
3 The experiment neither proved nor deproved Jessop's theory.
4 An exterior observer can often unintentionally erupt the behaviour of the subjects they are observing.
5 The method they initially chose to use was not a very reliant one, so he had to find an alternator.

27 Using sources

A Referring to source materials

Look at these extracts where writers are talking about their sources. Although the writers occasionally use 'I', many academic departments advise against doing this in writing if possible.

This paper begins with **a review of the literature on**[1] patient communication. The medical literature **suggests** that patients with serious illnesses tend to communicate poorly, especially if the 'disease' is not considered by the patient to be particularly threatening.

This essay draws its data from the most important **primary source**[2] of information on manufacturing in Nigeria: the Central Bank of Nigeria. I shall **make reference to**[3] this source throughout this essay. Several recent **secondary sources**[4] were also **consulted**.

For this project, I consulted the county **archives**[5] in an attempt to explain why there were so many deaths in 1840 and 1847. These proved a **valuable resource**. I also **surveyed the literature on**[6] agricultural production during the 1840s. However, I only directly **cite**[7] those works which are particularly relevant to the **present study**.

An extensive **body of literature**[8] exists on the effects of wildfires, ie fires that occur naturally, not caused by human action. Wildfires have burned across the western United States for centuries, but their effects are not fully known or **documented**[9]. The present study **draws primarily on**[10] the work of Gordon (1996), although information was also **retrieved**[11] from several relevant websites, all **accessed**[12] during the last six months.

As **noted**[13] in a recent report, Australia has been at the forefront of developments in e-learning. This success is **often attributed to**[14] Australia's geographical position, but the factors **catalogued**[15] in the report reveal a more complex picture.

[1] a summary and evaluation of all the important works written on a particular subject [2] an original document or set of documents giving information about a subject [3] slightly more formal alternative to *refer to* [4] books or articles about a subject, not original documents [5] a collection of documents of historical importance [6] searched for all the important works, summarised and evaluated them [7] refer to for illustration or proof [8] also 'body of knowledge/research'; note how it combines with *extensive* and *exist* [9] written about [10] uses information mainly from [11] found and taken from [12] opened in order to look at them [13] given special mention [14] people often say that this is the cause [15] recorded, listed

B More ways of referring to sources

Beeching's **seminal**[1] work **laid the foundations**[2] for the field of functional analysis.

Keynes's ideas were **set out**[3] in his book, *The General Theory of Employment, Interest and Money*, published in 1936. This work changed the way we look at how economies function. **Elsewhere**[4], Keynes claimed to be developing classical economic theory.

Design of compact heat exchangers is dealt with in Appendix A of the report, **treated**[5] separately from the **main body**[6] of the report.

[1] important and original work from which other works grow [2] created the first ideas from which a major set of ideas grew [3] gave all the details of his ideas, or explained them clearly (especially used about writing) [4] in another work by him
[5] more formal version of *dealt with* [6] the main part

Exercises

27.1 Match the beginnings and endings of the sentences.

1 The letters proved to be a valuable
2 An extensive body of
3 Newspapers are a good primary
4 The data are not given in the main
5 Plastics are not dealt with in the present
6 The thesis begins with a review of

☐ a study, which focuses on metals only.
☐ b body of the book; they are in the appendix.
☐ c the literature on intellectual property rights.
☐ d literature exists on human to animal communication.
☐ e source for the period 1980-1985.
☐ f resource for the study of the poet's life.

27.2 Rewrite the sentences using the words in brackets.

1 The article refers to the work of Hindler and Swartz (1988). (MAKES)
2 I consulted original government papers, and Schunker's book was also a useful critique for understanding the pre-war period. (SECONDARY)
3 Tanaka's book mainly uses data from several Japanese articles on galaxy formation. (DRAWS)
4 In a different paper, Kallen reports on his research into cancer rates among farm workers. (ELSEWHERE)
5 Han consulted the documents of historical importance in the Vienna Museum. (ARCHIVES)
6 Deneuve went to official websites during the period March to September 2015 and got out the relevant statistics to support his claim. (ACCESS / RETRIEVE)

27.3 Complete the sentences with the correct form of the verbs in the box.

note catalogue cite set out survey consult lay

1 In the first section of the book, Olsen .... the recent literature on the climate of Greenland. He then .... all the recent data on temperature and climate changes.
2 Labov's early work .... the foundations for modern sociolinguistics.
3 Reeves .... several Italian museum archives for her book on the history of violin-making and revealed some fascinating facts about the instrument.
4 This book .... the theory of planetary formation in language that ordinary people can understand.
5 Poliakov .... some interesting facts about the civil war that other scholars had overlooked.
6 Three contemporary critics are .... by Somerton to support her argument about the evolution of early 20th century poetry.

27.4 Complete the table. Do not fill the shaded boxes. Use a dictionary if necessary.

noun	verb	adjective	adverb
	attribute		
document			
	consult		
		primary	
catalogue			
foundation			
note			
	suggest		
		extensive	
	cite		

28 Analysing data

A Analysis in academic texts

Academic texts often include sections which deal with the analysis of data. In analysing a social or political issue, the writer may need to **come to / reach a conclusion** about the **advantages** or **disadvantages** of a particular **course of action**[1]. The writer may, for instance, conclude that the benefits **outweigh**[2] the **drawbacks**[3] or vice versa. An analysis may be a matter of **weighing up**[4] both sides of an argument, **taking into account** all the **relevant aspects**[5] of the issue and discussing all the **points raised**[6] by the research. When analysing the results of an experiment researchers must be **rigorous**[7] in their approach in order to be taken seriously by their peers. In their analysis scientists try to **deduce**[8] as much as is possible from their data, **drawing conclusions** that are **robust**[9] because they are **soundly**[10] based on their results.

[1] way of doing something [2] are of more importance than [3] disadvantages [4] thinking carefully about [5] (of a problem or situation) parts, features [6] ideas, opinions or pieces of information that have been presented in relation to the topic [7] extremely careful [8] reach an answer by thinking carefully about the known facts [9] reliable, able to stand up to close examination [10] completely, firmly

B Weighing up results

In the text in A did you notice an interesting metaphorical use of language – the image of **weighing up** ideas and of considering whether advantages **outweigh** disadvantages?

Arguments are, as it were, placed on each **side** of the scales and the judge or jury then have to **come down on one side** or the other. A particularly strong argument may **tip the scales in favour of** one side.

Language help

Noticing how language can be used metaphorically may help you to extend the use of the words you know. Make a note of any examples that you come across and try to find other examples of language based round the same metaphor.

C Interpreting results

The results **point to** an interesting trend. [show, indicate]

On the basis of our data we would **predict** continuing social unrest. [say something will happen in the future]

The survey provides some useful **insights** into the problem. [points that help us to understand more clearly]

We found that women **constitute** 40% of the workforce. [account for]

D Critical – several meanings

To analyse results properly a student needs good **critical thinking** skills. [the process of thinking carefully about a subject or idea, without allowing feelings or opinions to affect you]

The study begins with a **critical** review of the literature in the field. [giving opinions]

Most of our respondents were **critical of** the new law. [not pleased with, negative about]

The results suggest we are reaching a **critical** period in terms of climate change. [very important]

The results show the economy is in a **critical** condition. [serious]

It is **absolutely critical** that students check all their results carefully. [extremely important]

The tutor was **deeply critical of** our conclusions. [very negative about]

Language help

Remember how English words often have several distinct meanings. Note examples as you meet them.

Exercises

28.1 Complete each set of collocations with a word which can combine with all the words given.

1
come to
draw — a ....
reach

2
come down on one
be in favour of one — .... (s) of an argument
see both

3
.... — moment
review
comments

28.2 Complete the sentences using collocations from 28.1.

1 You should write a .... of the literature at the start of your dissertation.
2 It is difficult to .... any robust .... without a lot more data.
3 A good essay presents both .... and evaluates them properly.
4 There were some careless mistakes in my essay and the tutor made some .... on it.

28.3 Complete the extracts with the missing words. The first letter of each word is given to help you.

Which is better the night before an exam? To study longer and get less sleep or to study less and sleep longer? After [1]w.................. up the evidence, scientists have concluded that the advantages of getting more sleep [2]o.................. the [3]d.................. . Research has provided [4]i.................. into the link between sleep and memory development, suggesting that sleep is essential for memory. There are many variables to [5]t.................. into account in sleep and memory research – dreaming, phases of sleep and types of memories, for example – and recent research considers each of these in a [6]r.................. way [7]c.................. to conclusions that appear to be [8]r.................. . Dreams [9]c.................. about 25% of a typical eight-hour sleep, but research [10]p.................. to a connection between memory development and non-dreaming sleep time.

When considering energy conservation, we have to [11]t.................. i.................. account various [12]r.................. factors. But how do we relate a particular [13]c.................. of action to its outcome? For example, flying from London to Paris instead of taking the train is quicker but causes more pollution. You opt to cycle to work instead of driving in order to avoid adding to pollution. What can we [14]d.................. from the evidence? Do our individual choices make a difference? On the [15]b.................. of global data we can [16]p.................. that climate change will increase, but how much do personal choices affect the big picture? Could my choice to buy a second car tip the [17]s.................. and cause a global catastrophe?

28.4 Explain the meaning of *critical* or its related form in each sentence.

1 The hospital announced that the President remains critically ill.
2 Dixon was asked to write a critical review of contemporary Irish poetry.
3 The writer was imprisoned for his open criticism of the government.
4 It is absolutely critical all measurements are recorded every hour.
5 The development of critical thinking should begin at primary school.
6 The professor was deeply critical of his colleague's methodology.

28.5 Underline metaphorical uses of language in the sentences. Explain the metaphorical uses in your own words. Use a dictionary if necessary.

1 A recent survey has unearthed some interesting facts about commuting habits.
2 In predicting trends in inflation, economists often look at which direction the political winds are blowing.
3 Martin's controversial article on the causes of the crisis led to a storm of protest.
4 By digging into the archives, Professor Robinson was able to shed important new light on the history of the period.

29 Talking about ideas

A Talking about an idea or a collection of ideas

Look at the useful language for talking about ideas in the description of one idea below.

Article

Occasionally, in all **disciplines**[1] in both the arts and sciences, a **paradigm shift**[2] will occur which profoundly influences intellectual **thought**[3]. One such shift was represented by postmodernism, a (largely European) philosophical **movement**[4] of the late 20th century. As its name suggests, postmodernism followed and was a **reaction to**[5] 'modern' thought that had its origins in the 18th century (the period of the Enlightenment), when it was believed that logic, science and rigorous thinking would improve the world. The modernists believed in the existence of complete truth and objectivity and the search for the absolute **essence**[6] of things. The postmodernists rejected this way of thinking and **asserted**[7] that there is no objective reality or objective truth and that it is impossible to **generalise**[8] about human experience. Every individual **interprets**[9] the world in his or her own way, and that no interpretation should be considered more **valid**[10] than another.

[1] subjects [2] a time when the accepted way of doing or thinking about something changes completely [3] thinking in general [4] group of people sharing aims or beliefs [5] process of change stimulated by something else, often moving in the opposite direction [6] the most important quality or characteristics [7] said that something was true [8] present as something that is always true [9] decides what the meaning is [10] appropriate / which can be accepted

Common Mistake

You *discuss an idea* or *talk/write about an idea* but NOT ~~discuss about an idea~~.

Language help

In academic writing it is best to avoid *in my opinion* and to use a less personal expression like *It can be argued that …* or *Most (people) would agree that…*

B Some useful nouns relating to ideas

word	meaning	example
concept	principle, idea	The **concept** of honesty is understood differently in different cultures.
framework	system of rules, beliefs or ideas used as the basis for something	Mary is working on an analytical **framework** to help people design and evaluate training courses.
model	simple description useful for discussing ideas	The writer uses a Marxist **model** as the basis for his discussion of the economy.
notion	belief, idea	She doesn't agree with the **notion** that boys and girls should be taught separately.
perception	belief, opinion, held by many people	The novel had a powerful impact on people's **perception** of the war.
stance	way of thinking, often publicly stated	The government has made its **stance** on the boycott issue clear.
viewpoint	opinion, way of looking at an issue	The article provides a different **viewpoint** on this difficult topic.

Language help

A number of words that are useful for talking about ideas have irregular plurals: **criterion/criteria**, **phenomenon/phenomena**, **hypothesis/hypotheses**, **analysis/analyses**, **thesis/theses**.
They all originate from Ancient Greek. Perhaps this sentence will help you remember them. *There are several different hypotheses which claim to explain these phenomena and in his doctoral thesis Kohl offers an analysis of each hypothesis in accordance with a rigorous set of criteria.*

Exercises

29.1 Rewrite the underlined words and phrases using words and phrases from A opposite.

1. Many educators believe that different learning styles are equally acceptable.
2. In the UK a university faculty is a unit where similar subjects are grouped together.
3. The French impressionists were a key group with shared aims in European art.
4. The most important quality of international law is the application of a single standard for strong and weak nations alike.
5. Researchers spend much of their time trying to understand the meaning of their data.
6. Some 19th-century artistic styles were a direct response to the ugliness of industrialisation.
7. Harvey (2003) stresses that the findings of the study cannot be said to be always true, as only a small amount of data was used.
8. In the late 20th century, intellectual ways of thinking were greatly influenced by ideas of gender and race.
9. The article states to be true that internet gaming can provide a useful educational experience.
10. In my opinion, the theory of the big bang represented a complete change in our way of thinking about the universe.

29.2 Rewrite the sentences changing the underlined words from singular to plural or vice versa, as instructed. Make any other necessary changes.

1. There's an interesting PhD thesis on water resources in the library. (make plural)
2. What were your main criteria in designing your survey? (make singular)
3. She was interested in strange phenomena connected with comets. (make singular)
4. The hypothesis was never proved, as the data were incomplete. (make plural)

29.3 Match the beginnings and endings of the sentences.

1 We must never accept the notion	☐	a on the role of the United Nations in times of war.
2 The task of choosing an analytical	☐	b on gender and language use very clear.
3 The book expresses his viewpoint	☐	c of dark matter to explain certain observations.
4 Tannen has always made her stance	☐	d that intelligence is connected to race.
5 Consumers have different perceptions	☐	e of family healthcare which changed everything.
6 The report laid out a new model	☐	f of what low price and high quality mean.
7 Physicists developed the concept	☐	g framework is an important stage in any research.

29.4 Read the text and match the underlined words with the definitions. Use a dictionary if necessary.

Autonomy and creativity are two key concepts in the humanities which are often thought to be not part of scientific thinking. However, recent projects in the sciences suggest this is not true. For example, the attempt to load the components of human consciousness into a computer is a fundamentally creative activity which has profound implications for our understanding of what a human being is. Such science may make us change our way of thinking about moral and philosophical questions and may make it possible for those in the humanities to find a new grounding for their own work.

1. relating to standards of good or bad behaviour, what is right and wrong, etc.
2. felt or experienced very strongly or in an extreme way
3. a foundation or basis for something
4. ideas or opinions about something
5. the opposite of 'the sciences'
6. independence, or the right to think in your own way
7. knowledge about something

Over to you

Choose five words or expressions that you particularly want to learn from this unit and write sentences using them in relation to your own discipline.

30 Reporting what others say

A Reporting verbs

Reporting what others say is a key aspect of academic English. Notice the verb patterns.

In her latest article Morton **explains** how information technology is changing society.
Schmidt **describes** the process of language change.
Lee **states** that problems arose earlier than was previously thought. [says directly]
Uvarov **claims/asserts/contends/maintains/declares** that the causes of the revolution can be traced back to the 1800s. [says something is true, often used when others disagree]
Levack **observes/notes/comments/points out** that there are contradictions in Day's interpretation of the poem. [states but does not develop at length]
In the book Dean **mentions** some new research in the field. [refers to briefly]
Kim **demonstrates/shows** how Bach's music draws on earlier composers' work.
Gray **proves** there is a link between obesity and genes. [shows that something must be true]
Kon **suggests** that all poets are influenced by their childhood. [says indirectly or tentatively]
Van Ek **implies** that other historians have misinterpreted the period. [suggests indirectly]
Patel **argues** that governments should fund space research. [states with reasons]
Greenberg **emphasises/highlights/stresses** the importance of diet. [gives particular importance to]
McIntosh **pinpoints** the key features of the period in question. [focuses in on]
Vaz **advances/puts forward/proposes** a new theory. [used with *idea*, *theory*, *hypothesis*]
Davidson **casts doubt on** previous research in the field. [suggests it is inaccurate]
Gerhard **questions** previous interpretations of the play. [expresses doubts about]

B Reporting nouns

Academic writing frequently uses reporting nouns. Notice the verbs and patterns with each noun

Morton **provides an explanation as to** how information technology is changing society.
Schmidt **gives a description of** the process of language change.
Lee's **statement** that problems arose earlier than previously thought **has been challenged**.
Uvarov **makes the claim/assertion** that the causes of the revolution can be traced back to the 1800s.
Levack's **observation** that there are contradictions in Day's interpretation of the poem **has been supported** by a number of other scholars.
Kim gives a fascinating **demonstration of the way in which** Bach's music draws on the work of earlier composers.
Gray **provides proof of** the link between obesity and genes.
Kon's **suggestion** that poets are influenced by their childhood **is convincing**.
Van Ek **makes the** controversial **implication** that other historians have misinterpreted the period.
Patel **puts forward the argument** that governments should fund space research.
Greenberg **puts emphasis/stress on** the importance of diet. [Pl = emphases]

Common Mistake

According to is used when reporting others' viewpoints rather than your own. For example, *according to Greene and Willis* ... but *I would argue that* ... NOT ~~according to me~~.

Exercises

30.1 Cross out the word which is not possible in each sentence.

1 Sims *notes / observes / pinpoints* that commodity prices change depending on the season.
2 Grey *puts forward / proves / advances* a controversial theory to explain climate change.
3 Philipson *claims / questions / challenges* the accuracy of Malwar's figures.
4 Trail *stresses / emphasises / asserts* the importance of pilot testing before carrying out a survey.
5 Ripoll *advances / demonstrates / shows* how large-scale urban planning can go wrong.
6 Evans *declared / cast doubt / maintained* there was no causal link between the events.

30.2 Complete the table. Use a dictionary if necessary.

noun	verb	noun	verb
implication			describe
	observe	statement	
argument			emphasise
assertion			explain
	contend	demonstration	

30.3 Rewrite the sentences using nouns instead of the underlined verbs.

1 Harkov <u>contends</u> that population growth will be a serious problem, but this is not accepted by many scientists.
Harkov's *contention that population growth will be a serious problem is not accepted by many scientists.*
2 'Global symmetry' <u>states</u> that the laws of physics take the same form when expressed in terms of distinct variables.
'Global symmetry' is ...
3 The report <u>implies</u> that no individual government will ever be able to control the internet.
The report ...
4 Dudas <u>demonstrates</u> how dangerous genetic modification might be.
Dudas ...
5 Groot <u>emphasises</u> the role of schools in preventing teenage drug abuse.
Groot ...
6 Lenard <u>observes</u> that women use expressions such as 'you know' in English more than men but this was later proved to be inaccurate.
Lenard's ...
7 Plana <u>explained</u> the possible origins of the pyramids but this has been disputed by Ruiz.
Plana's ...
8 Wilson <u>describes</u> the ancient alphabet of the Guelcoga people.
Wilson ...
9 Wu <u>argues</u> that daylight-saving time should be extended throughout the year.
Wu ...
10 The President <u>asserts</u> that he cares about fighting poverty.
The President ...

30.4 Correct the mistakes in the sentences.

1 According to me, courses in academic writing should be compulsory for all new students.
2 It has not yet been proof that the virus can jump from species to species.
3 Richardson emphasises on a number of weaknesses in the theory.
4 Pratt makes a lot of emphasis on the relationship between geography and history.
5 Our latest results cast doubt to our original hypothesis.

Over to you

Find some examples of reporting what others say in an academic article or textbook in your own field. Do they use language from this unit? Copy out any interesting examples.

31 Talking about meaning

A The importance of meaning

Academic study in any subject inevitably requires precision with regard to the meanings of the **terms**[1] used. Many textbooks provide a **glossary**[2] of the **terminology**[3] of the subject and this should be referred to frequently, whenever the meaning of some new term is not **transparent**[4]. Often there are **subtle distinctions**[5] between the way in which a word is used in a non-academic context and the way in which it is used in a specific academic discipline and the student needs to be able to **distinguish**[6] between these different **senses**[7] of the same word. When writing an essay or an article it is often appropriate to begin by **defining**[8] the key terms relating to the topic. If this is not done, then the reader may find the writing **ambiguous**[9] and may **misinterpret**[10] the text. In lectures, too, the audience will require the lecturer to **clarify**[11] what they are saying by providing a definition of any unfamiliar terminology. This is essential if the lecturer is to communicate their meaning in a clear, **concise**[12] and **coherent**[13] way.

[1] individual words or expressions used in relation to a specific context [2] list of words/expressions with explanations of their meanings [3] a general word for the words/expressions used in relation to a specific subject [4] clear, often used when referring to meaning [5] small differences [6] understand the difference [7] meanings [8] explaining the meaning of [9] having more than one possible meaning [10] understand in the wrong way [11] make clear [12] expressing what needs to be said in a short and clear way [13] carefully organised and making sense

B The power of words

Writers may use words to **express** ideas or to **convey** a **message**[1] or to **evoke**[2] an **atmosphere**[3]. In scientific **discourse**[4], if words are not used precisely, then it is hard for the reader to **comprehend**[5] what the writer is trying to say. In literature, especially in poetry, the **connotations**[6] that words have may be at least as important, if not more important, than what those words **denote**[7]. The reader has to **infer**[8] the poet's meaning and this may involve being sensitive to **nuances of meaning**[9] and the ability to see things from the poet's **perspective**[10].

[1] key idea (e.g. in a book or film) [2] create a feeling or mood [3] feeling or mood [4] written or spoken texts [5] (formal) understand. In this context we can also say *apprehend* [6] associations [7] mean [8] form an opinion on the basis of indirect evidence [9] small differences in meaning [10] point of view

Language help

Use prefixes to help you work out the meaning of some words that initially look unfamiliar. For example, the prefix *mis-* carries the idea of wrongly or badly as in *misinterpret/misinterpretation*. Other examples include *mistranslate/mistranslation* and *misquote/misquotation*. (See Reference 5.)

Exercises

31.1 **Dr Babayan is advising Tomoko, one of his students who is about to start writing up her dissertation. Complete their conversation using words from A opposite.**

Dr Babayan: In the first chapter, you need a section where you [1]d.................. your [2]t.................. .

Tomoko: I'm sorry, what does that involve exactly?

Dr Babayan: You explain the [3]t.................., of your subject, the special technical words or phrases you're going to use and what precise meaning they have so that your text is [4]t.................., and every reader knows exactly what you mean when you use a word or phrase.

Tomoko: Does it have to be in the first chapter?

Dr Babayan: Well, usually, yes, though an alternative way of doing it is to provide an alphabetical [5]g.................. at the back of the dissertation where readers can look up the meaning. And remember, if you're using different [6]s.................. of the same word you must explain each one.

Tomoko: That's my problem. I sometimes find it difficult to [7]d.................. between the different meanings. There are so many [8]s.................. d.................. between words and between the different meanings of the same words in English.

Dr Babayan: Yes, I know, but all languages are like that; it's just that you don't notice it in your own language. Look, a dissertation is all about communicating your ideas in a clear, [9]c.................. and [10]c.................. manner. If you use words which are [11]a.................., your readers might [12]m.................. your text. So it's always important to [13]c.................. what you intend to say.

31.2 **Complete the text using the correct form of words from the box.**

denote perspective express comprehend evoke
nuance discourse convey infer connotation

'And it's a hard rain's a-gonna fall'

The American songwriter Bob Dylan is often considered to be as much a poet as a musician. He [1].................. his political ideas through folk songs in his early period. His melodies were often simple but his words [2].................. complex messages, often with subtle [3].................. of meaning. In one of his songs, he speaks of a 'hard rain' which will fall after a nuclear war. On one level the words [4].................. real, radioactive rain, but the [5].................. of the words are many: life will be hard, perhaps impossible. Perhaps the consequences will fall hard on the politicians who started the war too. There are many things we can [6].................. from these words. The song reflects the political [7].................. of the Cold War of the 1960s. It [8].................. an atmosphere of fear and hopelessness. Seen from the [9].................. of the post-Cold-War era, it may seem difficult to [10].................. such fear, but at the time, that fear was very real.

31.3 **Add negative prefixes *un-*, *in-* or *mis-* to the underlined words. Use a dictionary if necessary.**

1 The sign had been ....translated, so no one could understand what it meant.
2 I ....understood one of the exam questions and wrote about the wrong subject.
3 The text was quite ....ambiguous, so there was only one way of interpreting it.
4 Some of the totals had evidently been ....calculated, so the results were unreliable.
5 The essay was quite ....coherent, so it was almost impossible to follow the argument. There were also several ....quotations from well-known sources.
6 The law had been applied ....frequently and often ....appropriately before the government changed it in 2012.

32 Talking about points of view

A Commenting on others' views

No one can have a completely **objective**[1] point of view. Inevitably, we all see things to some extent **subjectively**[2]. It is impossible to be truly **impartial**[3]. We tend to be **biased in favour of**[4] things we're familiar with and **prejudiced against**[5] things we have little experience of. Of course, everyone believes their own views are totally **rational**[6].

[1] not influenced by personal beliefs or attitudes, based only on facts; opposite = **subjective** [2] in a way that is influenced by personal beliefs or attitudes [3] not supporting one person or group more than others [4] showing an unreasonable liking for something based on personal beliefs or opinions; opposite = **biased against** [5] showing an unreasonable dislike for, based on personal beliefs or opinions (stronger and more pejorative than *biased*); opposite = prejudiced in favour of [6] based only on reason; opposite = **irrational**

People's views tend to change as they grow older and begin looking at life from a different **standpoint**[1]. Young people are more likely to be **radical**[2] but then become more **reactionary**[3] or **conservative**[4] with age, considering their younger opinions **immature**[5].

[1] set of principles or beliefs on the basis of which opinions are formed [2] believing that there should be extreme political or social change [3] (disapproving) opposed to political or social change or new ideas [4] not inclined to trust change, especially if it is sudden [5] (disapproving) lacking in experience; opposite = **mature**

An **ideology** is a theory or set of beliefs or principles, particularly one on which a political system or organisation is based. It often has slightly negative associations in English, implying something that is rigid and restricting. A **philosophy**, on the other hand, suggests a set of beliefs that is much more thoughtful and serious.

B Word combinations relating to points of view

word combination	example	meaning
to hold views	My grandfather **holds** some surprisingly progressive **views**.	has ..... opinions
to adopt/take a stance	It is important that the university should **adopt** a principled **stance** towards research.	take a .... position
to change/shift your position	Luisa was initially totally opposed to the idea but she has slightly **shifted** her **position**.	changed her point of view a little
have ethical objections to	Increasing numbers of people **have ethical objections to** the war.	dislike for reasons relating to morality
the principles underlying	'Treat others as you would like to be treated' is a **principle underlying** much religious teaching.	basic idea lying behind something. You can also say **the underlying principles**.
to encounter prejudice	Female students in the 1920s **encountered** a certain amount of **prejudice**.	experienced unreasonable negative behaviour
deep-rooted prejudice	John does not share his father's **deep-rooted prejudices** against women.	strong, unreasonably negative views

Common Mistake

You can say *in my opinion* but NOT ~~in my point of view~~. You can say *from (someone's) point of view* but it means from that person's way of looking at something rather than in that person's opinion. ***From the language teacher's point of view**, it's good that all children have to learn a foreign language at school.*

Exercises

32.1 Replace the underlined words with words from A which mean the opposite.

1 The views she expressed were totally <u>rational</u>.
2 The committee seemed to be <u>biased against</u> applications from younger people.
3 The book is an <u>objective</u> account of life in a small town in the 1920s.
4 The club rules were <u>prejudiced in favour of</u> children.
5 The President's daughter was quite <u>mature</u> for her age.
6 He has rather <u>radical</u> views about marriage.
7 Her views on education are rather <u>radical</u>. (use a different word from 6)
8 In my opinion that judge always acts in a <u>biased</u> way.

32.2 Complete the sentences using the correct form of words from the box.

root	shift	adopt	encounter	underlie	philosophy	hold	ethical

1 The .... principles of Asian and European .... are very similar.
2 People tend .... a more conservative stance as they get older.
3 She has always .... the view that primary education should not start before the age of seven.
4 Many people have .... objections to investing in companies which support corrupt regimes.
5 Some employers still have a deep .... prejudice against employing older people, and many older people .... such prejudice when they apply for jobs.
6 The government seems to have .... its position recently.

32.3 Choose the correct word to complete each sentence.

1 Sandro majored in *philosophy* / *ideology* at Berkeley.
2 Most vegetarians do not eat meat because of their ethical *principles* / *objections* to killing animals.
3 After reading widely on the subject, I have *changed* / *adopted* my position with regard to the primary cause of the revolution.
4 It's worth spending plenty of time planning your essays, *in* / *from* my opinion.
5 Nothing will change unless people are prepared to *shift* / *take* a firm stance against injustice.
6 *In* / *From* the point of view of most local residents, the proposed new motorway would be a disaster.

32.4 Rewrite the sentences using the words in brackets.

1 The people of the area have some unusual views about nature. (HOLD)
2 Most young people seem not to like the proposals on student fees. (OBJECTIONS)
3 Examiners tend to prefer candidates with neat handwriting. (BIASED)
4 Girls look at their careers in a different way from their mothers. (STANDPOINT)
5 Let us now discuss the principles behind this approach. (UNDERLYING)

32.5 The following text contains some more words and phrases connected with points of view, opinions and ideas. Read the text and explain the meaning of the underlined words and phrases. Use a dictionary if necessary.

Academics have traditionally <u>taken the view</u> that their discipline is <u>intellectually independent</u> from all others. However, inter-disciplinary degrees are becoming more and more common, suggesting that <u>preconceptions</u> about what and how one should study may be somewhat <u>misplaced</u>. A more <u>liberal</u> view of education would <u>advocate</u> greater freedom to explore the links between different <u>fields of learning</u>, thus <u>pushing the frontiers of knowledge</u> in new and exciting directions. Many academics now feel that the future lies in this <u>blending of ideas</u> and the <u>cross-fertilisation</u> of <u>thought</u> which emerges from it.

33 Numbers

A Types of numbers

A **series** or **set** of numbers is a group of numbers together.

A **sequence** of numbers is a group of numbers in a significant order. For example, 1, 4, 9, 16, 25 is a sequence of numbers – it represents the numbers 1 to 5 **squared** ($1^2 = 1$, $2^2 = 4$, $3^2 = 9$, etc.)

1, 3, 5, 7 ... = **odd numbers**; 2, 4, 6, 8 ... = **even numbers**; 2, 3, 5, 7, 11 ... = **prime numbers** [numbers that cannot be divided by any other number, apart from themselves and 1].

The **maximum** is the highest number in a group and the **minimum** is the lowest number. *The room holds a maximum of 50 and we won't run the class without a minimum of 12 students.*

An **approximate** number is one which is roughly correct but is not the **precise** or **exact** number. *Work out the approximate answer in your head, then use a calculator to find the exact number.*

An **aggregate** is a number reached by totalling a set of numbers = the **total**. *The **average** exam mark is calculated by taking the **aggregate** of all the marks and dividing by the number of exam entries.*

A **discrete** number or unit is something which is separate and cannot be divided into smaller numbers or units of the same thing.

A **constant** number or quantity is one that does not change. *In the experiment we **varied** [changed] the amount of water in the beaker but kept the amount of salt added **constant**.*

A **random** number is one chosen by chance, i.e. you cannot predict it.

B Working with numbers

The word **figure** is often used to refer to the symbol used for a number. *Write the total number in words and **figures**.*

You can **calculate**[1] a number, **estimate**[2] a number, round a number **up/down**[3] and **total**[4] a set of numbers. Numbers can **tally**[5]. *My figures don't seem to **tally** with yours.* You can also **deduct**[6] one number from another number.

Values are individual numbers in a set of data. *The graph shows the temperature **values** for different months of the year.* **Variables** are characteristics that can take on different values for different members of a group or set being studied. *In investigating living standards you must take key **variables** such as social provision and cost of living into account.*

The **incidence** of something refers to how frequently it occurs. ***The incidence of** twins in the population is growing.* When talking about numbers, **magnitude** simply refers to the size of something, whereas in other contexts it indicates large size or importance. *Write down the numbers in **order of magnitude**, beginning with the smallest.*

When **making calculations** in, say, an exam, it is often a good idea to make an **estimate**[7] first of what the answer is likely to be. Then you will see if your final answer is **in the right area**[8] or not. Exam candidates are also often advised to show their **workings**[9] so that the marker can see how they **arrived at** their answer and they may get credit for their method even if the final answer is incorrect.

[1] work out [2] make a rough guess at [3] make a **fraction**, e.g. $\frac{1}{6}$ or 0.78 into the nearest **whole number** [4] add up [5] match, agree [6] take away, subtract [7] rough guess [8] approximately the same [9] all the calculations leading up to an answer

Common Mistake

Numbers between 1 and 2 (e.g. 1.6, one and a half, $1\frac{1}{4}$) are followed by a plural noun. *The population was studied over a period of one and a half years.* (NOT ~~one and a half year~~).

Exercises

33.1 Answer the questions.

1 What is five squared?
2 What is the next prime number after 19?
3 How is this sequence of numbers created? 3, 9, 27, 81
4 What is the aggregate of this set of test marks? 6, 8, 9, 5, 6, 7
5 If you round up 6.66, what number do you have?
6 $\frac{7}{9}$ and 4 – which is a whole number and which is a fraction?
7 In your country is tax automatically deducted from employees' earnings?
8 Is an accountant pleased or displeased if figures that he/she is checking tally?

33.2 Dr Syal is advising one of his dissertation students who is interested in pollution in road tunnels. Complete the conversation with the correct words.

Dr Syal: You could [1]c.................... the total number of private cars that use the tunnel each week, based on the day-to-day figures, and get an [2]a.................... figure for how much carbon they're all emitting.

Melissa: How [3]p.................... would that figure have to be?

Dr Syal: Oh, it doesn't have to be exact, you just need to [4]e.................... more or less what the total pollution will be. Then you can check to see if those figures [5]t.................... with the figures that have already been published for similar tunnels. And the figure won't be [6]c.................... of course; it'll go up and down depending on lots of factors such as weather conditions, average speed, etc.

Melissa: But can we say if the figures will be true for the future too?

Dr Syal: Well, we do know that traffic has been growing over the past ten years; it hasn't ever gone down, so I think you can make some useful predictions.

Melissa: Should I present each daily total as a [7]d.................... item or can I just put them all together into one figure for each week?

Dr Syal: A weekly total is fine, and you can [8].................... it up or [9].................... to the nearest 100.

Melissa: Right, OK. Thanks so much for your help.

33.3 Rewrite the sentences using the correct form of the word in brackets.

1 There were fewer accidents last year. (INCIDENCE) *The incidence of accidents declined last year.*
2 We made a rough guess at what the final figure might be. (ESTIMATE)
3 The graph shows the results from the lowest to the highest. (MAGNITUDE)
4 A computer program helped us work out the significance of the different variables. (CALCULATE)
5 Taking x away from y will help you arrive at the correct answer. (SUBTRACT)
6 The results from the first experiment were not the same as those we got from the repeat experiment. (TALLY)

33.4 Complete the email from a maths tutor using words from the box. There is one word you don't need. There is also one deliberate mistake in the email. Can you find it and correct it?

calculations variables
figures reached
area workings
values arrived

Hi everyone,
Just a quick note before you take the exam. Things to remember:
The exam lasts one and a half hour, so plan your time carefully.
Don't forget to show all your [1].................... as we want to see how you [2].................... at your results. Take great care when you make your [3]....................
– you'd be amazed at how many people submit answers that are hardly even in the right [4].................... . And please write legibly – we must be able to distinguish all your [5].................... . When doing graphs, plot the [6]....................
carefully and if asked to describe an experiment don't forget to take all significant [7].................... into account. Good luck!
Helen Ward

34 Statistics

A Basic statistical terms

A **normal distribution** of data means that most of the examples in a **set of data** are close to the **average**, also known as the **mean**, while relatively few examples tend to one extreme or the other. Normally distributed data shown on a chart will typically show a **bell curve**. It will often be necessary to work out the extent to which individuals **deviate**[1] **from the norm**[2] and to calculate the figure that represents **standard deviation**[3].

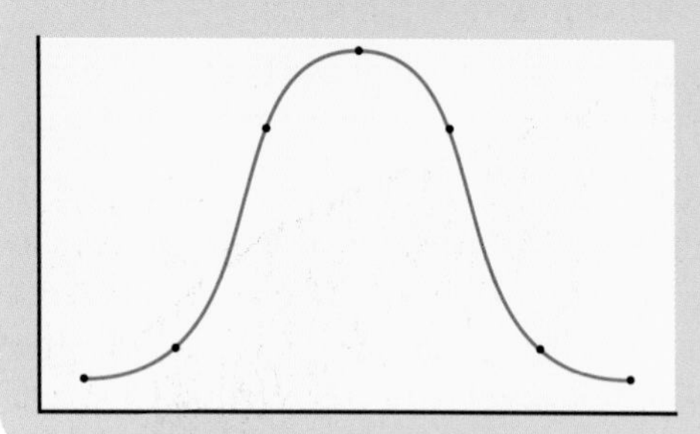

Six children are 7, 8, 8, 8, 11 and 12 years old. Their average or mean age is 9 years old (the **sum** of their ages divided by six). The **mode** (the most frequent value) is 8. The **median** is 9.5 (the **halfway point** between the two **extremes** of the **range**).

Statisticians are often concerned with working out **correlations**[4] – the extent to which, say, left-handedness **correlates with** intelligence. They must ensure that any data they collect is **valid**, i.e. that it is measuring what it claims to measure – all the subjects in the **sample**[5] must be appropriately and accurately assessed as left or right-handed, for example. The figures must also be **reliable**, i.e. they would be **consistent**[6] if the measurements were repeated. Usually, statisticians hope that their calculations will **show/indicate** a **tendency**, e.g. that left-handed people will be shown to be **significantly**[7] more intelligent than right-handed people.

[1] differ [2] the average [3] average difference from the norm [4] connections, often as cause and effect [5] the subjects of the experiment or group representing the total population measured [6] the same [7] noticeably

B A probability[1] problem

Sue picks a card **at random**[2] from an ordinary pack of 52 cards. If the card is a king, she stops. If not, she continues to pick cards at random, without replacing them, until either a king is picked or six cards have been picked. The **random variable**[3], C, is the total number of cards picked. Construct a diagram to illustrate the possible **outcomes**[4] of the experiment, and use it to calculate the **probability distribution**[5] of C.

[1] likelihood of something happening [2] by chance [3] number or element of a situation that can change [4] results [5] assessment of probabilities for each possible value of C

C Other useful nouns for talking about statistics

In a class of 8 women and 4 men, what **proportion**[1] are male? Answer: one third

In the same class what is the female to male **ratio**[2]? Answer: 2:1 (two to one)

The figures show a **trend**[3] towards healthier eating habits.

The study investigates the increase in the **volume**[4] of traffic on the roads.

Most of the students achieved marks between 45% and 65% but there were a couple of **outliers**[5] who got 32% and 84%

[1] number compared with another number [2] relationship between two numbers showing how much bigger one is [3] change in a particular direction [4] amount, quantity [5] figures very different from others in the set

Common Mistake

We say *10* ***per cent*** (NOT ~~the 10 per cent~~ or ~~10 percentage~~) of students got an A for the exam but the ***percentage*** of students achieving an A has increased.

Exercises

34.1 **Complete the sentences with words from A opposite.**

1 The six subjects who took the test scored 24, 22, 16, 16, 16 and 14 points out of 30. The .... was 16. The .... score was 19 and the .... or .... score was 18.
2 The .... of all donations to the charity in 2003 was $3,938. The smallest donation was $10 and the largest was $130. Most were around the .... point of $60.
3 The centre has recorded a wide .... of temperatures, with the two .... being 35° in the summer and -6° in the winter.

34.2 **Complete the text with words from the box. There are three words you don't need.**

distribution trends varieties significantly probability sample random correlate outcomes variables insignificantly

Life insurance companies base their calculations on the laws of [1] ...., that is they assess the likely [2] ...., given the different [3] .... such as age, sex, lifestyle and medical history of their clients. The premiums are therefore not chosen at [4] .... but are carefully calculated. The [5] .... of ages at which death occurs and causes of death are studied to see if they [6] .... with other factors to be taken into account in setting the premiums. Naturally, the companies also monitor social [7] .... and react to any changes which might [8] .... affect mortality rates.

34.3 **Answer the questions.**

1 There are 12 male students and 6 female students in the class. What is the ratio of males to females? And what proportion of the class is male?
2 If in a sample of 100 students, 98 evaluate a module as 5 or 6 out of 10 but 1 gives it 1 and 1 gives it 10, what are the scores of 1 and 10 called?
3 If my data show a tendency for students to choose the type of clothing their friends choose, does it mean that they always, often or rarely choose similar clothes?
4 If I repeat the same experiment three times and the results are not consistent, is my method reliable?
5 If 20 out of 200 students fail an exam, what proportion, in percentage terms, failed?
6 If the average score in a test is 56, and Barbara scores 38, by how many points has she deviated from the norm?
7 If the volume of court cases increases, what changes: the type of case, the size of each case or the total number of cases?
8 What does standard deviation tell us: (a) What the standard of something is, (b) what the norm is, or (c) what the average difference from the norm is?
9 If a general survey of teenage eating habits asks questions about what teenagers eat for breakfast and lunch, is the survey likely to be valid?
10 Here is a graph showing how many students got scores within each 10-mark band in a biology test. Do the scores show a normal distribution? What is the shape of the graph called?

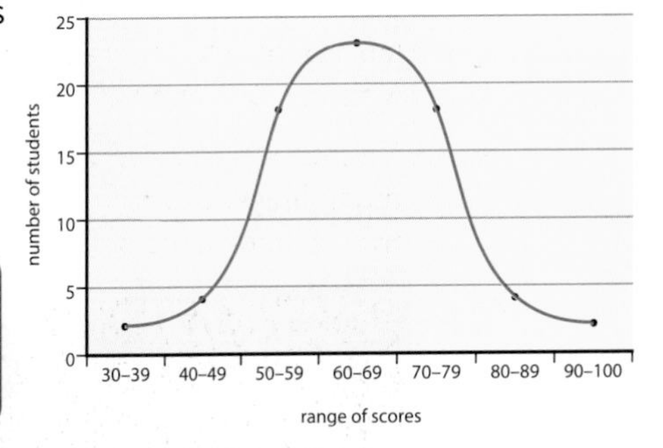

Over to you

What kinds of statistical data are likely to be discussed in your discipline? Find a relevant chart, graph or table and write about it using some terms from this unit.

35 Graphs and diagrams

A Types of diagrams

Diagrams are visual ways of **presenting data** concisely. They are often also called **figures**. In an academic article they are usually **labelled** Fig. (Figure) 1, Fig. 2, etc.

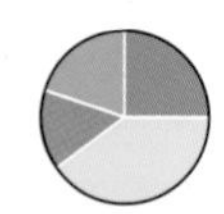

A **pie chart** is a circle divided into **segments** from the middle (like slices of a cake) to show how the total is divided up. A **key** or **legend** shows what each segment represents.

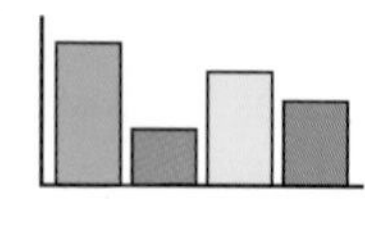

A **bar chart** is a diagram in which different amounts are represented by thin vertical or horizontal bars which have the same width but **vary** in height or length.

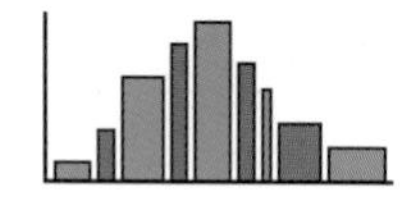

A **histogram** is a kind of bar chart but the bar width also varies to indicate different values.

Number	Amount
1	10
2	5
3	20

A **table** is a grid with **columns** and **rows** of numbers.

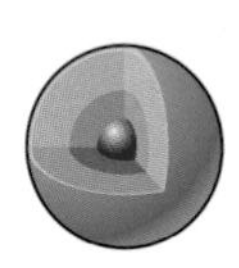

A **cross-section** is something, or a model of something, cut across the middle so that you can see the inside. A cross-section of the earth's crust, for example, shows the different **layers** that make it up. A **label** gives the name of each part of the cross-section. Cross-section can also be used to mean a small group that is representative of all the different types within the total group (e.g. *the survey looked at a cross-section of society*).

A **flowchart** is a diagram which indicates the **stages** of a process.

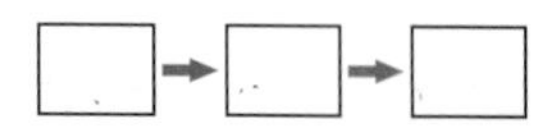

Common Mistake

Don't use the definite article (*the*) when referring to a specific diagram. *See Table 4 below.* (NOT ~~See the table 4~~ ...)

B A graph

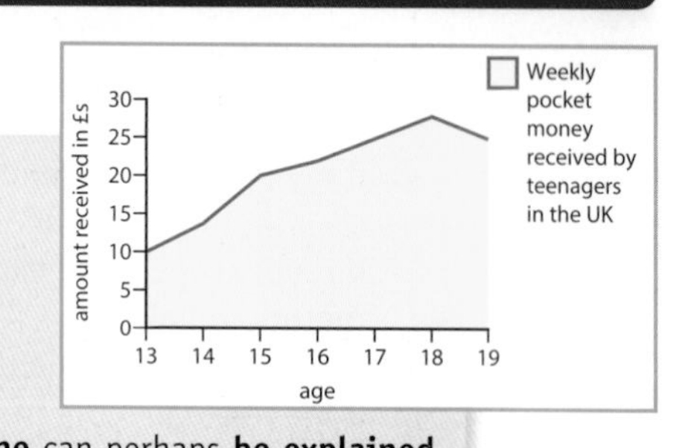

The **graph presents** data relating to teenagers and pocket money. A **random sample** of 1,000 teenagers were surveyed and the average pocket money received at each age has been plotted on the graph. The **x axis** or **horizontal axis indicates** age and the **y axis** or **vertical axis shows** the amount of money received per week. The **graph shows** that 15-year-olds receive twice as much pocket money as 13-year-olds. **From the** graph **we can see** that the amount received **reaches a peak** at the age of 18 and then starts to decline. This **decline** can perhaps **be explained by the fact that** many teenagers start earning and stop receiving pocket money at the age of 18.

Graphs are drawn by **plotting** points on them and then drawing a line to join **adjacent** points. If there are two separate lines on a graph, the lines can **cross** or **intersect** at various points. Lines that **run parallel** to one another never intersect.

Graphs show how numbers **increase** or **decrease**. Numbers can also be said to **rise** or **grow** and **fall**, **drop** or **decline**. Other verbs used about growth include **double**[1], **soar**[2], **multiply**[3], **appreciate**[4] and **exceed**[5] [another number].

[1] increase to twice the number or amount; opposite = **halve** [2] increase very quickly and by a large amount; opposite = **plummet** [3] increase to a very large number [4] increase in value; opposite = **depreciate** [5] increase to greater than a particular number or amount; opposite = **fall below**

Language help

The verbs *increase* and *decrease* are followed by *by* (e.g. *The population of the city has increased by 10%.*). The nouns *increase, rise, growth, fall, drop* and *decline, decrease*, are followed by *in* (to explain what is rising) or *of* (to explain the size of the change), e.g. *a rise / an increase* ***of*** *15%* ***in*** *the number of cars.*

Exercises

35.1 **Look at the chart and complete the text with the missing words.**

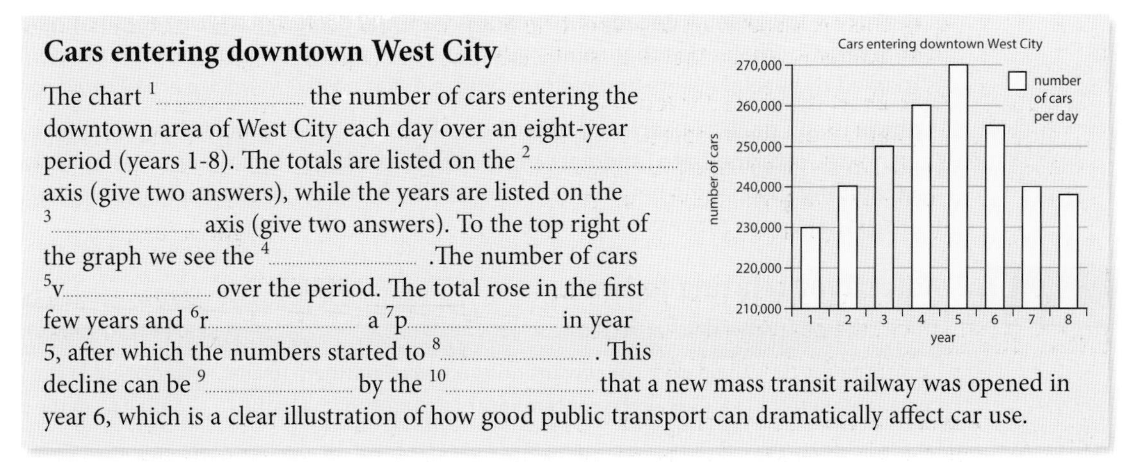

Cars entering downtown West City

The chart [1]............ the number of cars entering the downtown area of West City each day over an eight-year period (years 1-8). The totals are listed on the [2]............ axis (give two answers), while the years are listed on the [3]............ axis (give two answers). To the top right of the graph we see the [4]............ .The number of cars [5]v............ over the period. The total rose in the first few years and [6]r............ a [7]p............ in year 5, after which the numbers started to [8]............ . This decline can be [9]............ by the [10]............ that a new mass transit railway was opened in year 6, which is a clear illustration of how good public transport can dramatically affect car use.

35.2 **Answer the questions.**

1 Draw examples of a pie chart and a bar chart.
2 What is the best type of diagram to present the different layers of rock in the Grand Canyon?
3 In a table, what is the difference between columns and rows?
4 What would be the best type of diagram to present the different stages in a research project you did?
5 How many segments are there in the pie chart in A opposite?
6 If you look at two adjacent columns in a table, are they next to each other or separated?
7 What is another name for a legend in a diagram?
8 What type of data collection are you doing if you survey the first 50 people you come across?
9 What do two lines on a graph do if (a) they intersect and (b) they run parallel to each other?
10 Choose the correct sentence: (a) There was an increase in 12% of smart phone sales last year. (b) There was an increase of 12% in smart phone sales last year.

35.3 **Replace the underlined words with more precise, academic words.**

1 The different <u>bits</u> of the pie chart show the numbers of people in each age group.
2 She kept a record by <u>marking</u> the midday temperature on a graph for a month.
3 People's salaries usually reach their <u>highest point</u> when they are in their late 40s.
4 This flowchart shows the different <u>bits</u> of our project over the next five years.
5 The two lines on the graph <u>cross each other</u> at point A.
6 Draw a line connecting the points that are <u>next</u> to each other.
7 The government's popularity in the opinion polls is beginning to <u>go down</u>.
8 If you look along the third <u>line</u> of the table you can see the figures for the 1950s.

35.4 **Rewrite the underlined words and phrases using words from B opposite. There is also a deliberate mistake in one of the sentences. Can you find it and correct it?**

1 Populations of some bird species in South Asia have <u>crashed</u> by 97% in recent years. The number of cases of death by poisoning has <u>increased</u> sharply.
2 In 2007 the child mortality rate <u>fell to lower than</u> 60 deaths per 1,000.
3 The average family car in the UK <u>goes down in value</u> by 20% per year. This means its value has <u>fallen by more than half</u> after just three years.
4 A typical piece of land on the edge of the city will <u>go up in value</u> by 15% per year, and house prices have <u>gone up rapidly by a large amount</u> in the last six months.
5 Business courses have <u>increased greatly in number</u> while science programmes have <u>gone down</u>.
6 The temperature <u>rose higher than</u> 45°C in some parts of the country. See the figure 3.
7 Between 1983 and 2006, the number of this species of eagle <u>went up</u> from 22 pairs to 58. Other bird populations have <u>gone up to twice the number</u> in the same period.
8 The numbers of old soldiers attending regimental reunions are <u>becoming smaller</u> each year.

36 Time

A Periods of time

A **century** = 100 years. A **decade** = 10 years. An **annual** conference is one that happens every year. A **quarterly** journal is one that comes out four times a year. An **era** is a particular period of time that is marked by special events or developments, e.g. *the post-war era, an era of rapid social change*.

A **phase** is any stage in a **series of events** or process of development. A project can be at an **initial** [beginning], **intermediate** [middle] or **final phase or stage**. A phase or stage may also be described as **preceding** [happening before now], **current** [happening now], **critical** [particularly important] or **transitional** [in the process of change].

B Adjectives relating to time

Adjective	example	meaning
concurrent	There were **concurrent** riots in several northern towns.	occurring at the same time
contemporary	I studied all the **contemporary** accounts of the battle I could find. Jo is researching **contemporary** music.	dating from the same period existing now
eventual	The **eventual** cost of the project is likely to exceed €10 million.	happening or existing later; after effort or problems
forthcoming	My article will be published in the **forthcoming** issue of the *New Scientist*.	happening soon
ongoing	Helen has a number of **ongoing** projects.	happening now
simultaneous	There were **simultaneous** concerts in several cities.	happening at the same time
subsequent	The book examines the war and the **subsequent** changes in society.	happening after something else
successive	**Successive** governments would face similar problems.	happening immediately after something else
temporary	Georgia got a **temporary** position at the university.	not for a long period; not **permanent**

C How times change

In recent times/years – particularly the last three decades – society has **gone through a period** of considerable change. **Prior to** the 1990s very few people had access to a home computer. **Nowadays**[1] the majority of homes have at least one computer. This expansion in home computing has **coincided with**[2] the **emergence**[3] of internet technology. **At the moment** we are at a stage where the situation is still **evolving**[4]. Subsequent generations will live in a very different world although we do not know exactly how things will develop **in the near future**[5], **over the next few years**, let alone **in the long term**[6].

[1] at the present time (used to compare with the past, particularly in spoken English or more informal writing) [2] happened at the same time as [3] appearance [4] gradually changing [5] at a time which is not far away; opposite = **in the distant future**; [6] at a period of time in the distant future opposite = **in the short term**

Common Mistake

Sometimes words, e.g. *early*, *late*, *daily* can be both adverbs and adjectives, e.g. *a(n) early/late/daily meeting, we met early/late/daily*. But *nowadays* is only an adverb. We talk about *present/present-day/current* problems NOT ~~nowadays problems.~~

Exercises

36.1 **Complete the emails to university staff with the missing words. The first letter of each word is given to help you.**

Plans have now been finalised for the new sports centre and the [1]i.................... p.................... of the construction will begin on 1st March. From that date until completion of the works, the West Car Park will be closed. A [2]t....................car park will be available during the period at Campus East, and a new, [3]p.................... car park will be opened when the [4]f.................... stage of construction of the centre is completed.

Please inform your Department Secretary of all staff publications for the [8]c.................... academic year, including [9]f.................... papers and books (with the expected date of publication). These are needed for the University's [10]a.................... report. Include any publication from the [11]p.................... year which was not listed in last year's report.

Due to [5]o.................... technical problems, emails with large attachments may not be accepted by the university's server. This is likely to continue during the [6]t.................... phase of the project while the new server is being installed. This will reach a [7]c.................... stage next week, when problems may be greatest. We apologise for the inconvenience.

The University today celebrates a [12]c.................... of research. 100 years ago this month, the Centre for Medical Research was officially opened. In the last [13]d....................alone, five major new research centres have opened, a record for a ten-year period. We look forward to the start of a new [14]e.................... of research over the [15]n.................... f.................... years.

36.2 **Choose the correct words to complete each sentence.**

1 *In* / *At* the moment, I'm writing up my thesis. I hope to finish in the *near* / *next* future.
2 Our research is *at* / *in* an *intermediate* / *ongoing* stage – we now need to analyse our data.
3 The *emergency* / *emergence* of internet technology has transformed the travel industry.
4 The university has *gone* / *got* through a period of great change in the *latest* / *last* decade.
5 In the *far* / *distant* future, scientists may be able to cure almost all common diseases.
6 Anti-social behaviour is *a nowadays problem* / *a problem nowadays* in many big cities.
7 A *series* / *serial* of events occurred in 1986 which changed the political climate in the country. In *consequent* / *subsequent* years, two new parties were formed which became engaged in *concurrent* / *eventual* attempts to win over voters.
8 Prior *of* / *to* 2012, the industry was unregulated. In *recent* / *the last* years, however, the government has introduced new regulations.
9 In 1968, a monetary crisis coincided *with* / *to* a huge budget deficit, and most *contemporary* / *temporary* political commentators warned that the *eventual* / *forthcoming* cost to the nation would be enormous.
10 The Prime Minister asked people to put up with austerity in the *short* / *future* term, promising that they would reap the benefits in the *distant* / *long* term.

36.3 **Complete the table. Do not fill the shaded boxes. Use a dictionary if necessary.**

noun	verb	adjective	adverb
		eventual	
		successive	
	evolve		
emergence			
	coincide		
period			

Over to you

Write five sentences relevant to your discipline using words from 36.3.

37 Cause and effect

Cause and effect is often described using conjunctions like *because*, prepositional expressions like *due to* and *because of* and adverbs like *therefore* and *consequently*. In this unit we focus on verbs and nouns relating to cause and effect. Pay particular attention to the prepositions they are used with.

A Verbs relating to cause and effect

You are probably already familiar with these verbs relating to cause and effect: *make, cause, create, do, produce, force*. Here are some other useful verbs.

Her grandmother **influenced/had a considerable influence on** Sarah's choice of career.

Parental attitude largely **determines** how well a child adapts to school. [is the main factor affecting it]

A good teacher **motivates** their students. [makes them want to do something positive]

The flow of traffic through the town is **facilitated** by the one-way system. [made easier]

His speech **provoked** an angry response. [caused, usually something negative]

The explosion was **triggered** by the heat. [started, usually something sudden and negative]

The tilting of the earth on its axis **accounts for** the change in the seasons. [explains]

Sid's determination **springs/stems from** his desire to improve the world. [is the result of]

The country's victory **gave rise to** a new mood in society.

Mobile technology **contributed to** the information revolution. [was one factor influencing]

Their child was given drugs to **stimulate** growth. [cause something to develop or function]

Her exhibition **generated** a lot of interest. [caused something to happen or exist]

The drugs may **induce** nausea. [cause, often used in a medical context]

A teacher's presence can often **inhibit** teenagers' discussions. [prevent them from being as free as they might otherwise have been]

A number of benefits can be **derived from** this situation. [gained as a result of something]

B Nouns relating to cause and effect

noun	example	meaning/comment
chain reaction	The incident set off a **chain reaction** which affected us all.	set of related events in which each one causes the next one
consequence	The war had major **consequences**.	results
effect, impact	The **effect**/**impact** of the film **on** the audience was very powerful	influence
end	Does the **end** justify the means?	note how end here means aim or goal
origin/source	The accident was the **origin**/**source of** her later problems.	beginning or cause
outcome	The **outcome of** the discussions was very positive.	result or effect of an action
precedent	There are several **precedents for** taking such a decision.	something that already happened and provides a reason for doing the same
reason	What was the **reason for** his success / why he succeeded?	note how reason is often followed by for or why

Common Mistakes

1 While *cause* can be both a noun and a verb, *effect* is usually a noun. The equivalent verb is *affect. Her father's problems* ***affected*** *her deeply. Her father's problems had* ***a*** *profound* ***effect*** *on her.*
2 The preposition that follows *reason* is *for. What was the reason for the decline in the population?* (NOT ~~the reason of the decline~~ …)

Exercises

37.1 Choose the best verb to complete each sentence.

1 Researchers are investigating why chocolate *provokes / induces* headaches in certain people.
2 Wilson's most recent paper has *motivated / generated* a great deal of interest among sociologists.
3 The drug *triggered / facilitated* headaches and dizziness among a number of subjects in the test.
4 Having an end-of-term prize *contributes / motivates* students to do well in their class tests.
5 Intensive farming has *contributed to / provoked* the decline of bird populations.
6 The missile test *stimulated / provoked* an immediate and very strong response from neighbouring governments and from the United Nations.
7 Astrologists believe that people's lives are *motivated / determined* by the planets and stars.
8 The barrier *inhibits / induces* the flow of water into the area to prevent flooding in the rainy season.
9 A leak in the tank *stemmed from / accounted for* 40% of the fuel loss, and evaporation took away another 5%.
10 The renovated college buildings have wider doors to *influence / facilitate* the use of wheelchairs.
11 The Minister cut taxes in an attempt to *stimulate / trigger* the economy, which was performing poorly.
12 Britain has *facilitated / derived* many economic benefits from membership of the European Union.

37.2 Match the beginnings and endings of the sentences.

1 The article explores the origins
2 One small explosion set off a chain
3 The confusion probably stemmed
4 The proposed new tax could have
5 The disastrous events of 2003 gave
6 The judge explained that there were

☐ a major consequences for larger families.
☐ b precedents for his decision.
☐ c rise to a widespread sense of disillusionment.
☐ d of the concept of democracy.
☐ e reaction, causing massive damage.
☐ f from a lack of communication.

37.3 Complete the sentences with the missing words. In one sentence, it is not necessary to add a word.

1 De Routa's work in the 1970s influenced .... the development of computer science.
2 The acid seemed to have no .... whatsoever on the plastic, which remained unchanged.
3 Everyone hoped that the outcome .... the meeting between the two governments would be a new and better trade agreement.
4 The reason .... the failure of the project was a lack of funding.
5 The impact of global warming .... the polar ice caps is now understood more clearly.
6 There is no precedent .... this kind of decision.

37.4 Write the nouns related to these verbs. Use a dictionary if necessary.

motivate influence trigger contribute induce

37.5 Complete the sentences using the correct form of nouns from 37.4.

1 Byron's poetry had a significant .... on the work of other Romantic poets.
2 Tree pollen can be a .... for hay fever attacks in vulnerable people.
3 All the political parties illegally offered people .... to vote for them, such as cash payments, free tickets for sports events, etc.
4 The .... made by the burning of fossil fuels to global warming is now beyond dispute.
5 The .... to get a good job and to travel and see the world is often more effective than the teacher or the teaching material in language learning.

Over to you

Find a text describing a major event or series of events (e.g. an accident, a war, a social change) and note all the verbs and nouns in it relating to causes and effects or results. Write your own example sentences using these words.

38 Classifying

Classifying means dividing things into groups, according to their type.

A Useful nouns when classifying

word	example	meaning
category	Each of our students **falls into** one of three **categories**.	a group that shares some significant characteristics
component	Milk is an essential **component** of any young child's diet.	a part which combines with other parts to create something bigger
existence	The **existence** of 'dark matter' in the universe was first proposed in 1933.	the fact that something or someone is or exists
feature	Effective use of metaphor is a **feature** of the poet's style.	typical part or quality
hierarchy	Humans can be described as being at the top of a **hierarchy** with amoebas on the bottom level.	system in which people or things are arranged according to their importance or power
nature	The **nature** of her work means that she is under a lot of stress.	type or main characteristic of something
structure	In this unit we shall be looking at the **structure** of the heart.	the way in which the parts of a system are arranged
type	The lion is one **type** of large cat.	group with similar characteristics, a smaller division of a larger set

B One example of a classification system

There is an enormous **variety/diversity** of living things (or organisms). To help study them, biologists have **devised**[1] ways of naming and classifying them according to their **similarities** and **differences**. The system most scientists use puts each living thing into seven groups organised from most **general** to most **specific**. Therefore, each species **belongs to**[2] a genus, each genus belongs to a family, each family belongs to an order, etc. Species are the smallest groups. A species **consists of**[3] all the animals of the same type who are able to breed and produce young of the same kind; each species is **distinct from**[4] all other species. Biologists **allocate**[5] all organisms to a position in this system.

[1] thought of, invented [2] is part of [3] includes, is made up of [4] significantly different from
[5] place (also **assign**)

C Categorising people

When categorising people, it is often necessary to take age, **gender**[1], **social class, occupation, marital status** and **ethnic background**[2] into account. It may also be appropriate to consider the **urban-rural**[3] **dimension**[4]. Age, for example, is important in that different **generations** tend to have different attitudes and other **characteristics**. Social class can be **described** in different ways;
the term **blue collar** may be used to mean working class while **white collar denotes**[5] middle class. The categories of student, **homemaker** (i.e. housewife/househusband), and **senior citizen**, as well as types of **employment**[6] are **subsumed**[7] under the **heading**[8] of occupation or **occupational background/status**.

[1] sex, male or female [2] racial background [3] city versus countryside [4] aspect, way of considering something [5] means [6] paid work [7] included as part of a larger group [8] title summing up a group

Exercises

38.1 Complete the extracts from a lecture and a class using the words in the boxes.

belong categories components consist distinct diversity fall feature structure type

Computer programming languages usually [1]........................ into one of four [2]........................: imperative, functional, object-oriented and logic. These languages are [3]........................ from one another in how they operate. The [4]........................ of imperative languages is based on commands, you know, "do this, do that thing". Languages such as Fortran and COBOL [5]........................ to this [6]......................... Functional languages [7]........................ of mathematical functions . The [8]........................ of object-oriented languages are commands which are combined with the data to create "Objects". The main [9]........................ of logic languages is that they state facts or relations between things. Now, in the case of human languages, [10]........................ is considered a good thing. In the case of programming languages, it suggests we still haven't found the best one!

blue collar class devise employment ethnic gender generations homemakers occupational senior citizens

For your end-of-year project, you must carry out a survey of consumer preferences for one product or a type of product. You'll need to [11]........................ a questionnaire and you'll need to take a lot of factors into account. These include [12]........................, that is how many males and/or females are in your sample, social [13]........................, and so on. And also different [14]........................; will it just be adults, or young people too? And what about [15]........................? They may be retired, but they still buy a lot of things. Also, what about [16]........................ status? 'Are you going to separate [17]........................ and white collar workers? Or are you also interested in people who are not in [18]........................ such as [19]........................, but who are often the ones who buy the goods? And in our multicultural society, don't forget [20]........................ background.

38.2 Complete the table. Do not fill the shaded boxes. Use a dictionary if necessary.

noun	verb	adjective	adverb
		similar	
		different	
	allocate		
	describe		

38.3 Complete the sentences using the correct form of words from 38.2.

1 It is hard to .... between these two .... plants. They hardly .... at all.
2 The professor persuaded the university to .... more resources to his department.
3 There are some magnificent .... passages in the writer's later novels.
4 In your essay comment on the .... and the .... between the two poems.

38.4 Cross out the word that does not fit in each sentence.

1 It is difficult to *categorise / classify / devise* human emotions as we know little about their true *nature / structure / characteristics.*
2 Sensation and action can both be *included / subsumed / allocated* under the term 'behaviour'.
3 The atmosphere of the planet *consists / is made up / includes* of different gases.
4 The wildlife in this area is characterised by its *variety / hierarchy / diversity.*

39 Structuring an argument

A Developing an argument: what it is about

Read these extracts from the opening paragraphs of student essays. Note the prepositions.

This essay is **based on** findings from recent research into cold fusion.

The arguments I shall **put forward** are **relevant to** our understanding of Newton's laws.

The final section will **focus on** childcare, **paying attention to** the pre-school years in particular.

For the purposes of this essay, two opposing theories will be examined. I shall **refer to** Ashbach's and Linn's work, respectively.

The first section reviews recent literature, **with reference to** the arguments concerning social policy.

The political arguments concerning population control are **beyond the scope of** this essay.

Many articles have been published **on the subject of** genetic modification of crops.

B Adding points to an argument

Bad diet and high stress levels, **as well as** lack of exercise, are key factors in causing heart disease, **along with** smoking and high alcohol consumption.

In addition to the questionnaire, we also conducted interviews with some of the subjects.

A **further** argument in support of raising the retirement age is that life expectancy is increasing. **Moreover/Furthermore**[1], many people enjoy working; **for example** / **for instance**[2], in a recent survey, 68% of people said they would like to work till they were at least 70.

[1] *moreover* is much more frequently used in academic style than *furthermore* [2] *for example* is much more frequently used in academic style than *for instance*

C Qualifying: limiting and specifying an argument

Dr O'Malley is leading a class discussion on human rights.

O'Malley: OK. 'Human rights are rights which you possess simply because you are human.' **To what extent** can we say that? What are the **pros and cons**[1] of this view?

Anna: Well, I think it's too simplistic, **in the sense that**[2] it ignores the rights of victims and everyone else's right to life. So, **provided that** we remember this, then we can give people basic rights, **albeit**[3] with limitations.

Kirsten: Mm, that's **all very well, but**[4] if you say human rights depend on, **say**, government decisions about national security, then they're no longer *rights*, are they? They become privileges. **Having said that**[5], it's a complex issue with no simple answer. **Even so**, I still think we must be careful not to give our rights away.

O'Malley: OK. Fine. **Apart from** victims' rights, are there other arguments for restricting rights? I mean we could look at protecting property, ending a chronically sick person's life, **and so on** / **and so forth**[6]. Let's talk about **the degree/extent to which** these are relevant.

Ricardo: Every sick person has the right to life, but **at the same time** / **by the same token**[7], we should be free to decide when we want to die.

O'Malley: Well, a lot of sick people can't make that decision for themselves, **despite the fact that** we may respect their right to a dignified death.

Ricardo: Hmm. **Nevertheless/Nonetheless**[8], I think it's a key issue.

[1] advantages and disadvantages [2] used to explain precisely what has just been said [3] (formal) although [4] indicates a partial agreement, followed by a disagreement [5] said when you wish to add a point which contrasts with what has just been said [6] and similar things; the two phrases can be used separately or together (and so on and so forth) [7] what you are about to say is also true, for the same reasons as what you have just said [8] however

Exercises

39.1 **Complete the text about the first wife of King Henry VIII of England (1491–1547) with the correct prepositions from A opposite.**

This essay examines the early life of Catherine of Aragon (1485–1536), focusing particularly [1] .... the period of her brief marriage to Prince Arthur, his death at the age of 15 and her subsequent marriage to his brother Prince Henry, later to become King Henry VIII of England. [2] .... the purposes of this essay, I shall pay little attention [3] .... either the earlier or the later periods of her life. Her eventual divorce from King Henry is, thus, [4] .... the scope [5] .... this essay. Much more has already been written [6] .... the subject [7] .... this later period of her life. The literature [8] .... reference [9] .... the period is extensive but my essay is largely based [10] .... a couple of sources which are particularly relevant [11] .... any discussion of this period, and I shall refer [12] .... these throughout.

39.2 **Complete the phrases with the correct words.**

1 the pros and ....
2 at the same ....
3 and so on and so ....
4 put .... (arguments)
5 that's all very well, ...
6 the extent to ....
7 in addition ....
8 as well ....

39.3 **Replace the underlined phrases in the text with phrases from the box with a similar meaning.**

nevertheless advantages and disadvantages the degree for instance as well as furthermore provided that

There are a number of <u>pros and cons</u> to take into account when considering the purchase of a hybrid (gasoline-electric) car. Such cars are, <u>for example</u>, undoubtedly better for the environment in the sense that they cause less air pollution. <u>Moreover</u>, <u>the extent</u> to which they rely on oil, a natural resource which is rapidly becoming depleted, is much less than is the case with conventional cars, <u>Nonetheless</u>, hybrid cars are not without their problems. Cost may be an issue <u>and also</u> the technical complexity of the engine. <u>As long as</u> you take these factors into account, there is no reason not to buy a hybrid car.

39.4 **Choose the correct word or phrase to complete each sentence.**

1 She wrote an excellent essay, ... with a certain amount of help.
A even so B albeit C despite the fact
2 A .... point must also now be made against a change in law.
A furthermore B moreover C further
3 He is an important poet, ... his work has had a great influence on other writers.
A in the sense that B to what extent C provided that
4 Prices have continued to rise .... costs have been falling.
A for instance B despite the fact that C so
5 The riots resulted in much damage. ...., we should not ignore the fact that the disorder brought benefits to some.
A As well as B With reference to C Having said that
6 But there is a negative side to new technology. .... the advantages, we also need to consider a number of disadvantages.
A Be that as it may B Apart from C all very well but
7 The internet has provided immense benefits, but, ..., it has enabled criminals and terrorists to exploit new media and means of communication.
A however B by the same token C the extent to which
8 Bangladesh is one of the world's most densely populated countries, ... smaller states such as Malta and Singapore.
A respectively B along with C with reference to

40 Organising your writing

A Openings

Look at these openings from students' written work, and note the items in bold.

This assignment will **address** the problem of socio-economic data in health studies.

This dissertation **is concerned with** individual differences in the ability to connect thoughts and emotions.

The **aim** of this paper is to **explore** constant acceleration formulae, **with a focus on** motion along a slope.

The **purpose** of this essay is to **investigate** the use of focus group interviews.

This thesis **consists of** four parts. Each part **presents** and **discusses** a different set of experiments.

This assignment **is divided into** three sections, with each section **devoted to** a different aspect of world trade.

B Organising the main points

useful when ...	Items	examples
working through a list of different things	• first(ly), secondly, thirdly • next • lastly/finally	**First(ly)**, let us look at the history of the problem. [*Firstly* is more formal than *First*] **Next**, there is the issue of air resistance. **Finally**, let us consider increased taxation as a possible solution.
changing topics / bringing in new points	• we now turn to • let us turn to • at this point	**We now turn to** the question of which model provides a better explanation of the phenomenon. **At this point** it is important to look again at the data.
referring forward in the text	• below • in the next section • later • the following	We shall see **below** that depopulation has been a major factor. [lower on the page or later in the essay/article] **Later**, I shall look at other possible reasons for this. The **following** example comes from Hillson (1998).
referring back to something	• above • in the preceding section • earlier • (as) we saw / have seen	The **above** figures indicate a significant decrease. Three hypotheses were listed **in the preceding section**. [the section immediately before this one] I noted **earlier** that lack of fresh water was a serious problem. **As we saw** in section 2, this is a complex topic.
referring to examples, diagrams, pages, etc.	• see • consider • take, for example, • as can be seen in	For the complete results, **see** Appendix A, page 94. **Consider** Figure I, which shows changes from 1976–8. **Take, for example**, Sweden, where industrialisation was rapid, **as can be seen in** Figure 2.
referring separately to different people or things	• respectively • the former • the latter	Groups A and B consisted of 14-year-olds and 16-year-olds, **respectively**. [i.e. group A was 14-year-olds and group B was 16-year-olds] Rostov and Krow both studied the problem. The **former** wrote a book; the **latter** published two papers. [the first and then the second person or thing mentioned]

Common Mistakes

Don't confuse, *first(ly)* with *at first*. *At first* means 'at the beginning' and refers to situations which change: *At first there was no increase in temperature, but later, the temperature rose by 0.5 °C*. See Unit 49 for the difference between *lastly* and *last*.
Say *as can be seen in Figure 1*, NOT ~~as it can be seen in Figure 1~~.

See Units 16 and 47 for more useful expressions for organising your writing.

Exercises

40.1 Complete the introduction to a paper with words from A opposite. There may be more than one possible answer.

The [1]............................ of this paper is to consider the nature of moral education in Soviet children's literature. It is particularly [2]............................ with the moral values presented in books published with the [3]............................ of teaching reading at primary school. The thesis [4]............................ of four parts. The first part attempts to [5]............................ a number of general questions relating to children's literature from any historical period. Parts 2, 3 and 4 are [6]............................ specifically to the Soviet example. Part 2 is [7]............................ into three main sections, the first of which discusses the nature of the Soviet value system with a particular [8]............................ on the work ethic.

40.2 Read the sentences and answer the questions.

1 Tolstoy's most famous novels are *War and Peace* and *Anna Karenina*, the former being first published between 1865 and 1869 and the latter between 1875 and 1877.

Which of Tolstoy's novels was published in the 1860s?

2 More precise data can be found in Table 3 below.

Does Table 3 appear before or after this sentence?

3 Let us now turn to the question of the country's economic situation.

Has the writer already begun discussing the country's economic situation or not?

4 The brothers, Olaf and Erik, would go on to become professors of archaeology and Greek, respectively.

Which brother taught archaeology?

5 The preceding example is taken from Atakano (2014).

Does the example come before or after this sentence?

40.3 Choose the correct word to complete each sentence.

1 *Take / Put / Look*, for example, the case of Megginson which was described in Chapter 2.
2 *At first, / Firstly*, I would like to discuss the nature of 16th-century English and then the impact that this had on the works of Shakespeare.
3 The article *concerns / devotes / addresses* the issue of religion in the modern world.
4 Look at Figure 3 *under / below / beneath* for more detailed information.
5 In the *following / preceding* section we shall deal with this issue in more detail.
6 For more detailed information *see / go / turn* Appendix B.
7 Let us *now deal / see / consider* Figure 2.1.
8 This aspect of the problem will be discussed *latter / later / lastly* in this article.

40.4 Rewrite the underlined parts of the sentences using the word in brackets.

1 As Table V shows, there has been an increase in the numbers of students. (SEEN)
2 In Section 3 we take up again some of the arguments from Section 2. (PRECEDING)
3 Now let us turn our attention to developments in Constantinople. (POINT)
4 The dissertation consists of six chapters. (DIVIDED)
5 Let us now consider the issue of the reunification of Germany. (TURN)

Over to you

Choose an essay topic relevant to your own discipline. Write an introductory paragraph using expressions from A opposite. Then write sentences that could go in an essay using vocabulary from B.

41 Processes and procedures

A General nouns and verbs

Note the prepositions which follow the nouns in bold.

The next **stage in / step in / phase of** the data collection was the administration of the questionnaire.

The **procedure**[1] **for** Experiment B was different from that of Experiment A.

The **application**[2] **of** Thoren's method produced some interesting results.

They studied the **behaviour of** large corporations during periods of economic crisis.

The team carried out a computer **simulation**[3] **of** climate change over the next 30 years.

Twenty-five subjects were **selected**[4] **from** the first group to take part in the second analysis.

She **designed** a course to train students to **utilise**[5] self-motivation strategies.

The article sets out to **unify**[6] some concepts in the theory of economic growth.

Three case studies were carried out to **supplement**[7] the statistical data.

The experiments were repeated, in order to **verify**[8] the results observed in the original data.

[1] carefully controlled set of actions [2] using it for a practical purpose [3] a model of a problem or course of events [4] (formal) chosen [5] (formal) use something in an effective way [6] bring together/combine [7] add something to something to make it larger or better [8] make certain that something is correct

B Social/political/economic processes

example with noun	equivalent verb	meaning
The **emergence** of nation states changed Europe in the 19th century.	Nation states **emerged** in the 19th century.	process of appearing or starting to exist
The paper is a study of water **consumption** in Brazil during 2001.	Millions of litres of bottled water are now **consumed**.	process of using fuel, energy, food, etc.
Ratification of the trade agreement took place in 2004.	The agreement was **ratified** in 2004.	process of making an agreement official
Before the **advent** of computers, scientific analysis was a slow process.	Before computers were **developed/ invented**, analysis took a long time.	arrival of an invention (the noun has no verb form)

Language help

Research into academic writing shows that using the noun forms of the words in B above is typical of formal writing and often leads to higher grades in exams and assessments.

C Technological processes and procedures

Look at these questions on a college website dealing with computer problems.

Is there any way to **automate**[1] the process of converting text files to PDF format?

How can I **display**[2] different values on the same bar in a bar graph?

How can I **export**[3] data from my REFS software to a list of references in my dissertation?

Is there a fast way to **input**[4] questionnaire results into a database?

How can I **insert**[5] a footnote into my essay?

How can I save the numerical **output**[6] from the BIGSTATS program as a text file?

[1] make it be operated by machines, instead of by humans [2] arrange them so that they can be seen [3] copy it either to a different part of the computer's storage space or to another form of storage [4] put them into the computer's system [5] add [6] results produced by the programme

Exercises

41.1 Choose the best word to complete each sentence.

1 It is sensible to *unify / select / verify* your results before publishing them.
2 Hip replacement is usually a simple medical *application / procedure / behaviour*.
3 Many students *supplement / utilise / verify* their scholarships by doing some part-time work.
4 A computer *stage / procedure / simulation* shows what will happen if the ocean current does indeed change direction and start flowing from the Arctic to the West Indies.
5 As the next *step / behaviour / application* in our study we plan to carry out interviews.
6 Her aim is to *form / design / function* a radically different type of electric engine.
7 The team sought permission to *verify / utilise / unify* a large telescope at the local observatory.
8 The first *behaviour / phase / process* of the project ended in 2014.
9 You should *select / verify / supplement* the most suitable type of chart for your data.

41.2 Rewrite the underlined words and phrases using more formal words and phrases from B and C opposite.

1 It is hardly surprising that people <u>use</u> far more electricity than they did ten years ago.
2 The <u>arrival</u> of mobile technology transformed the way people manage their social and professional lives.
3 A number of talented new designers have <u>appeared</u> this year.
4 You've missed out a letter in this word here – you need to <u>add</u> a p between the a and the t.
5 He spent many years trying to <u>create</u> a machine that would automatically sort large numbers of coins.
6 The team had to <u>put in</u> a huge amount of data to run the experiment.
7 We spent many months trying to <u>make</u> the process of recording the temperature <u>automatic</u>.
8 The <u>information that came from</u> the system was automatically <u>sent</u> to a spreadsheet.

41.3 Complete the tables. Add the preposition which usually follows the verb or noun where you see (+). Use a dictionary if necessary.

verb	noun
apply (+)	(+)
behave	(+)
simulate	(+)
(+)	selection (+)
	design (+)
ratify	(+)
(+)	insertion

verb	noun
	verification (+)
	utilisation (+)
emerge (+)	(+)
consume	(+)
(+)	input
display	(+)

41.4 Complete the sentences using words from 41.3.

1 The article traces the .... of South Korea as a major economic force.
2 Because of the drought everyone has been asked to reduce their water ....
3 I think it would be a good idea to .... some tables into the results section of your article.
4 It took considerable negotiations before all parties consented to the .... of the treaty.
5 This course will focus on the .... of theory to practice.
6 It took me a long time to .... all the data from the survey into the new software. The old software was quicker.
7 Most psychology students choose to do a course on animal ....
8 The book offers useful advice on the .... of experiments.

Over to you

Use a dictionary to find some typical word combinations for these words: *process*, *procedure* and *stage*. Then write five sentences about aspects of your own subject using five of the word combinations.

42 Facts, evidence and data

Being able to use the vocabulary in this unit well will help you avoid repetition in your writing.

A Facts

Fact is a countable noun.

Researchers try to **establish** the facts. They hope that the facts will **bear out**[1] or **support** their hypothesis. Most carefully **check** their facts before **presenting** them to others although there are, of course, dishonest people prepared to **distort**[2] the facts in order to claim that these facts are **interesting**, **relevant**[3], **undeniable** or **little-known**.

Notice how *fact* is also often used in sentences like the following:

It is hard to **account for the fact that** share prices rose over this period. [explain why]

The problem **stems from the fact that** there is a basic conflict of interests. [has arisen because]

The lecturer **drew attention to the fact that** the economy was now improving. [emphasised that]

[1] confirm [2] change [3] connected to the topic being discussed

B Evidence

Evidence is uncountable - you can refer to one **piece/item of evidence** or to the **body of evidence** [large amount of evidence].

Researchers	**look for** **collect** **examine** **consider**	evidence.	Evidence	**exists**. **comes to light**[1]. **accumulates**[2]. **emerges**.	Evidence may	**suggest** **point to** **confirm** **support** **demonstrate**	a conclusion.

Irrefutable[3], **abundant**[4], **convincing** or **growing** evidence pleases the researcher.

Flimsy[5], **conflicting**[6], **scant**[7] or **inconclusive**[8] evidence is a problem for the researcher.

Researchers aim to **provide** or **offer** enough **hard evidence**[9] to support their theories.

[1] becomes known [2] builds up [3] which cannot be denied [4] plenty of [5] not strong
[6] contradictory [7] not much [8] neither proving nor disproving in a clear way
[9] evidence which is reliable and can be proven, used mainly in spoken English

C Data

Some people consider **data** as a plural noun – *these data show an unexpected trend* – while others consider it as uncountable – *this data differs from last year's. This is a particularly interesting piece/item of data*. The tendency is increasingly to use *data* as an uncountable noun, but you will see both forms and may use it whichever way you prefer yourself.

Data can be **reliable**[1], **comprehensive**[2], **accurate**, **extensive** or **empirical**[3].

You **organise**, **analyse**, **interpret**, **record**, **obtain** or **collect** data.

Data **suggests**, **reflects**, **indicates**, **shows** or **demonstrates** something.

[1] can be trusted [2] full, complete [3] based on practical observation rather than theory

D Giving examples

You often need to **give** or **provide an example** to **illustrate the facts** you're presenting. A good example can be described as **striking**, **clear**, **vivid**, **illuminating** or **telling**. Sometimes, particularly in written English, the word **instance** is used as an alternative to **example**. *There is a striking instance of the author's use of metaphor in the final poem. We shall analyse one specific instance of this problem.*

Say can be used in informal English to mean *for example. Try and finish the report by, say, next Friday.*

Exercises

42.1 Read the extract from a university seminar on forest conservation. Some students are questioning aspects of a presentation given by Sandra, one of the group. Complete the extract with the missing words. The first letter of each word is given to help you.

Aidan: I enjoyed your presentation, and you've [1]e.................. some interesting facts about the loss of forests year on year, and it's [2]u.................. that tropical forests are in danger. But I think the evidence you [3]o.................. for your claim that sustainable forest exploitation is failing is very [4]f.................. and not very [5]c.................. at all. We need to [6]c.................. a lot more data. Right now there's a lot of [7]c.................. evidence, so we can't say for certain that it's not working.

Sandra: If you want [8]h.................. evidence, just look at the International Tropical Timber Organisation, and read their latest report. Their evidence [9]d.................. that only three per cent of tropical forests are being managed properly.

Petra: Well, I've read the ITTO report, and actually it [10]d.................. attention to the fact that their previous report had found only *one* per cent of forests were properly managed, so you may be [11]d.................. the facts a little by just looking at one year. And also, there's a lot of [12]l.................. k.................. work being done with local people to encourage them to conserve the forests, so you could say there's [13]g.................. evidence that things are getting *better.*

Dr Li: Hmm, I don't think we're going to agree on this. I think, as usual, it's a question of how you [14]i.................. the data. Thanks, anyway, for your presentation, Sandra.

42.2 Replace the underlined words with words or expressions with similar meanings. There may be more than one possible answer.

1. The data show that the drug education project has been successful.
2. The data in the latest study are more complete than in the earlier one.
3. This is the most interesting piece of data in the whole thesis.
4. What a clear example this is of the power of the human mind!
5. Unfortunately, the facts do not bear out the hypothesis.
6. We cannot explain the fact that attitudes are more negative now than five years ago.
7. The problem arises from the fact that the software was poorly designed.
8. The article gives examples of different methods which have been used over the years.
9. New evidence has emerged that the cabinet was not informed of the Minister's decision.
10. We need to examine the evidence before we can reach a conclusion.
11. The evidence suggesting that sanctions do not work is plentiful and impossible to deny.
12. A considerable amount of evidence now exists, but we always try to get more.
13. We have a lot of observed data which suggest the problem is on the increase.
14. This is a clear example of how conservation can benefit local people.

42.3 Cross out the word which does not fit in each sentence.

1. Thorsen's aim was to *establish / check / bear out / present* the facts.
2. The evidence *suggests / points to / supports / emerges* a different conclusion.
3. Lopez *collected / reflected / obtained / recorded* some fascinating data.
4. The writer provides some *growing / telling / striking / illuminating* examples.
5. The evidence Mistry presents is *convincing / flimsy / vivid / conflicting.*
6. Unfortunately, there is only *scant / hard / inconclusive / flimsy* evidence in support of my theory.
7. Some interesting new evidence has *come to light / considered / emerged / been collected* recently.
8. Make sure your data are *accurate / reliable / contradictory / comprehensive* before you publish them.

Over to you

Look at any text from your discipline and see what words are used with *facts, data* and *evidence*. Are they the same as the ones in this unit? Note any different ones.

43 Making connections

A Connecting data and evidence

Read how a scientist used 14 cameras to study his baby son learning language.

In a child's life the progression from just making noises to using words meaningfully is still not completely understood. So an American scientist has collected 24,000 hours of video, **complemented**[1] **by** 33,000 hours of audio, of his baby son. The scientist hopes computers will **reveal links**[2] **between** the child's activities and his learning of language. He has divided each room into sections such as sink, table, fridge and stove. The computer picks out **combinations of** movements between these sections which are repeated. Researchers then **piece together**[3] how these fragments **correlate with**[4] specific activities, such as making coffee or doing the dishes. Eventually the computer will **bring** all the information **together** and provide statistics on how often the child observed an activity before finally producing a word **related to** it.

[1] which has made the video better or more useful [2] show connections not seen before [3] understand by looking [4] are connected with and influenced by

B Expressing links and connections between people and things

Nowadays, the term 'hacker' is **synonymous with**[1] a criminal who attacks computer systems. Originally, the word **referred to**[2] a skilled programmer, and only later did it become **associated with**[3] malicious attacks.

In humans and in chimpanzees, hand movements **accompanied by** speech or vocal sounds are made more often with the right hand than the left hand. **Taken together**, the data suggest that this phenomenon may date back as far as 5 million years ago.

In the 1980s, the wages of less-skilled US workers fell **relative to**[4] those of more-skilled workers. The **mutual**[5] influence of the inflow of less-skilled immigrants and the growth in US imports is also important.

Scientists have found **evidence of** an animal that can shrink and then grow again. Galapagos marine iguanas seem to grow smaller or larger, possibly **reflecting** changes in the food supply.

The book examines the development of the **bond**[6] between children and their parents. The **relationship between** individual development and the strength of the bond varies between sons and daughters.

In questionnaire A, zero **corresponds to** 'disagree strongly' and 5 indicates 'agree strongly'. In questionnaire B, the **reverse**[7] is true, **in that**[8] 5 is **equivalent to** 'disagree strongly'.

The prefix ***inter-*** indicates a link or relationship between things (see Reference 5).

Interaction[9] between learner and learning material is a defining characteristic of education.

He studied the **interrelated**[10] effects of families and peers on African-American youths.

The article is concerned with the **interplay**[11] between emotions and logical thinking.

[1] the two are so closely connected that one suggests the other [2] related to [3] connected in people's minds [4] varying according to the speed or level of something else [5] influencing each other [6] close connection [7] opposite [8] used before giving an explanation for something [9] communication with or reaction to [10] connected and having an effect on each other [11] the effect two or more things have on each other

Common Mistake

Remember that *evidence* is an uncountable noun. Do not make it plural. *The surface of the material showed* ***evidence*** *of wear and damage*. NOT ~~evidences~~ of …

Exercises

43.1 Match the beginnings and endings of the sentences and complete the sentences with the correct prepositions.

1 The study revealed links
2 Jill's thoroughness is complemented
3 Musical talent correlates
4 The sculpture is an unusual combination
5 The conference has brought
6 The team are trying to piece
7 Peter's new study is closely related
8 The term 'hacker' used to refer

☐ a .... gentle curves and sharp angles.
☐ b .... scholars from all over the world.
☐ c .... information from a range of sources.
☐ d .... his previous research.
☐ e .... a computer programmer.
☐ f .... use of the drug and heart problems.
☐ g .... her co-researcher's originality.
☐ h .... mathematical ability.

43.2 Correct the mistakes in the sentences.

1 There is usually a very strong bind between a mother and her child.
2 Salaries have fallen over the last few years, not in real terms but relative of inflation.
3 The report on care for the elderly revealed evidences of neglect by health professionals.
4 In the experiment, group A performed best on the manual dexterity test and least well on the memory test, whereas for group B the reversal was the case.
5 'Malicious' is more or less synonym with 'nasty'.
6 The problems discussed above are all closely interrelationship.
7 Took together, the studies by Kim and Li suggest earlier theories on the cause of the disease were flawed.
8 The research is original in this it approaches the topic from a completely fresh angle.
9 The painter loved to explore the interplaying between light and shade.
10 In speech, verbal language is typically acompanied by body language.

43.3 Complete the text using words from the box.

associated interaction corresponds mutual equivalent
reflects evidence relationships reveals

[1] .... within a chimpanzee community is the theme of Gavros's fascinating new book. It describes the various different [2] .... between the animals, and [3] .... how an individual's behaviour [4] .... his or her position in the community, showing how the older females in particular offer each other [5] .... support. The book also provides [6] .... to suggest that chimpanzees use sounds in systematic ways to communicate with each other. One particular sound, for example, clearly [7] .... to the human cry of 'Watch out!' while another would seem to be the [8] .... of 'Help!' Certain gestures also seem to be [9] .... with specific meanings.

43.4 The following sentences contain some more words beginning with *inter-*. Use your knowledge of what the prefix means to explain the meaning of the words in their context.

1 Alf won a prize in an inter-university chess competition.
2 Interstate highways in the USA are usually wide and well-maintained.
3 Our economic interdependence means that recession in the US also affects us.
4 Intermarriage throughout the centuries had meant that most European monarchs at the beginning of the twentieth century were quite closely related.
5 The world wide web has enormously facilitated the interchange of information between scholars.
6 The design was a complicated construction of interconnecting parts.

Over to you

Are there any terms that begin with the prefix *inter-* in your discipline? Make a list of them and be sure you know what they mean by checking in a dictionary if necessary.

44 Describing problems

A Introducing a problem

As the mining operations became deeper and deeper, **the problem of** flooding **arose**[1].

In a recent survey, 14% of customers **experienced difficulties with** online buying.

Walsh's paper discusses the **controversy**[2] **surrounding** privatisation of health services.

Conservation driven by market forces seems to be a **contradiction in terms**[3].

The topic is inadequately treated, and several **errors are apparent**[4] in the analysis.

Integrating the new member states **poses**[5] **a challenge to** the European Union.

The research **raises**[6] **the issue of** rainforests and the people who live in them.

The patient **had difficulty in** remembering very recent events.

Most theories of the origin of the universe **contain inconsistencies**[7].

The results **revealed shortcomings**[8] **in** the design of the questionnaire.

[1] *question/issue/difficulty/controversy* also combine with *arise* [2] a lot of disagreement or argument about something [3] a combination of words which is nonsense because some of the words suggest the opposite of others [4] can be seen [5] *threat/problem/danger* also are often used with *pose*; the verb *present* can also be used with these nouns [6] *question/problem* also are often used with *raise* [7] have different parts that do not agree [8] faults or a failure to reach a particular standard

B Responding to a problem

word	example	meaning
react (v) reaction (n)	It was a study of how small firms **react** to the problem of over-regulation.	act in a particular way as a direct result of
respond (v) response (n)	The Minister's **response** to the problem of inflation was to impose a price freeze.	his/her reaction to what has happened or been said
deal with	How should training courses **deal with** the issue of violence in the healthcare setting?	take action in order to solve a problem
tackle	Governments do not seem to be able to **tackle** the problem of urban congestion.	try to deal with
address	Governments need to **address** the problem of waste from nuclear power plants.	(formal) give attention to or deal with
mediate (v) mediation (n)	The community leaders attempted to **mediate between** the police and the people.	talk to the two groups involved to try to help them find a solution to their problems

C Solving a problem

The researchers **solved the problem** by increasing the temperature.

The team **came up with / found a solution to the problem** of water damage.

By using video, the researchers **overcame the problem** of interpreting audio-only data.

The treaty **resolved the problem** of sharing water resources. [more formal, solved or ended]

A successful **resolution to** the crisis came in 2014. [noun form of resolve]

The **answer to** the problem **lay in** changing the design of the experiment.

The book was entitled: '**Conflict Resolution**: the Management of International Disputes'.

Common Mistake

We say *have difficulty (in) doing* NOT ~~have difficulty to do~~ *We had some difficulty assembling the apparatus.*

Exercises

44.1 Match the beginnings and endings of the sentences. Use the words in A opposite to help you.

1 Students always seem to have difficulty
2 Ford pointed out that the methodology had
3 The need to find replacement fuels poses
4 The media continue to focus on the controversy
5 In the figures he presented several errors were
6 On their way across Antarctica they experienced
7 The results of the opinion poll raise
8 Problems caused by pollution in this area

☐ a surrounding the President.
☐ b apparent.
☐ c some important questions for the Party.
☐ d many difficulties.
☐ e arose fairly recently.
☐ f in remembering this formula.
☐ g a number of inconsistencies.
☐ h considerable challenges for scientists.

44.2 Complete the sentences by adding a preposition in the correct place.

1 It is no easy task mediating unions and management.
2 In this lecture I plan to deal the later novels of Charles Dickens.
3 The answer to most problems in agriculture lies the soil.
4 He thought for a long time but was unable to come with a solution.
5 Green tourism may initially feel like a contradiction terms.
6 I wonder what the professor's reaction the article will be.
7 The company has experienced a number of difficulties the computer operating system.
8 Have you found a solution the problem yet?

44.3 Complete the table. Use a dictionary if necessary.

noun	verb	noun	verb
	solve	resolution	
reaction			respond
	contain	contradiction	
	reveal		mediate

44.4 Complete the sentences with the correct form of words from 44.3.

1 The professor was furious that the student .... him so rudely in public.
2 New investigations have led to the .... of a major fraud.
3 I hope someone will eventually come up with a .... to the problem of global warming.
4 The diplomats are hoping to .... between the two sides and so prevent a conflict.
5 The library .... many rare and beautiful books.
6 I am still waiting for the committee's .... to my request for an extension for my dissertation.
7 At the beginning of the new academic year Marie .... to make much more effort with her assignments.
8 The lecturer .... very angrily when I questioned one of her conclusions.
9 The title of the article made it sound interesting but its .... were disappointing.
10 Specialists in conflict .... were brought in to try to calm the situation.

Over to you

Much academic work is based on asking questions or raising problems and finding solutions to them. Find an article relating to your own discipline which discusses a problem. Note down any interesting vocabulary that you find there.

45 Describing situations

A Existence and location

Look at these extracts from history lectures.

The **existence** of a large population of migrant workers put pressure on the country's **infrastructure**[1].

We need to look at all the **circumstances**[2] **surrounding** the events of 1926.

Historians noted the **absence**[3] of a clear political ideology in the actions of the workers.

Looking at events in their social **context** means taking all the factors of a person's social **environment** into account.

The **conditions** in which the poorest sector of the population lived were bad.

The **status**[4] of women was not a serious subject of debate until the 1960s.

[1] basic systems and services, such as transport and power supplies [2] facts or events that make the situation the way it is [3] opposite = **presence** [4] official position, especially in a social group

Common Mistake

Be careful with the spelling of *environment* and *circumstances*.

B Factors affecting situations

word	examples	notes
constrain (v) constraint (n)	Scientists are **constrained** by the amount of funding they can obtain / are **subject to the constraints of** funding.	being controlled and limited in what they can do
restrain (v) restraint (n)	Growth in car ownership could be **restrained** by higher taxes. High land prices are a **restraint on** the expansion of private housing in the city.	limiting the growth or force of something
minimum (n/adj) (opp) maximum minimal (adj)	The **minimum**/**maximum** temperature was recorded at each stage. Damage to buildings was **minimal**.	smallest/largest amount allowed or possible very small in amount
confine (v)	Major industrial pollution is **confined to** the big cities in the north of the region.	limited to
restrict (v) restriction (n)	The government took measures to **restrict** the sale of tobacco products to young people. To fight traffic congestion, the city **imposed a restriction of** one car per household.	limiting something and reducing its size or preventing it from increasing
intrinsic (adj) (opp) extrinsic	English language is an **intrinsic** part of the college curriculum.	extremely important and basic characteristic of it
integral (adj)	Users' experiences are **integral to** the way libraries measure their performance.	necessary and important as a part of a whole
finite (adj) (opp) infinite	Oil is a **finite** resource; it will run out one day. There is evidence to suggest the universe may be **infinite** in size.	having a limit or end /ˈfaɪnaɪt/ having no limit or end /ˈɪnfɪnət/
stable (adj) (opp) unstable stability (n) (opp) instability	It takes decades to create a **stable** democracy. Political **instability** is a threat to the whole region.	if something is stable, it is firmly fixed or not likely to move or change

Language help

Remember that noun phrases are an important feature of academic style. Note in particular the ways of expressing verbs using noun phrases in the table above.

Exercises

45.1 Complete the sentences with words from A opposite.

1 To understand the problem, we need to look at all the many factors which may influence development in the child's social and physical ....
2 It has been claimed that the .... of teaching as a profession is not as high as it used to be or as it should be.
3 The infrared aerial photograph seems to show the .... of a large village around 1,000 years ago.
4 The company's president died in rather suspicious .... and his son took over.
5 In the .... of any instructions from above, I think we should decide ourselves how to proceed.
6 The country can never become a major economic player unless it improves its ...., especially the roads and railways.
7 I can't tell you what the word means unless you tell me it in .... Was it in an academic text?
8 Students today live in very luxurious .... compared with students in the past.

45.2 Replace the underlined words with their opposites.

1 The economy has been stable for several years.
2 Stability has been a feature of government in the country for the last decade.
3 The northern region possesses an apparently finite supply of uranium.
4 The presence of cholera in the area was noted by scientists in 1978.
5 A minimum temperature of 20 degrees must be maintained at all times.

45.3 Choose the best word to complete each sentence.

1 The government has introduced legislation to *restrict* / *constrain* smoking in public places.
2 Learning from your mistakes is an *infinite* / *intrinsic* part of making progress.
3 Her attempt to *confine* / *restrain* the children from making a noise in the library met with little success.
4 The professor always insists that even the most junior research associate is an *unstable* / *integral* part of the team.
5 What are the *minimum* / *minimal* requirements for getting a place on the course?
6 During the exam period restrictions are *opposed* / *imposed* on visitors to the college.
7 There were some rather curious *circumstances* / *contexts* surrounding the case.
8 The level of taxation in the country is a major *constraint* / *restraint* on foreign investment there.

45.4 Rewrite the sentences using the words in brackets.

1 In the 1960s the government restricted the amount of money people could take out of the country. (RESTRICTION)
2 The problem exists only in the capital city. (CONFINED)
3 Oil is a resource which will run out one day. (FINITE)
4 In the accident there was very little damage to the car. (MINIMAL)
5 All research is constrained by funding decisions. (SUBJECT/CONSTRAINTS)
6 The fact that the country is socially unstable deters investors. (SOCIAL)
7 Normally we would not behave in this way. (CIRCUMSTANCES)
8 Most small children believe that fairies exist. (OF/FAIRIES)

Over to you

Find a news article about a scientific development and read the description of the situation which led to it (often to be found in the introduction). Note any useful **nouns** used there (and any prepositions that follow them).

46 Comparing and contrasting

A Prepositional expressions

Look at the prepositional expressions in these titles of journal articles.

expression	notes
Problems in pain measurement **a comparison between** verbal **and** visual rating scales **A comparison of** different methods and approaches to homeschooling	*Between* is used when two different things are being compared. *Of* is used when different examples of the same thing are being compared.
Mobility in the EU **in comparison with** the US The effects of risk on private investment: Africa **compared with** other developing areas An exploration of the average driver's speed **compared to** driver safety and driving skill	*With* and *to* are both used nowadays with similar meanings in these expressions. American English generally prefers *compared with*.
Reduced rate of disease development after HIV-2 infection **as compared to** HIV-I	This expression indicates that there is indeed a difference between the things which are compared.
Some psycho-physical **analogies between** speech and music	Comparisons between things which have similar features; often used to help explain a principle or idea [by **drawing an analogy with** something]
Differences and similarities between mothers and teachers as informants on child behaviour **Differences in** ethical standards between male and female managers: myth or reality?	*Between* is used with difference when different groups of people or things are compared. *In* is used when different aspects of one thing are compared (here 'ethical standards').
Is globalisation today really **different from** globalisation a hundred years ago?	*Different to* is also used in UK academic usage, but *different from* is more frequent. *Different than* is often found in US English. Verb = **differ from**
Contrasts between urban and rural living	*Contrast* suggests an obvious difference. Typical adjectives – **marked/sharp/stark contrast**
Children's understanding of the **distinction between** real and apparent emotion	A *distinction* is a difference between two similar things.

B Linking expressions

46% of the male subjects responded negatively. **Similarly/Likewise**, 46% of the female subjects said they had never voted in any election.

The poet's early work is full of optimism. **In/By contrast**, his later work is melancholy.

Older teenagers were found to be more likely than younger teenagers to purchase clothes. **Conversely**, younger teenagers purchased more video games. [in an opposite way]

Unlike Scotland at that time, Ireland had mortality rates that were relatively low.

Verb endings in some languages can show present, past or future tense, **whereas** / **while** in English, verb endings can only show present or past.

A recent study suggested that building a network of good friends, **rather than** maintaining close family ties, helps people live longer into old age.

On the one hand, critics accuse the police of not protecting the public from crime. **On the other hand**, people also complained that the police were too oppressive. [used to compare two different facts or two opposite ways of thinking about a situation]

In the north, the rains are plentiful. In the south **the reverse is true** and drought is common.

Common Mistake

Remember to say *the same as*, NOT ~~the same that~~, or ~~the same than~~. Say *similar to*, NOT ~~similar as~~. Don't confuse *on the other hand* (see above) with *in contrast*. *In contrast* expresses a marked opposition between two ideas: *Chan sharply condemned the diplomatic moves*; ***in contrast**, his deputy, Tiong, saw them as an attempt to create political stability.*

Exercises

46.1 Complete the sentences with the missing words. There may be more than one possible answer.

1 The study looked at the different life chances of working-class children .... to those of middle-class children.
2 The results showed a marked .... between the two groups of plants being tested.
3 The title of her paper was: 'Retail price differences in large supermarkets: organic foods .... to non-organic foods'.
4 My project was a .... of different styles of industrial architecture in the 1990s.
5 The result of the second experiment was very different .... that of the first.
6 It would be interesting to do a .... between the musical skills of teenage girls and those of teenage boys.
7 The physicist drew an .... between the big bang and throwing a stone in a pond.
8 Gronsky believes cold fusion will soon be achieved in the laboratory. .... , his colleague Ladrass believes cold fusion is simply theoretically impossible.

46.2 Rewrite the underlined words using the word in brackets.

1 The two groups were not the same as each other. (DIFFERENT)
2 The three liquids had many things in common with one another. (SIMILAR)
3 The data revealed that the informants' responses were different. (DIFFERENCES)
4 The title of her paper was 'A comparison of male attitudes and female attitudes on the subject of prison sentencing. (COMPARED)
5 The economy of the north is booming, and, in a similar way, the south is also enjoying an economic upturn. (SIMILARLY)
6 The Gaelic spoken in Ireland differs from the Gaelic spoken in Scotland. [SAME]
7 Lecturers often explain a difficult concept by comparing it with something familiar. [ANALOGY]
8 In the 1950s, public transportation enjoyed a boom but nowadays it is little used. [REVERSE]

46.3 Rewrite the pairs of sentences as one sentence, using the word in brackets.

1 The south of the country has little in the way of forests. The north of the country is covered with thick forests. (UNLIKE)
Unlike the south of the country, which has little in the way of forests, the north is covered with thick forests.
2 A questionnaire is good. In this case, face-to-face interviews are better. (RATHER)
3 Asian languages such as Vietnamese are quite difficult for learners whose first language is a European one. The opposite is also true. (CONVERSELY)
4 Oil is plentiful at the present time. It will run out one day. (HAND)
5 Boys tend to prefer aggressive solutions to problems. Girls, on the other hand, prefer more indirect approaches. (WHEREAS)

46.4 Decide if the statements are true (T) or false (F). Use a dictionary to check the meaning of the bold words if necessary. If the statements are false, explain why.

1 If two things are **mutually exclusive**, one makes the other impossible. T F
2 If two methods of doing something are **compatible**, they cannot both be used. T F
3 If two things are **equated**, they are said to be similar or the same. T F
4 If there are **parallels** between two phenomena, they are very different from each other. T F
5 If there is an **overlap** between two things, they share some properties. T F

47 Evaluation and emphasis

A Adjectives for evaluating: opening sentences from science articles

The first **comprehensive**[1] survey of coral reefs is being carried out in the Indian Ocean.

Fundamental[2] problems exist in current theories of the universe, a physicist claims.

A **groundbreaking**[3] discovery has been made in research into ageing and death.

Important new information about the planets has been gained from the Orbis space probe.

Working hours have increased and pressures at work have become more **intense** in the UK.

A **crucial** stage in global warming could be reached within ten years, scientists say.

The search for a unified theory of the human mind is **misguided**[4], says a psychologist.

The discovery of a dinosaur-like bone fossil in Africa is **unique**, according to scientists.

In 1997, Irkan published a **significant** piece of research on open structures in bridges.

Current responses to the global energy crisis are **inadequate**, a scientist has warned.

[1] complete, including everything that is necessary [2] basic, from which everything else originates
[3] very new and a big change [4] based on bad judgement or on wrong information or beliefs

B Teachers' evaluations of student assignments

Good! The only **criticism** I have is that there is a **notable**[1] lack of **key** references to work before 1990. You should have **given credit to**[2] earlier work by Wilson and Healey.

I am concerned about the **validity**[3] of some of your analysis, and as a result, some of your conclusions may be **invalid**. **Significantly**, you had problems in Section C.

I don't think the two different analyses you did are **compatible**[4]. **It is not surprising that** you had problems matching the two results, which **could be viewed as** almost **contradictory**.

There are some **solid**[5] arguments in Section A, but I think your conclusion in B is **mistaken** and lacks **hard**[6] evidence. Your data are rather **limited**.

[1] important and deserving attention [2] stated the importance of [3] basis in truth or reason
[4] able to exist successfully together [5] of a good standard [6] clear, able to be proven

C Other evaluative expressions

It is **noteworthy** that Holikov (1996) also had difficulty explaining the phenomenon.

It is worth recalling[1] **that** three previous studies failed to find a link between the two events.

We should **recognise/acknowledge** how difficult it is to interpret these data.

These results **are borne out by**[2] two other studies: Hermann (1998) and Morello (2001).

In his **seminal**[3] work, Abaka **challenges**[4] current techniques, revealing **flaws**[5] in data interpretation.

[1] *recall* is more formal than *remember* [2] confirmed, shown to be true [3] containing important new ideas, very influential [4] questions whether they are correct [5] faults, mistakes or weaknesses; we can say a method is **flawed** (adj)

D Emphasising

The research **underlined/highlighted** the need for a new social policy for childcare.

When used at the beginning of a sentence for extra emphasis, negative expressions are followed by inversion of the subject and verb. A form of *do* is used when there is no other auxiliary or modal verb.

Under/In no circumstances / On no account is it acceptable to video people without consent.
Seldom / Rarely would such data be considered appropriate for normal research purposes, and **in no way / by no means** should anyone regard data gathered in this way as meeting the university's ethical criteria. **Only** when full consent had been given in writing did the researcher commence filming.

Exercises

47.1 **Answer the questions about the adjectives in A opposite.**

1 Which two adjectives have negative associations?
2 Which adjective sounds most positive and exciting and means 'new and changing our understanding'?
3 Which two adjectives can be quite close synonyms and could be used, for example, in the phrase *to play a(n) .... role in the development of?*
4 Which adjective has a similar meaning to the adjectives in 3 but is stronger or more extreme?
5 Which adjective means 'the only one of its type'?

47.2 **Complete the sentences using words from the box.**

acknowledged evidence limited borne flawed mistaken challenged flaws seminal credit crucial groundbreaking validity viewed

1 Nierinck gave .... to the input of her research associates and .... that they had played a .... role in the project.
2 Unfortunately, these results are not .... out by other work in the field and you are .... to claim that there is hard .... to support your theory. There are .... in some of your calculations, and they need redoing.
3 Herbert .... Evensson on the .... of his conclusions, claiming that his data were .... and were too .... to be reliable.
4 This superb article can be .... as a .... piece of work which has made .... discoveries about the nature of cancerous cells.

47.3 **Choose the best word to complete each sentence.**

1 The study *highlights / gives credit* the need for more research.
2 I don't find your arguments either *hard / solid* or convincing.
3 Unfortunately, the two studies came up with results which were not *compatible / limited.*
4 She wrote the first *contradictory / comprehensive* study of this *key / misguided* period of Vietnamese history.
5 It is *borne out / worth recalling* that his work was initially criticised for being too *limited / flawed* in scope.
6 The article *underlines / is viewed as* the importance of literacy and numeracy skills in early education.

47.4 **Complete the second sentence so it means the same as the first.**

1 It is by no means certain that all the students will pass their final exams.
By no means ....
2 Rarely had he met such an outstanding student.
He ....
3 The country has seldom witnessed such a display of public feeling.
Seldom ....
4 In no way will we be able to halt the process of global warming.
We ....
5 Students will not be allowed to defer the completion of their dissertation for longer than six months under any circumstances.
Under no circumstances ....
6 We will only know the answer when we gather a lot more data.
Only when we ....

Over to you

Think of one discovery or development in your discipline which is usually considered groundbreaking and write a sentence about it. Name one article or book which most people in your discipline would consider seminal. Why is it viewed as such?

48 Describing change

A Historical changes and their effects

The **transition**[1] from agriculture **to** industry challenged the economic and political **status quo**[2] in many countries. Millions of people **abandoned**[3] villages and rural areas and moved into cities. The **shift**[4] **away from** self-sufficiency meant most people became dependent to some degree on large corporations and had to **adapt**[5] **to** new social environments and **adjust**[6] **to** new ways of doing things. A **move**[7] **towards** smaller, nuclear families brought about **fundamental**[8] changes in family patterns. **Maintaining**[9] the old ways became **increasingly**[10] difficult. On the other hand, the **elimination**[11] **of** diseases such as smallpox **transformed**[12] millions of people's lives, and the **expansion**[13] **of** healthcare in many countries saved countless lives. Technology **enhanced**[14] life in various ways. For many people, nonetheless, the negative **impact**[15] **of** technology **on** the environment **altered**[16] the way we think of our relationship with nature, and **sustainable**[17] **development**, rather than development for its own sake, became an important goal for a number of countries.

[1] change from one form to another [2] the situation as it was at that time [3] left for ever [4] change in position or direction [5] change to suit different conditions [6] become more familiar with a new situation [7] action taken to achieve something [8] in a very basic way [9] not allowing them to change [10] more and more [11] removal of [12] changed completely [13] increase in size or extent [14] improved the quality of [15] powerful effect [16] changed slightly [17] causing little or no damage to the environment and therefore able to continue for a long time

B More verbs for describing change

The exchange rate between the euro and the dollar has **fluctuated** recently. [changed or varied, especially continuously and between one level and another]

The technicians **modified** the flow of oil through the engine. [changed it slightly to improve it]

The company's lawyers **amended** the contract to take account of the new situation. [changed the words of a text, typically a law or a legal document]

Seven power plants were **converted from** oil **to** gas. [caused to change in form or character]

After 20 years of trading in the US, the firm **transferred** their operations **to** Brazil. [moved]

The economy **recovered** after three years of depression. [returned to a satisfactory condition]

Oil supplies are **diminishing** rapidly so that **acquiring** new supplies is vital for many countries. [becoming less; (formal) obtaining, getting]

We need to **refine** our analysis to obtain more accurate results. [improve it, especially by removing unwanted material]

The government **relaxed** controls **on** imports in 1997. [make less strict or severe]

Plans have been drawn up to **restore** 50,000 acres of wetland to their former state. [return something or someone to an earlier good condition or position]

C Adjectives which often describe change

There was a **gradual change** in attitudes in the 1990s. [slow, over a long period of time]

A **sudden change** in the temperature of the liquid occurred after some minutes.

There is a **marked change** in how people perceive antisocial behaviour. [very noticeable]

There was **no perceptible change** in the learning outcomes. [which could be noticed]

Sweeping changes were introduced in the legal system. [important and on a large scale]

Common Mistake

A *change in* temperature/behaviour, etc. suggests a process by which the thing has become different.
A *change of* approach/government/clothing, etc. suggests the substitution of one thing for another.

Exercises

48.1 Answer the questions.

1 If prices fluctuate what do they do?
2 If a disease is eliminated, how much of it remains?
3 If interest in something is diminishing, is it becoming less or more?
4 If there is a marked change in someone's behaviour, is it a big or a small change?
5 If most people think smartphones enhance their lives, do they feel that their lives have become better or worse?
6 If controls on imports are relaxed, do they become more or less strict?

48.2 Choose the best word to complete each sentence.

1 The economy now seems to be *recovering / amending*.
2 Many people now are *converting / transforming* to using solar power.
3 Our survey did not succeed in getting all the information we need and so we shall have to *diminish / refine* our questions a little.
4 Why do some people *abandon / shift* their families and disappear without a word?
5 It takes most people some time to *alter / adjust* to living in a new country.
6 In recent years most societies have seen a major change in the *transition / status quo*.
7 It is increasingly hard to *adapt / maintain* traditions in the face of progress.
8 There have been some attempts to *restore / alter* the environment to its original state.
9 The government introduced *sweeping / fluctuating* changes to healthcare delivery.
10 The change in the chemical's colour was so *marked / gradual* that many students failed to notice it.

48.3 Complete the phrases with the correct prepositions.

1 a change .... the climate
2 to transfer money .... a Swiss bank account
3 a shift .... the countryside towards the towns
4 to have an impact .... the cost of living
5 to relax controls .... immigration
6 to adjust .... changes
7 the transition .... one period to the next
8 to adapt .... a new way of life
9 to bring a change .... shoes on the field trip
10 to observe the impact .... the weather .... people's moods.

48.4 Complete the sentences using a word formed from the word in brackets. Use a dictionary if necessary.

1 There has been an enormous .... in aviation in recent years. (EXPAND)
2 Economists are increasingly concerned that development should be .... (SUSTAIN)
3 There has been no .... change in the patient's condition. (PERCEIVE)
4 The survey found that most people feel that modern life is becoming .... difficult. (INCREASE)
5 Industrial .... has, of course, transformed people's working lives. (DEVELOP)
6 The group's aims include the .... of famine and poverty. (ELIMINATE)
7 The apparatus worked well after we had made some .... to it. (MODIFY)
8 With increasing unemployment many people have had to make .... to their lives. (ADJUST)
9 Many linguists have studied first language ...., or how people learn their mother tongue. (ACQUIRE)
10 There is unlikely to be any .... of controls in the near future. (RELAX)

49 Summarising and concluding

A Conclusions and summaries

Summarising is concerned with expressing the most important facts or ideas about a topic in a short and clear form.

Concluding is concerned with (a) stating your position or opinion after considering all the information about something, or (b) stating that you have come to the end of something.

Recapitulating is concerned with briefly repeating your main points.

Read these openings of the final paragraphs of academic articles. Note the useful expressions.

As we have seen / As has been shown, the data are consistent across the three separate tests. **To conclude / In conclusion**, it seems that women's greater risk of depression is a consequence of gender differences in social roles.

From these comparisons **we may draw/come to the following conclusions**. As was expected, there are large differences between Russia and the two Nordic countries (Finland and Sweden).

To recapitulate[1] the findings of the present experiments: mothers' speech to young children was simpler than their normal speech.

To sum up / To summarise / In summary[2], in the case of high achievers in all professions, emotional competence is twice as important as purely mental abilities. **In short**[3], emotional competence is the key.

To bring this paper to a close[4] I summarise **the main points**[5] here: siblings influence the development of behaviour, and problems among siblings are linked to other problems.

[1] a less formal alternative is the short form *to recap* [2] (more formal) can also be ***in sum***
[3] used before describing something in as few words and as directly as possible [4] or **bring this paper to an end** [5] or **the key points**

B Other useful words and expressions for summarising and concluding

We may summarise the findings **in a few words**: conserving wetland is an urgent priority.

The **final** point to stress is that pay is rarely the only factor in industrial disputes. **To put it briefly** / **Stated briefly**, complex motives contribute to strikes. [*final* is more formal than *last*. *Stated briefly* is more formal than *to put it briefly*]

Praditsuk (1996) **provides/gives a (brief) summary** of Asian economic cooperation.

In their **abstract**, the authors claim to have made a breakthrough in cancer research. [shortened form of an article, book, etc., giving only the most important facts or arguments]

The government only published a **précis** of the report, not the full report. [/'preɪsi/ a short form of a text which briefly summarises the important parts]

In this essay, I have **attempted** to review **concisely** the arguments in favour of intellectual property rights in relation to the internet. [in academic style it is common to say that you have attempted/tried to argue or demonstrate something instead of directly saying you did it; *concisely* means in a short and clear way, without unnecessary words]

On balance, the **overall** picture seems to be that the political climate influences corporate strategy. [after thinking about the different facts or opinions; general rather than in particular]

In the final/last analysis/Ultimately, the only safe prediction is that the future is likely to be very different from the present. [said when talking about what is most important or true in a situation]

Common Mistake

Don't confuse *lastly* and *at last*. *Lastly* refers to the final point or item in a list or a series of points being discussed, and is similar to *finally*. *At last* refers to something which happens after people have been waiting for it for a long time.
Remember: *eventually* does NOT mean 'perhaps'. It means 'in the end, especially after a long time or a lot of effort, problems, etc.'

Exercises

49.1 Rewrite the underlined parts of the sentences using the words in brackets.

1 To conclude, the tests suggest the drug has no dangerous side effects. (CONCLUSION)
2 In short, losing the war was a humiliating defeat for the country on a number of different levels. (SUMMARISE)
3 To sum up, it is impossible to blame the disaster on one person alone. (SUMMARY / SUM – give give two answers)
4 From the survey we can conclude that advertising has a stronger effect on teenage girls than on other groups of the population. (DRAW / COME – give two answers)
5 To recap, there were a number of different reasons why the experiment was less successful than had been hoped. (RECAPITULATE)

49.2 Complete the sentences using words from the box.

abstract key analysis balance close eventually main provide put end words ultimately

1 On .... it would seem that more people are against the proposed law than for it.
2 Authors submitting an article for the journal are requested to provide a brief .... outlining the contents of their article.
3 To .... it briefly, General Pachai's attempts to manipulate the situation to his own advantage .... / .... led to his own downfall. (give two alternatives)
4 Most theses .... a summary of the literature in the field in their opening chapter.
5 In the final .... no one can be completely certain as to what caused the crash.
6 To summarise the problem in a few ....: manufacturing in the country has declined drastically in the last ten years.
7 Let us now recap the .... / .... points of the discussion. (give two alternatives)
8 Before bringing this paper to a(n) .... / ...., I should like to suggest some areas requiring further research. (give two alternatives)

49.3 Complete the sentences with *lastly* or *at last*.

1 After several months of negotiations, the two sides have .... reached agreement.
2 First, we shall consider the causes of the war, then we shall look at the events of the war and, ..., we shall discuss the consequences of the war.
3 She decided not to apply to Melbourne University. First and foremost, her marks were not likely to be good enough but also her parents did not want her to apply there. ...., none of her friends were considering going there.
4 My brother was very relieved when, ..., he finished writing his dissertation.

49.4 Explain the difference in meaning between *in the end* and *at the end* in the two sentences. Use a dictionary if necessary.

1 In the end, the government realised that the tax law had been a mistake and abolished it.
2 At the end of the book, Tao states that privatisation of public services is the solution.

49.5 Correct the six mistakes in the paragraph.

The art of writing a précise is to remember, first and foremost, not to include anything that was not in the original text. Stated brief, it is your job to tempt to capture the original writer's ideas conceasely, to provise a summary and, in the final analyse, to give your reader a shortcut to the original text.

50 Making a presentation

A Introducing the presenter

Let's **welcome** Carmen Gregori, who's going to talk to us today **on the subject of** 'Healthcare in Paraguay'.

Now I'd like to **call on** Mieko to **make/give her presentation**. Mieko, thank you.

OK, thank you everybody. Now, Dr Ulla Fensel is going to **present her research** to us.

I'd like to introduce Dr Li Meiju, who's going to **address**[1] **the topic** of 'Preventive medicine'.

[1] rather formal; we can also say formally *speak to the topic of X*, or, less formally, *talk about X*

B Getting started

In this presentation I'd like to **focus on** recent developments in biomass fuels. I'll speak for about 45 minutes, to **allow time for** questions and comments. **Feel free to**[1] interrupt if you have any questions or want to make a comment.

First I'll **give a brief overview of** the current situation **with regard to** intellectual property rights, then I'd like to **raise** a few **issues** concerning the internet. I'll try to **leave**[2] **time for questions** at the end.

I'd like to begin by looking at some previous studies of ocean temperatures. There's a handout **going round**[3], and there are some **spare**[4] **copies** here if you want them.

In this talk I'll **present the results of** a study I **did**[5] for my dissertation. I'll try to **keep to** 20 minutes and not **go over time**.

[1] an informal way of giving permission [2] less formal than allow time [3] a more formal version would be **(which is) being distributed** [4] extra [5] or, more formal, **carried out** / **conducted**

C During the presentation – and closing it

Now let's **turn to** the problem of workplace stress.	begin to examine or talk about
Moving on, I'd like to look at the questionnaire results **in more detail**.	going on to the next point less formal than **in greater detail**
I also want to talk about the supply of clean water, but I'll **come back to** that later.	or, more formal, **return to**
I'd just like to **go back to** the previous slide.	or, more formal, **return to**
As this slide shows, there's been a **clear drop in** popular support for the government.	or, more formal, a **marked decline in**
Anyway, **getting back to** / **to return to** the question of inflation, let's look at the Thai economy.	**getting back to** is less formal than **to return to**
The results were not very clear. **Having said that**, I feel the experiment was worthwhile.	a less formal way of saying **nevertheless**
You can **read more about this** in my article in this month's issue of World Geography.	or, more formal, my article ... **discusses this topic in more depth**
In our study we **draw on work done by** Sinclair and Owen, aiming to take it **a bit further**	or, more formally, ... **carried out by** .... or more formally, ... **develop it**.
I'll **skip** the next slide **as time is (running) short**.	**skip** (informal) = leave out / omit;
To sum up, then, urban traffic has reached a crisis. **That's all I have to say*. Thank you for listening.**	* informal - not used in writing
Well, I'll stop there as I've **run out of time**. Thank you.	have no time left
Dr Woichek will now **take questions***. Are there **any questions or comments**?	* rather formal = accept and answer questions

Exercises

50.1 Complete the introductions to presentations with words from A opposite.

1 Dr Anwar Musat will now .... his research on soil erosion in Malaysian forests.
2 I'd now like to .... on our next speaker, Eva Karlsson, to .... (give two answers) her presentation.
3 Ladies and gentlemen, let's .... our next speaker, Professor Prodromou from the University of Athens.
4 Thanks, everybody. So, Masanori is going to talk to us now .... the subject .... 'Mental health issues in Japan'.
5 I'd like to introduce today's speaker, Dr Krishnan Guptar, who is going to .... the topic of metal fatigue in rail tracks.

50.2 Replace the underlined words with less formal words and phrases.

1 We need to consider family income too, but I'll <u>return</u> to that later.
2 So, <u>to proceed to the next point</u>, I'll <u>omit</u> item 4 on the handout and instead talk about number 5 in <u>greater</u> detail.
3 I'll try to finish by 3.30, but <u>don't feel you need to ask permission to</u> leave if you have a class or other appointment to go to.
4 There is a handout <u>being distributed</u> and I have some <u>more</u> copies too if anyone wants them.
5 I'll finish there as my time has <u>come to an end</u>.
6 We didn't want to make people uncomfortable by having a camera in the room. <u>Nevertheless</u>, we did want to video as many of the sessions as possible.
7 I'd like to <u>return to</u> a point I made earlier about river management.
8 So, I believe our experiments have been successful. <u>I shall end there</u>. Thank you.
9 <u>To return to</u> the problem of large class sizes, I'd like to look at a study <u>carried out</u> in Australia in 2002.
10 I'll try not to <u>exceed my time</u>, so I'll speak for 30 minutes, to <u>allow</u> time for questions at the end.

50.3 Complete the sentences with the correct prepositions.

1 I'd like to focus .... waterborne diseases in this presentation.
2 The situation .... regard .... exports has been very good in recent years.
3 I'd now like to turn .... a different problem.
4 I always find it difficult to keep .... just 30 minutes, so please tell me when I have five minutes left.
5 I'd like to begin .... asking you all to do a small task.
6 I plan to allow ten minutes .... questions at the end of my presentation.
7 We can discuss this .... more depth later if you would like.
8 Our work draws heavily .... some research carried .... by the University of Salford.

50.4 Write six sentences you might hear during a presentation using appropriate combinations of the words in boxes A and B. You may use words in box A more than once.

Box A
present take raise draw
make give show

Box B
issue presentation results overview
comment slide questions work

I shall present the results of some studies done recently.

Over to you

A lot of lectures and presentations are available online. Choose one in a subject relevant for your studies and make a note of any useful words or expressions the speaker uses.

Reading and vocabulary 1

This section will give you further practice in the kinds of vocabulary you have studied in this book and will help you to become more aware of academic vocabulary as you read. The texts will be useful for you, whatever discipline you are studying.

Read the text. Use a dictionary if necessary but note that it is not essential to understand every word. Then do the exercises.

HOME
HEALTH
FITNESS
NUTRITION
EXERCISE

Nutrition for elite athletes

Becoming an elite athlete requires good genes, good training and conditioning and a sensible diet. Optimal nutrition is essential for peak performance. Nutritional misinformation can do as much harm to the ambitious athlete as good nutrition can help.

Athletes benefit the most from the amount of carbohydrates stored in the body. In the early stages of moderate exercise, carbohydrates provide 40 to 50 per cent of the energy requirement. Carbohydrates yield more energy per unit of oxygen consumed than fats. Because oxygen often is the limiting factor in long duration events, it is beneficial for the athlete to use the energy source requiring the least amount of oxygen per kilocalorie produced. As work intensity increases, carbohydrate utilization rises.

Complex carbohydrates come from foods such as spaghetti, potatoes, lasagna, cereals and other grain products. Simple carbohydrates are found in fruits, milk, honey and sugar. During digestion, the body breaks down carbohydrates to glucose and stores it in the muscles as glycogen.

During exercise, the glycogen is converted back to glucose and is used for energy. The ability to sustain prolonged vigorous exercise is directly related to initial levels of muscle glycogen. The body stores a limited amount of carbohydrate in the muscles and liver. If the event lasts for less than 90 minutes, the glycogen stored in the muscle is enough to supply the needed energy. Extra carbohydrates will not help, any more than adding gas to a half-full tank will make the car go faster.

For events that require heavy work for more than 90 minutes, a high-carbohydrate diet eaten for two to three days before the event allows glycogen storage spaces to be filled. Long distance runners, cyclists, cross-country skiers, canoe racers, swimmers and soccer players report benefits from a precompetition diet where 70 per cent of the calories comes from carbohydrates.

1 Find words in the text to match the meanings.

1 the best possible
2 not extreme
3 produce (verb)
4 use (noun)
5 changed in form
6 continuing for a long time

2 Explain how the prefix affects the meaning of the base word in these words from the text. Note down three other words using the same prefix.

1 misinformation
2 kilocalorie
3 half-full
4 precompetition

3 Find five words in the text that fit in each of the following categories.

1 types of carbohydrate food
2 types of sports people

4 Complete the table. Use a dictionary if necessary.

noun	verb	adjective
	require	
		limiting
		beneficial
intensity		
		simple
digestion		

Language help

Once you have read and understood the content of a text, look over it again and check that you know the different forms of important words in it, as in the table above.

Reading and vocabulary 2

Read the text. Use a dictionary if necessary but note that it is not essential to understand every word. Then answer the questions.

The Solar System

Until very recently, many scientists held the view that the Solar System was unique. In part this was due to the fact that carbon-based life had evolved on Earth, and in part because astronomers had been unable to detect any other planets in our Universe. Today, however, planetary systems have been discovered elsewhere in our own Galaxy and must, by any kind of logic, exist in others. There is thus little reason to suppose that some form of life has not developed there also, and that Homo sapiens and the other forms of life that flourish here, are not unique.

The Solar System comprises a central star – the Sun – and a large number of much smaller, denser, bodies that include the eight planets: Mercury, Venus, Mars, Earth, Jupiter, Saturn, Uranus and Neptune, together with their moons, dwarf planets and large numbers of meteoroids, asteroids and comets.

Most of the smaller bodies orbit the Sun in the same plane – known as the ecliptic – and the entire system rotates and moves through Space. In fact the Sun and its attendant family take roughly 200 million years to rotate around the centre of our Galaxy, known as the Milky Way.

Stars usually are composed of hydrogen, deuterium, tritium, helium, and lithium and have a mass that is sufficient to sustain stable fusion reactions. Because of these nuclear reactions, they emit massive amounts of electromagnetic radiation at a wide range of wavelengths. Planets, on the other hand, are usually relatively cool and stable, and much smaller. They may be small, rocky bodies, such as the terrestrial planets, dwarf planets, and asteroids, or much larger bodies, known as giant planets, composed predominantly of gases and ices.

Planets, being relatively non-massive, are gravitationally bound to more massive stars, which is the situation in our own Solar System. During the early stages of its evolution, many of the planets captured smaller bodies that now orbit around them; these are their moons. Amongst them are Earth's Moon, the Galilean satellites of Jupiter and many others. Such bodies have a wide range of size and composition.

Once there were considered to be nine planets, the outermost, Pluto, being discovered as recently as 1930. However, astronomers were not sure about Pluto's mass until the discovery in 1978 of an attendant companion, named Charon. Calculations on the orbital behaviour of the two enabled astronomers to establish that Pluto had a diameter of 2400 km, which was puzzling, as it was far too small to cause certain orbital perturbations that had been observed. However, powerful new ground- and space-based observations have completely changed our understanding of the outer Solar System. Instead of being the only planet in its region, Pluto and its moon are now known to be examples of a collection of objects that orbit the Sun within the Kuiper Belt, a region that extends from the orbit of Neptune out to 55 astronomical units. Astronomers estimate that there are at least 70000 icy objects in this region similar in composition to Pluto, and many of these are more than 100km across. As a consequence, Pluto/Charon was demoted to the class of dwarf planet.

1 Underline word combinations in the first four paragraphs of the text which match the meanings.

1 were of the opinion
2 it therefore seems very unlikely
3 a great many
4 generally called
5 in contrast
6 mainly made up of

2 Find words in the last two paragraphs that could be replaced by the following words.

1 comparatively
2 case
3 thought
4 allowed
5 ascertain
6 perplexing
7 group
8 stretches
9 calculate
10 downgraded

3 Explain the meaning of these words in the text.

1 evolve
2 flourish
3 comprise
4 orbit
5 rotate
6 emit

Over to you

Use a search engine on the web to find a recent article relating to astronomy. Make a note of any interesting new facts and vocabulary that you find there.

Reading and vocabulary 3

Read the text. Use a dictionary if necessary but note that it is not essential to understand every word. Then answer the questions.

GRAPHOLOGY

Graphology, in its linguistics sense, is the study of the system of symbols that have been devised to communicate language in written form. It must be clearly distinguished from the psychological sense of the term, which refers to the study of handwriting as a guide to character and personality. It also needs to be seen in contrast with graphetics, the study of the physical properties of manuscript, print and other forms of graphic expression. Linguistic graphology is an abstract study (as is its counterpart in the study of speech, phonology), dealing with the kinds of elements used in a language's writing system, the number of elements there are and how they interrelate, and the rules governing the way these elements combine in written texts.

The term graphology was coined by analogy with phonology, and several of the phonological notions used in the study of speech have also been applied to written language. In particular, the idea of a grapheme has been developed, analogous to phoneme. Graphemes are the smallest units in a writing system capable of causing a contrast in meaning. In English the switch from cat to hat introduces a change; therefore c and h represent different graphemes. The main graphemes in English are the 26 units that make up the alphabet. Other graphemes include the various marks of punctuation and such special symbols as @, & and £.

Graphemes are abstract units, which may adopt a variety of forms. The grapheme a may appear as A, a, ɑ or in other forms, depending on the handwriting style or typeface chosen. Each of these possible forms is known as a graph (cf phone in speech).

The analogy between graphology and phonology is important but there is no identity of function. Graphemes may signal phonemes, but they may also signal words or word parts (as with the numerals where each grapheme 1, 2 etc is spoken as a word that varies from language to language). Graphemes of punctuation show links and boundaries between units of grammar that may have nothing to do with the sounds of speech (notably the use of the hyphen). And several of the morphological relationships between words are conveyed by graphology more clearly than phonology: for example the link between sign and signature is closer in writing than in speech (where the g is pronounced in the second word but not in the first) and the same applies to such sets as telegraph, telegraphy, telegraphic, where there are several stress and vowel changes in speech but none in writing.

1 Complete the notes about forensic linguistics using words from the text.

Graphology = the study of written [1] .... devised to communicate written language.

Grapheme = the smallest [2] .... in a writing system [3] .... of causing a change in meaning. It may be written in different forms [4] .... on handwriting style or typeface chosen. These different forms are [5] .... as graphs.

Graphemes can [6] .... phonemes, words, word parts or relationships between words.

2 Complete the phrases with the correct prepositions from the text.

1 to be distinguished .... something else
2 refers .... something
3 to be seen .... contrast with something
4 coined .... analogy .... something
5 analogous .... something
6 depending .... something
7 relationships .... things
8 the same applies .... something else

3 Write the abstract nouns based on the same roots as these verbs from the text. Use a dictionary if necessary.

1 communicate
2 distinguish
3 refer
4 use
5 govern
6 combine
7 apply
8 develop
9 introduce
10 represent
11 include
12 adopt
13 appear
14 know
15 speak
16 pronounce

Over to you

Find a description of your own subject areas or one specific aspect of it. Write it out. Does it include any of the more general vocabulary from this text? What other interesting words and expressions does it use?

Reading and vocabulary 4

Read the text. Use a dictionary if necessary but note that it is not essential to understand every word. Then answer the questions.

Measuring time

ACCORDING TO ARCHAEOLOGICAL EVIDENCE, the Babylonians, Egyptians and other early civilizations began to measure time at least 5,000 years ago, introducing calendars to organize and coordinate communal activities and public events, to schedule the shipment of goods and, in particular, to regulate cycles of planting and harvesting. They based their calendars on three natural cycles: the solar day, marked by the successive periods of light and darkness as the earth rotates on its axis; the lunar month, following the phases of the moon as it orbits the earth; and the solar year, defined by the changing seasons that accompany our planet's revolution around the sun.

Before the invention of artificial light, the moon had greater social impact. And, for those living near the equator in particular, its waxing and waning was more conspicuous than the passing of the seasons. Hence, the calendars developed at the lower latitudes were influenced more by the lunar cycle than by the solar year. In more northern climes, however, where seasonal agriculture was important, the solar year became more crucial. As the Roman Empire expanded northward, it organized its calendar for the most part around the solar year.

The Egyptians formulated a civil calendar having 12 months of 30 days, with five days added to approximate the solar year. Each period of 10 days was marked by the appearance of special star groups (constellations) called decans. The cosmic significance the Egyptians placed in the 12 decans led them to develop a system in which each interval of darkness (and later each interval of daylight) was divided into a dozen equal parts. These periods became known as temporal hours because their duration varied according to the changing length of days and nights with the passing of the seasons. Summer hours were long, winter ones short; only at the spring and autumn equinoxes were the hours of daylight and darkness equal. Temporal hours, which were adopted by the Greeks and then the Romans (who spread them throughout Europe), remained in use for more than 2,500 years.

Ingenious inventors devised sundials, which indicate time by the length or direction of the sun's shadow, to track temporal hours during the day. The sundial's nocturnal counterpart, the water clock, was designed to measure temporal hours at night. One of the first water clocks was a basin with a small hole near the bottom through which the water dripped out. The falling water level denoted the passing hour as it dipped below hour lines inscribed on the inner surface. Although these devices performed satisfactorily around the Mediterranean, they could not always be depended on in the cloudy and often freezing weather of northern Europe.

1 Answer the questions about the text.

1 What did early civilisations use calendars for?
2 What did they base their calendars on?
3 Why did the lunar calendar have more significance in the tropics?
4 How do temporal hours differ from 'normal' hours?
5 Why do sundials and water clocks work less well in northern latitudes than round the Mediterranean?

2 Complete the word combinations.

1 to base calendars .... natural cycles
2 periods of .... and darkness
3 the waxing and .... of the moon
4 to divide something .... equal parts
5 temporal hours varied .... to the changing lengths of day and night
6 remained in .... for a century

3 The following words have different meanings in this text from their more familiar everyday meaning. Explain their meanings (a) in this text and (b) in a non-academic context.

1 cycles
2 revolution
3 waxing
4 civil
5 marked
6 adopted

Language help

After studying a text, read through it again, paying particular attention to word combinations. Write down any interesting or useful ones that you notice.

Reading and vocabulary 5

Read the introduction to a book on archaeology and medicine. Use a dictionary if necessary but note that it is not essential to understand every word. Then answer the questions.

Introduction

Not everything we do is documented in writing, particularly the routine activities of our daily lives, because records in both the written and oral traditions tend to be generated for extraordinary, unusual, and big events. The written record is, nonetheless, the basis upon which the subject of history, of all types, is investigated. Archaeological remains, meanwhile, can be studied and used to access unrecorded and mundane activities that have a significant impact on how people lived and understood their world. The aim of this book is to look beyond and behind texts and to explain how artefacts and structures associated with medical practices in the Greco-Roman world can be examined to determine past perceptions of health care, healers, and objects and spaces associated with treatments that might not be described in textual sources. It will be shown that archaeology is not simply a means of cataloguing artefacts and digging through layers of soil, but an insightful and critical scholarly discipline that can be used to ask vital and interesting questions about past lifestyles and social regulations that guided people's behaviours and, in this case, medical practices. The examples given in this study are period specific, but the methods and theories introduced through them can be used or adapted to study other eras in history. Scholars and students unfamiliar with archaeological data and their interpretation will gain an ability to make critical analyses of archaeological studies for themselves, draw upon material remains for their own research, and become familiar with the complex interpretations that can be derived from objects.

Social rules regarding actions and behaviours are largely realized and understood through habitual performance rather than through explicit statements. For instance, it is common for visitors to a foreign country to make a social faux pas when they are unfamiliar with the conventions of the culture. If a visitor thinks to ask someone native to the region why activities are performed in certain manners that differ from those with which he or she is familiar, responses tend to be vague, such as "it is the polite thing to do" or "it is common sense", but trying to ascertain why an action is polite or a matter of common sense can be difficult. Medically related activities and feelings about the ill are replete with culturally informed norms that are not verbally acknowledged, such as spacing one's self at specific distances away from the ill, keeping silent in a doctor's office, constructing hospitals in certain manners, discarding medical waste in specific ways, and fearing certain diseases and illnesses over others. Such reactions to the ill, along with spaces and objects associated with them, will generally vary from one society to another.

1 Find words in the first paragraph that could be replaced by the following words.

1 spoken
2 created
3 foundation
4 routine
5 influence
6 objects
7 ways of understanding
8 method
9 different levels
10 perceptive
11 academic subject
12 modified

2 Explain the meanings of these words in the second paragraph.

1 explicit
2 faux pas
3 conventions
4 ascertain
5 replete with
6 norms
7 constructing
8 discarding

3 Underline all the adjectives in the first paragraph. Then underline the nouns they are combined with.

4 Underline all the adjectives in the second paragraph. Write the nouns formed from the same root.

Over to you

Search in an online encyclopedia for an article on either archaeology or the history of medicine. Read the text and make a note of any useful adjective + noun combinations.

Reading and vocabulary 6

Read the text. Use a dictionary if necessary but note that it is not essential to understand every word. Then answer the questions.

SEEING THINGS DIFFERENTLY

Visualisations surround us as we work, play and learn. Enter a typical classroom and you will find the walls covered with pictures, photographs, cartoons, diagrams, maps and graphs. But the world is changing. Interactive whiteboards are now commonplace and teachers project animations onto them while annotating and describing the images for the students. Textbooks are no longer predominantly textual, but are rich with images, and their digital versions burst with videos and multimedia. Graphs need not only be constructed by calculating values from an equation, organising them in a table and then translating them to paper. Now anyone can draw them using software. We can even grab part of the line and see the equation change as a result. And students in the classrooms do not just consume visualisations produced by others, but sketch their ideas, upload videos they have created and summarise their understanding using mind-mapping software. It is perhaps only within formal assessments that we continue to place so much emphasis on written expression.

Given the multiplicity and ubiquity of visual representations, it seems sensible to ask whether this is a good thing for education. Are students benefiting from visualisations as they learn languages, study mathematics or develop their understanding of scientific practices? Or, instead, have we dumbed down and prettied up education without considering the consequences?

As ever, the answer is nuanced. There are distinct benefits to learning with visualisations, but it is more complicated than simply asserting that 'a picture is worth a thousand words' and hoping for the best. As we continue to move into an increasingly visual digital future, what do we know about learning with visualisations that can help us design better educational experiences?

Treated broadly, a visualisation is a representation of something that preserves, at least in part, some of the inherent visual or spatial information of the original, such as its shape, colour, texture, size, or spatial orientation. This information might be represented quite directly, in the case of road maps or diagrams for constructing furniture, or more abstractly, as is seen with line graphs or Venn diagrams.

Visualisations are always selective and can also exaggerate or add extra information. When we look at a road map, for example, we do not want to see every bend and twist in the road, nor every tree or house a street passes by, but we do value artificial colouring to indicate whether it is a narrow or wider road.

There are cognitive advantages to this. Visualisations can augment our memory, for example. When we represent information externally, rather than trying to remember it, we free up our short-term memory so that it can be used more efficiently. Imagine trying to remember a series of directions when finding your way around a new city, rather than simply looking at a map. We also tend to remember things that have been represented visually as well as verbally over the long term.

Visualisations organise information more efficiently, grouping relevant elements by physical proximity or by other forms of visual cues such as colour or connecting lines. As a consequence, when we inspect a visualisation as opposed to written description, we do not have to work hard to find related information, and any inferences seem to emerge, rather than having to be laboriously constructed.

1 Explain the meanings of these words in the text.

1 commonplace
2 annotating
3 predominantly
4 consume
5 multiplicity
6 ubiquity
7 dumb down
8 pretty up
9 asserting
10 selective
11 cognitive
12 augment
13 proximity
14 inferences
15 emerge
16 laboriously

2 Read this paragraph from the text. Try to complete it with the missing words without looking back at the text.

Treated broadly, a visualisation is a [1]............ of something that preserves, at least in [2]............, some of the inherent visual or spatial information of the [3]............, such as its shape, colour, texture, size, or spatial orientation. This [4]............ might be represented quite directly, in the [5]............ of road maps or diagrams for constructing furniture, or more abstractly, as is seen with line graphs or Venn [6]............

3 Choose ten words and expressions from the text that you would like to learn. Write them in your vocabulary notebook in a way that will help you learn them – in a context that is personally meaningful, perhaps.

Language help

When you work on a text, prepare some exercises of your own to help you learn vocabulary from it. These could focus on meanings, on word combinations or on words formed from the same root as words in the text. Do the exercises a few days after reading the text as useful revision of its language.

Reference I

Formal and informal academic words and expressions

There are many differences between formal, neutral and informal vocabulary in English. Here we list a number of words and expressions that are frequent in academic contexts and which may present problems in terms of choosing between formal, neutral and less formal alternatives.

You may often hear some of the informal words and expressions during classes, seminars, etc., but be careful not to use them where they are not appropriate, for example in formal essays or dissertations. Use a good dictionary which gives information about formality if you are in doubt. Where words are informal, we make a special note here. Space is provided at the end for you to add further examples of your own.

(n) = noun (v) = verb (adj) =adjective

formal	neutral (or informal where indicated)	example or comment
accord	agreement	an accord/agreement between two countries
acquire	obtain, get (less formal)	See Unit 48
address (v)	give attention to	address / give attention to a topic / an issue
address, speak to	speak/talk about	See Unit 50
adjudicate	judge	adjudicate/judge a contest/dispute
administer	give	administer/give a drug/medicine to a patient
advantages and disadvantages	pros and cons (informal)	See Unit 28
advocate (v)	support, encourage	We do not advocate/support/encourage the use of questionnaires with young children.
aim	set out (to do X)	In this paper, we aim/set out to challenge some current assumptions.
albeit	although	See Unit 39
appeal for	ask for	The police are appealing/asking for any information the public can offer.
attempt	try, have a shot at (informal)	See Units 1, 3, and 15
attire	clothes	She always wore rather old-fashioned attire/clothes.
be accepted / be offered a place	get in (informal) (for entry into a university or college)	I hope to get in / be accepted / be offered a place to study engineering.
call on	ask (somebody to do something)	See Unit 50
catalogue (v)	list	See Unit 27
characteristic (adj)	typical	See Unis 1 and 4
check	go through	See Units 6 and 42
compose	write	e.g. a poem/letter/symphony
conduct	carry out, do (less formal)	(an experiment / research / a study) See Units 3, 6 and 26
conduct (n)	behaviour (in the social sense)	Such conduct/behaviour is unacceptable.
consist of	be made up of	See Units 6, 38 and 40
constitute	make up	See Units 6 and 28
consult (v)	read, look at	e.g. a document/archive See Unit 27

contest (v)	argue against, disagree with	contest / argue against / disagree with a judgement
convention	agreement	No written convention/agreement existed until 1984.
cordial	friendly	cordial/friendly relations between governments
correct	right	It took hours of calculations to arrive at the correct/right answer.
deliver	give	deliver/give a talk/lecture
demonstrate	show	See Units 3, 12, 30 and 42
describe	set out	See Units 3, 6, 30 and 38
diminish	decrease, grow smaller	The population has diminished/decreased / grown smaller.
discuss	go into	See Units 3, 6, 12 and 40
dispose of	get rid of	dispose of / get rid of nuclear waste
document (v)	record, write about	See Unit 27
dormitory	dorm	BrE = hall of residence See Unit 19
dwelling	house, flat, apartment	There were originally 50 dwellings/houses/ flats/apartments on the site.
endure	last	The dynasty endured/lasted for eight centuries.
examination	exam (slightly informal)	(formal test) degree examinations/exams
examine	take, have a look at(informal)	See Units 3, 12 and 42
exceed	be more, higher; greater than	See Unit 35
exchange	swap (informal)	The tube was exchanged/swapped for one of a larger calibre.
final	last	See Unit 49
hierarchy	pecking order	e.g. in an institution
highlight	point up	See Units 6 and 30
improper	wrong	improper/wrong procedure
in excess of	over, higher than	See Units 7 and 16
in greater detail	in more detail	See Units 16 and 50
in respect of, with respect to	with regard to, as far as X is concerned, as far as X goes (informal)	See Unit 16
in sum, in summary	in short, to sum up, summing up	See Units 1 and 49
inappropriate	unsuitable	inappropriate/unsuitable form of words
incorrect	wrong (rather more direct than incorrect)	The totals in column 3 are incorrect/wrong.
incur	result in, experience	incur costs/expenses
instigate	initiate, start something	See Unit 24
instruct	direct, order	instruct/direct/order somebody to carry out a task
investigate	look into (slightly informal)	investigate / look into a problem

laboratory	lab	See Unit 26
maintain	keep	See Unit 30
make reference to	refer to	See Unit 27
negotiations	talks	negotiations/talks between governments
nevertheless	having said that	See Units 39 and 50
observe	point out	See Units 6, 26 and 30
occasion	time	It happened three times / on three occasions.
occupation	job, profession	(on a questionnaire) Question 3: What is your occupation/profession?
omit, not attend to something	skip (informal)	skip a lecture, skip/omit a chapter
pledge	promise	as a noun or as a verb
pose	ask	pose/ask a question See Unit 12
postgraduate	postgrad (informal)	See Unit 19
present	put forward	an idea/view/theory, etc. See Units 6 and 40
primarily	mainly	See Units 1 and 5
recapitulate	recap	See Unit 49
recently	lately	These animals have not been seen recently/lately.
representative	rep (informal)	She's the student representative/rep on the Departmental Committee.
resign	quit (informal)	The President resigned/quit in 1986.
resolve	solve, end	resolve/solve a problem, resolve/end a conflict
rest on	be based on	See Unit 14
return to	come back, go back, get back	See Unit 50
revise	look back over, go over	See Units 6 and 22
sanction (v)	permit	The government cannot sanction/permit law breaking.
secure (v)	obtain, get (informal)	secure/obtain/get oil supplies
sole(ly)	only	See Units 1 and 5
somewhat	slightly, a little, a bit (informal)	See Unit 5
speak of	talk of, talk about (less formal)	See Unit 14
spouse	husband, wife	The President's spouse/husband/wife attended the ceremony.
substantial	large, big	a substantial/large number/amount See Unit 7
treat	deal with	This issue was not treated / dealt with fully in Holstedt's earlier work.
undergraduate	undergrad (informal)	The undergrads/undergraduates mostly live in halls of residence.
undertaking (n)	promise	an official undertaking/promise to do something
utilise	use something effectively	utilise/use a resource/method
virtually	almost, more or less	See Unit 1
write of	write about	See Unit 14

X is not possible / not correct	There's no way X... (rather informal)	See Unit 1
Yours faithfully	Yours sincerely, Best wishes (less formal), best (informal)	way of ending a letter or email

Reference 2

Numbers, units of measurement and common symbols

You know how to say all the numbers in English. Here we look at how combinations of numbers are said aloud.

BrE = British English AmE = North American English

For spelling differences between BrE and AmE, see Reference 4.

A Fractions

Fractions are normally spoken as in these examples:

$\frac{1}{2}$	a (one) half
$\frac{1}{4}$	a (one) quarter
$\frac{3}{4}$	three quarters
$\frac{1}{5}$	a (one) fifth
$\frac{2}{3}$	two thirds
$\frac{1}{4}$ km	a quarter of a kilometre
$\frac{1}{2}$ cm	half a centimetre

Complex fractions and expressions of division are usually said with *over*.

$\frac{27}{200}$	twenty-seven over two hundred twenty-seven divided by two hundred

B Decimals

Decimals are normally spoken as in these examples:

0.36	*nought point three six* (BrE) *zero point three six* (AmE)
5.2	*five point two*

C Percentages

Percentages are spoken as *per cent*.

16.3%	*sixteen point three per cent*

D Calculations

Calculations are normally said in the following ways:

7 + 3 =10	*seven and three is/are ten* (informal) *seven plus three equals ten* (more formal)
28 – 6 =22	*six from twenty-eight is/leaves twenty-two* (informal) *twenty-eight minus six equals twenty-two* (more formal)
8 x 2 =16	*eight twos are sixteen* (informal BrE) *eight times two is sixteen* (informal) (the most common form in AmE) *eight by two is/equals sixteen* (informal) *eight multiplied by two equals/is sixteen* (more formal)
27 ÷ 9 =3	*twenty-seven divided by nine equals three*
500 ± 5	*five hundred plus or minus five*
>300	*greater than three hundred*
<200	*less than two hundred*
$3^2 = 9$	*three squared is/equals nine*
√16 = 4	*the (square) root of sixteen is four*
$3^3 = 27$	*three cubed is/equals twenty-seven*

$\sqrt[3]{8} = 2$	*the cube root of eight is two*
$2^4 = 16$	*two to the power of 4 is/equals sixteen* (AmE = two to the fourth power ...)

E Units of measurement

Although the metric system is now common in the UK and other English-speaking countries, non-metric units are still used in many contexts, especially in the USA.

Units of length and distance are normally spoken as follows:

3 in, 3"	*three inches*
2 ft 7 in, 2' 7"	*two feet seven inches* (or, very informally, *two foot seven inches*)
500 yds	*five hundred yards*
3m (AmE = 3 mi.)	*three miles*
500mm	*five hundred millimetres* (or, more informally, *five hundred m-m*)
1.5 cm	*one point five centimetres*

Units of area are normally spoken as follows:

11 sq ft	*eleven square feet*
5 sq m, $5m^2$	*five square metres*
7.25 cm^2	*seven point two five square centimetres*

Units of weight are normally spoken as follows:

3 oz	*three ounces*
5 lb	*five pounds*
300 g	*three hundred grammes*
18.75 kg	*eighteen point seven five kilograms*

Units of volume, capacity and temperature are normally spoken as follows:

300 cc	*three hundred cubic centimetres* (or, less formally, *three hundred c-c*)
5 pt	*five pints*
3.2 gal	*three point two gallons*
75 cl	*seventy-five centilitres*
200 l	*two hundred litres*
20°	*twenty degrees*

F Common symbols

&	'ampersand' - this symbol is read as 'and'
*	asterisk
©	copyright symbol
TM	trademark symbol
®	registered trademark
•	bullet point
✓	BrE = tick; AmE = check
✗	BrE = cross; AmE = an 'X'
#	BrE = hash or hash-tag (Note: in American English, this symbol is used for numbers, e.g. #28 AmE; no. 28 BrE)
@	this symbol is read as 'at' – used in email addresses
.	a full stop is said as 'dot' in email and web addresses
/	this is said as 'forward slash' in web addresses
∞	infinity symbol
"	this symbol is read as 'ditto' – used in lists to avoid writing a word if the same word is written immediately above it

Reference 3

British and North American academic vocabulary

There are numerous differences in vocabulary between the English of the UK and Ireland and the English of the USA and Canada, the two dominant areas which have historically influenced English in many other parts of the world. However, there is also a great amount of mixing, and Americans and Canadians are often familiar with British and Irish usages, and vice versa. So the table below is for general guidance only. Also, nowadays, thanks to the global media and the internet, American vocabulary is influencing and being imported into British, Irish and international English more and more. Other important varieties of English, such as Indian, Australian, African, Caribbean, etc., also have their own words and phrases, but have probably, for historical reasons, had less influence overall on international usage or academic usage in particular.

The first column of the table shows words and phrases that are commonly used in North American English, but which are not used, or used to a far lesser extent, in British and Irish English, and which are likely to occur in academic texts or in general college and university contexts and student life. Be prepared to meet others in everyday life in English-speaking countries.

See also Unit 19 of this book. Space is provided at the end for you to add further examples of your own.

For differences between British and American grammar, see the special chapter in the *Cambridge Grammar of English* (published by Cambridge University Press).

AmE = North American English BrE = British/Irish English

North American	British/Irish	comment
airplane	aeroplane	
alternate (adj)	alternative	e.g. Section 7 presents an alternative approach to this issue. *Alternate* (adj) in BrE means 'every other', e.g. The drug was administered on alternate days.
antenna	aerial	
apartment	flat	Both forms are heard increasingly in BrE.
apartment building	block of flats	
attorney	lawyer	
ATM (automated teller machine) cashpoint	cash machine	from which one can get money. The AmE forms are also used in BrE.
bill	note	e.g. a 100 dollar bill, a 50 euro note
cafeteria	canteen	Both are common in BrE.
candy	sweet(s)	
cart	trolley	used in a supermarket to carry one's shopping
cell phone	mobile phone	
checking account	current account	bank account for day-to-day use
chips	crisps	
coach class	economy class	cheapest class of air travel
condominium, condo (informal)	block of flats	
cookie	biscuit	small, flat cake
cord	lead, cable	electrical cable joining an appliance to a power connection

co-worker	workmate	
crosswalk	pedestrian crossing	
dirt road	unpaved road, track	
district attorney	public prosecutor	
divided highway	dual carriageway	
doctor's office	surgery	
downtown	town centre, city centre	
(the) draft	conscription	compulsory military service
drug store	chemist's, pharmacy	
eggplant	aubergine	vegetable
elementary school	primary school	
elevator	lift	
emergency room	A and E (accident and emergency)	at a hospital
eraser	rubber	object used to delete writing in pencil
fall	autumn	
faucet	tap	for water
field	pitch	a sports area, e.g. football pitch/field
flashlight	torch	a light powered by batteries
freeway	motorway	
(French) fries	chips	long, thin pieces of fried potato, eaten hot (see *chips* vs *crisps*)
furnace	central heating boiler	
garbage, trash	rubbish, refuse (more formal)	
gas	petrol	fuel for motor vehicles
grounded	earthed	electrical
high school	secondary school	
highway	main road	*Highway* in BrE is normally only used in technical and legal/official contexts.
intersection	crossroads	
intermission	interval	e.g. break in a cinema/theatre performance.
interstate (highway)	main/major road, motorway	
jack	socket	connection for a telephone land line
kindergarten	nursery school	In AmE, *kindergarten* refers to school for five-year old children, the year before entering first grade. In BrE, *nursery* refers to a special room for babies, while *nursery school* refers to a school for children aged 2-5 (also called *pre-school*).
legal holiday	bank holiday	
license plate, license tag	number plate	on a vehicle
line	queue	
locker room	changing room	for sports
mail	post	letters and packages delivered to a home or place of business

mall	shopping centre	*(Shopping) mall* is used more and more in BrE.
mass transit, public transportation	public transport	
movie	film	*Movie* is also common in BrE.
movie theatre	cinema	
normalcy	normality	
operating room	operating theatre	in a hospital
outlet	socket	place to connect for electrical power -BrE also uses *power point*
overpass	flyover	in a road system
parentheses	brackets	In AmE, the word *brackets* refers to [ ].In AmE, *parentheses* are ( ).
parking garage	multi-storey car park	
parking lot	car park	
penitentiary	prison	
period	full stop	referring to punctuation
petroleum	crude oil	oil when it comes out of the ground
prenatal	ante-natal	'before birth'; concerning mothers-to-be
private school	private school, public school	A *public school* in the UK is a private secondary school; schools run by the government are called *state schools*.
railroad	railway	
recess, break	break e.g. gap between activities, for lunch, etc.	
restroom, bathroom, washroom (Canada)	toilet, loo (informal)	*Restroom* is used for public facilities, whereas *bathroom* also refers to facilities in a home.
resumé	curriculum vitae (or CV)	
round trip	return	e.g. a round trip / return ticket
running shoes, sneakers	trainers	
sales clerk	shop assistant	
sales tax	VAT (value added tax)	tax added to goods and services at the point of purchase
schedule	timetable	
scotch tape	sellotape	adhesive tape
server	waiter, waitress	*waitress* is less common; *waiter* is increasingly used for male and female.
senior	pensioner, senior citizen	
sidewalk	pavement, footpath	
social security number	national insurance number	individual personal number used by officials in connection with tax, social benefits, etc.
stop lights	traffic lights	
store	shop	
subway	underground (railway)	A *subway* in BrE is an underground tunnel or passageway for pedestrians to cross a road.

takeout	takeaway	meals, food
teller	cashier	person who serves customers in a bank
thumbtack	drawing pin	e.g. used to fix a notice to a noticeboard
tractor-trailer	articulated lorry, juggernaut	
trashcan	(dust)bin	
truck	lorry, truck, wagon (informal)	
two weeks	fortnight	
vacation	holiday	*Vacation* is used in BrE universities to mean the periods when no teaching takes place. In AmE, *holiday* refers to a national day of observance, for example New Year's Day.
zee	zed	last letter of the English alphabet
zucchini	courgette	vegetable
zip code (USA), postal code (Canada)	postcode	

Reference 4

Spelling variations

Some words are spelt differently in different varieties of English. The main contrasts are between British/Irish and US English. Other varieties of English tend to opt for either predominantly UK/Irish or predominantly US spelling. The US spelling tends to be simpler and a clearer reflection of the way the word is pronounced. You can, of course, use whichever spelling you prefer but it is sensible to be consistent. The main patterns of spelling variation are shown below.

Space is provided for you to add further examples of your own.

Word-processing and other computer programs often have spellcheck features that check the spelling of what you write. You can usually set these to either UK, US or Australian spelling. However, remember that it is not sensible to rely on the computer to check and correct your spelling for you. A spellcheck program will not pick up the spelling errors in this sentence, for example: *I don't no weather their are two many mistakes inn yore righting ore knot.*

pattern of variation	examples of British + Irish spelling	examples of US spelling	comment
words with *-our/or*	labour, honour, behaviour, endeavour, favourable, rumour	labor, honor, behavior, endeavor, favorable, rumor	In some words UK spelling uses the *-or* form, e.g. humorous, honorary, glamorous.
words ending with-*er/re*	centre, theatre, centimetre, litre, lustre	center, theater, centimeter, liter, luster	UK spelling distinguishes between metre (l00 cms) and meter (measuring device).
verbs ending in single *l* when they add a suffix	cancelling, labelled, marvellous, counsellor	canceling, labeled, counselor, marvelous	Sometimes the *ll* spelling will also be found in US texts.
other words with single or double l	fulfil, enrol, enrolment, instalment, skilful, wilful	fulfill, enroll, enrollment, installment, skillful, willful	The verb *to install* can be written with either *l* or *ll* in both UK and US English, although *ll* is more common.
words ending with *-ogue/og*	analogue, catalogue, dialogue	analog, catalog, dialog	The *-gue* ending can also be found in US texts.
verbs ending with *-ise*/ize and nouns ending with *–isation/ization*	emphasise, minimise, globalise, colonise, organise, standardise, globalisation, colonisation, organisation, standardisation	emphasize, minimize, globalize, colonize, organize, standardize, globalization, colonization, organization, standardization	Some verbs always end in *-ise*, e.g. advertise, advise, apprise, arise, comprise, compromise, despise, devise, disguise, enfranchise, enterprise, excise, exercise, improvise, incise, premise, revise, supervise, surmise, surprise. With other words the *–ize/ization* endings will also sometimes be found in UK texts.

verbs ending with *-yse/yze*	analyse, catalyse, paralyse	analyze, catalyze, paralyze	The nouns *analysis*, *catalysis* and *paralysis* are spelt the same in both UK and US texts.
some words ending with –*ce/se*	defence, offence, pretence, practise (verb) and licence (noun)	defense, offense, pretense, practice (verb and noun), license (verb and noun)	UK spelling distinguishes between *practice* and *licence* (nouns) and *practise* and *license* (verbs).
some words with -*ae* or -*oe* in UK English	anaesthetic, gynaecology, haemorrhage, orthopaedic, manoeuvre, oesophagus	anesthetic, gynecology, hemorrhage, orthopedic, maneuvre, esophagus	Words in this category are all of Greek origin and most occur in medical contexts.
miscellaneous	aluminium, cheque, grey, kerb, mould, plough, programme (e.g. TV/research programme), pyjamas, storey (of building), (car) tyre	aluminum, check,gray, curb, mold, plow, program, pajamas, story, tire	In UK spelling note the spelling of computer *program*. In UK spelling *check*, *curb*, *story* and *tire* have distinct meanings from *cheque*, *kerb*, *storey* and *tyre*.

Reference 5

Word formation

One advantage of English vocabulary is that many words are formed from the same root. As a result, if you know the word *friend*, it is easy to understand other words from the same root such as *friendly*, *friendship*, *unfriendly* and *befriend*. Learning what prefixes (for example *un-*, *mis-*, *extra-*) and suffixes (*-ify -ship*, *-less*) mean can help you to extend your vocabulary in a relatively effortless way. When you meet a new word, it is a good idea to write it down with other words using the same root + different prefixes and suffixes. Thus, you might write down together, for example, *amoral*, *morality*, *immoral*, *morally*, *moralise*, *moralist*, *moralistic*. See Unit 17 for more work on prefixes and suffixes.

Variation occurs in the use of hyphens, especially in newspapers and popular magazines. For example the prefix *de-* may or may not be followed by a hyphen (*decontaminate*, *de-escalate*), but some prefixes are almost always used with a hyphen (e.g. *ex-*, *semi-*). Train yourself to be aware of any prefixes which regularly occur in your academic area and make a note of how they are usually written. Note that North American English makes much less use of a hyphen after prefixes than British English.

The following table includes some of the major prefixes and suffixes that are useful as far as academic vocabulary is concerned. Familiarising yourself with these will not only help you to work out what unfamiliar words mean but will also help you to remember those words. Space is provided for you to add further examples of your own.

prefix	meaning	examples	further examples of your own
a-	without	amoral /ˌeɪˈmɒrəl/, apolitical /ˌeɪpəˈlɪtɪkəl/, atypical /ˌeɪˈtɪpɪkəl/]	
ante-	before	antecedent, antedate	
anti-	against, opposing	anti-establishment, anti-globalisation, anti-inflammatory	
arch-	more extreme	arch-capitalist, arch-rebel	
auto-	self	auto-dial, auto-rotate	
bi-	two, twice	biped, bisect	
circum-	round	circumnavigate, circumvent	
co-	with	co-pilot, co-edit	
col-, com-, con-	with	collaborator, compose, concur	
contra-, counter-	against, opposing	contra-revolutionary, contraception, counter-measure, counter-intuitive	
de-	opposite action	decentralise, declassify	
dia	across	diagonal, diameter	
dis-	opposite action or state	disagree, disprove, distrust, disbelief, disproportionate	
dys-	abnormal	dyslexia, dysfunctional	
e-	electronic	e-literate, e-book	

eco-	relating to the environment	eco-disaster	
equi-	equal	equidistant, equilateral	
ex-	previously	ex-president, ex-student	
extra-	very	extra-bright, extra-strong	
extra-	outside	extra-curricular, extra-sensory	
hyper-	having too much	hypersensitive	
il-, im-, in-, ir-	not	illiterate, improbable, indecision, irrelevance	
in-	movement to or towards the inside of something	input, inset, intake, import	
inter-	between, connected	interactive, interbreed	
intra-	within	intra-generational, intramuscular	
kilo-	thousand	kilogram, kilowatt	
macro-	large in size or scope	macro-economics, macro-scale	
mal-	badly	maladjusted, malnutrition	
micro-	small in size or scope	micro-economics, micro-scale	
mis-	wrongly	mistranslate, misunderstanding	
mono-	one	monochrome, monoculture	
multi-	many	multicultural, multi-level	
neo-	based on something older but in a new form	neo-classical, neo-conservative	
non-	not	non-believer, non-competitive	
out-	more, to a greater extent	outnumber, outlive	
over-	too much	over-abundance, overflow, overexcited	
post-	after	post-examination, post-modern	
pre-	before	pre-existing, pre-pay	
pro-	in favour of	pro-liberal, pro-feminist	
pseudo-	false	pseudo-intellectual, pseudo-science	
quasi-	almost, not quite	quasi-academic, quasi-legal	
re-	again	rediscover, redefine, rename	
retro	backwards	retrogressive, retrospective	
semi-	partly	semi-organic, semi-precious	
sub-	under, lesser	sub-heading, sub-species	
super-	above, bigger	superpower, supersonic	
trans-	across	transcontinental, transcribe	
ultra-	extreme	ultra-sensitive, ultrasound	

un-	not	uncertain, unusual, unscrew, unplug	
under-	insufficient	underemployed, undernourished	
well-	useful, successful	well-designed, well-written, well-established	

suffix	meaning	examples	further examples of your own
-able, -ible	can be	understandable, undeniable, comprehensible, indefensible	
-ant	having an effect	pollutant, accelerant	
-based	forming a major part of	computer-based, oil-based	
-cy	state or quality	complacency, literacy, appropriacy	
-ee	person affected by something	interviewee, evacuee, addressee	
-free	without	debt-free, pain-free	
-hood	state, condition, period	boyhood, motherhood	
-ic	connected with	photographic, electric	
-ics	study of	genetics, electronics	
-ify	give something a quality	beautify, solidify, simplify	
-ism	belief, behaviour	radicalism, impressionism	
-ist	person with specific beliefs or behaviour	socialist, pessimist	
-ize, -ise	bring about a state or condition	characterize/characterise, formalize/formalise	
-less	without	hopeless, meaningless	
-like	resembling	warlike, hook-like	
-ness	quality or state	effectiveness, hopefulness	
-ocracy	type of ruling body	meritocracy, bureaucracy	
-ocrat	person ruling	technocrat, aristocrat	
-ology, -ological	study of	biology, biological, geology, physiological	
-proof	protected against, safe from	windproof, dustproof	
-ship	state or experience of having a specific position	professorship, leadership	

Key

Unit 0

0.1 Personal answers

0.2 *Possible answers:*

1 university:
to apply to university; a world-famous university [typical word combinations]
a university, not ~~an university~~ [special note]
the university of life [other use]

2 academic:
I'm studying academic vocabulary. [example of word in use]
an academic institution; academic standards; the academic year; academically gifted [typical word combinations]
can also be a noun for a person who teaches at a university [special note]
an academy; academia; non-academic [additional vocabulary]

3 degree:
My brother is studying for a degree in zoology. [example of word in use]
an honours degree, an arts degree, to do a degree in..., a post-graduate degree [typical word combinations]
a degree of risk 38 degrees Celsius; a matter of degree [other uses]

0.3 2 note down an interesting expression or note an interesting expression down
3 come across an interesting expression

0.4 *Possible answers:*

1	2
to write up	special
to conduct	secondary
to design	further
to do	adult

0.5 *Possible answers:*

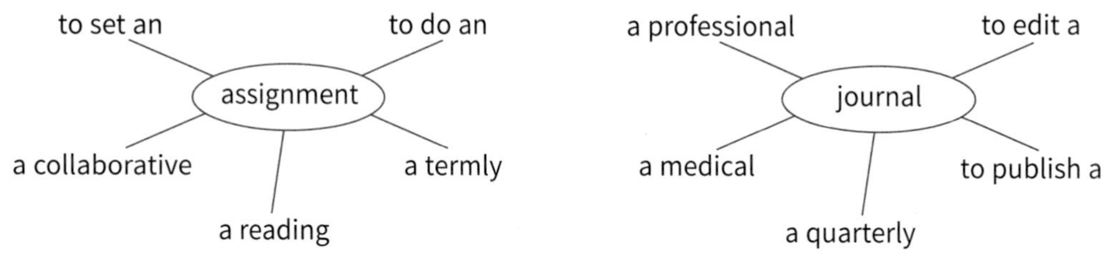

0.6 Personal answers

1.1 Unit 1

2 focus, focus
3 confirmed, confirms / confirmed
4 generates, generates
5 indentified, identified
6 turn, turn
7 underlines, underlines / underlined
8 solid, solid

1.2
1 The book is **primarily** concerned with the problem of policing the internet.
2 **Virtually** every school in the county had reported problems with the new system.
3 The work of the Institute is not **solely** devoted to cancer research.
4 **Fundamentally**, we believe we have demonstrated a significant link between the two events.
5 Several research teams have **attempted to solve** the problem, without success.
6 The reaction is **characteristic of** the way large corporations keep control of their markets.

1.3
1 depends heavily, be produced cheaply
2 relatively easily
3 production, reliance, discovery, claim
4 new and different from previous ways

1.4
2 development of, revolution
3 solution, alteration
4 exploration, challenges

Unit 2

2.1
1 of
2 on (on the subject/issue/topic of)
3 beyond the scope of

2.2
1 issues
2 topics
3 theory
4 theme
5 model
6 Principle

2.3 1 g 2 f 3 h 4 e 5 b 6 a 7 d 8 c

2.4
1 Recent research that was carried out
2 a strong case for boosting
3 Its methodology
4 their views on how best to prevent crime
5 beyond the scope of the study
6 raising awareness of the issue

2.5
1 Nature
2 Significance
3 Features
4 Assessment
5 Patterns
6 Identification
7 Perspectives
8 Principles

Unit 3

3.1
affect – influence
attempt – try
calculate – compute
challenge – question
demonstrate – show
identify – distinguish
include – involve
investigate – study
provide – give

3.2
1 be seen
2 accounted
3 classifying
4 present
5 show
6 develop
7 establish
8 attempted

3.3
1 Sentence A means that Greig's work backs up that of Park; in other words, it comes to the same conclusions. Sentence B means that Greig's work questions Park's conclusions.
2 Sentence A asks someone simply to say what the new tax regulations are. Sentence B asks someone to give their opinion with regard to the new tax regulations.
3 Sentence A means that Lodhi's work is the source of some new data. Sentence B means that Lodhi discusses new data, giving his opinion as to their implications and significance.
4 Sentence A means that Titova did the experiments himself. Sentence B means that Titova considered some experiments which others had carried out.
5 Sentence A means that Lee was able to prove why such changes occur. Sentence B means that Lee tried to find out why such changes occur but we do not know how successful he was in this.
6 Sentence A means Okaz accepted this without proof or questioning. Sentence B means Okaz did something to show that the data were giving a true picture of something.
7 Sentence A means show how it works in some way, e.g. by drawing a graph or an illustration of some kind. Sentence B means discover it by doing calculations.
8 Sentence A means the events caused economic development to happen. Sentence B means the events had an influence (perhaps positive or negative) on economic development.

3.4 Erikson's (2005) book [1]**offers / gives / provides an explanation of / for** the changing patterns of educational achievement in children of poorer families. She [2]**undertakes / carries out an exploration of** the relationship between income, family background and achievement at school and in further education. The book [3]**gives / provides a description of** a study carried out in 12 inner-city neighbourhoods. Erikson's research [4]**places / put emphasis on** the importance of support within the home.

3.5
1 investigation
2 illustration
3 analysis
4 effect (note the change in the first letter)
5 attempt
6 classification

Unit 4

4.1
1 A lengthy discussion of the advantages of solar power is not **relevant to** this essay topic.
2 It is **typical of** the disease for it to start with an itchy rash.
3 This methodology is not **appropriate to** the kind of research you are planning.
4 The use of original metaphors is **characteristic of** the writer's style.
5 **Relative to** previous explanations, this theory is quite persuasive.
6 Dark hair and eyes are **common to** all people from the region.

4.2
1 apparent discrepancy
2 principal cause
3 rigorous methodology
4 potential problem

4.3
1 inaccurate
2 complex
3 precise
4 an insignificant
5 concrete
6 qualitative

4.4
1 specific
2 rigorous
3 potential
4 qualitative
5 complex
6 rough

4.5

adjective	noun	adjective	noun
appropriate	appropriacy	complex	complexity
significant	significance	accurate	accuracy
precise	precision	rigorous	rigour

4.6
2 The slight discrepancy in the two sets of figures **has no significance**.
3 **The complexity of the poet's language / The complexity of the language used by the poet** makes his work difficult to interpret.
4 **Precision is essential** when taking measurements.
5 The later part of the book **will have more relevance** for next year's course.
6 The tutor was pleased with **the simplicity and appropriacy of our research proposal**.

Unit 5

5.1
1 Sentence A means that Heinrich's experiments were largely criticised or criticised on the whole on ethical grounds. Sentence B means that Heinrich's experiments were criticised on ethical grounds more than on for any other reasons.
2 Sentence A means that the results were rather or fairly surprising in view of the circumstances. Sentence B means that the results were particularly or greatly surprising in view of the circumstances. In other words, the results in the second sentence surprised the writer more than those in the first sentence.
3 Sentence A means that the new rules have a direct impact on first year students as opposed to students from other years, who may either be indirectly affected or not affected at all. Sentence B means that the new rules affect first year students more than students from other years, even though other years may be affected.

4 Sentence A means that urban alienation is the main focus of the study. Sentence B means that urban alienation was probably not the initial focus of the study but it turned out in the end to be its most significant theme.
5 Sentence A means that the team finally, after a long time of trying, obtained some results which they had not predicted. Sentence B means that the team often obtained results which they had not predicted.

5.2
1 essentially
2 simply
3 basically
4 simply
5 generally

5.3
1 exactly
2 infrequently
3 eventually
4 roughly
5 implicitly
6 generally
7 precisely
8 indirectly

5.4 *Suggested underlinings:*

Marine conservationists are currently attempting to save the world's coral reefs. One plan is to literally glue the damaged reefs back together, using coral artificially raised in underwater laboratories. Reefs are increasingly under attack from human activity as well as from events which occur naturally, such as hurricanes and tsunamis. A recent UN report warns that 30% of the world's coral reefs have been completely destroyed or are severely damaged.

Scientists have recently discovered that ants can remember how many steps they have taken. By carefully shortening or lengthening the legs of ants, the team observed that short-legged ants apparently became lost and could not easily find their way home to the nest. Similarly, ants with longer legs typically travelled 50% further than they needed to and were also temporarily unable to find the nest. It seems ants can definitely count their steps.

1 similarly
2 artificially/naturally and apparently/definitely
3 recently
4 increasingly
5 severely
6 temporarily

Unit 6

6.1
1 We **carried out** a series of experiments to test out our hypothesis.
2 Before the test you should **go / look back over** Chapters 7 and 8 of your textbooks.
3 In his article on the American Civil War Kingston **goes into** the reasons why the situation developed in the way it did.
4 Cole **puts forward** some fascinating theories on the development of language in his latest book.
5 The psychologist **pointed out** that it was very unusual for a young child to behave in this way.
6 Please **go through** your work carefully before handing it in.
7 Simpson's book **sets out** to prove that the Chinese reached America long before the Vikings.
8 Women now **make up** over half the student population in universities in this country.

6.2
1 on
2 out
3 up
4 out
5 up
6 forward
7 on
8 out

6.3 1 f 2 a 3 e 4 b 5 c 6 d

6.4 *Possible answers:*
1 an experiment, a survey
2 your results, your research, a report
3 an idea, an argument
4 flaws, errors, mistakes
5 your notes, your work, figures
6 an experiment, a research project

Unit 7

7.1
1 surprising
2 excessive
3 Considerable
4 reasonable
5 substantial
6 excess
7 total
8 handful
9 fewer
10 significant

7.2
1 A vast amount of
2 a huge amount of
3 a small number of
4 An enormous amount of
5 results
6 has been

7.3
1 large/huge
2 All of + have been
3 small-scale
4 more and more
5 small

7.4
1 For some years
2 a massive number of
3 the first few microseconds of
4 After no more than
5 more or less

Unit 8

8.1
1 a
2 d
3 e
4 c
5 b
6 g
7 f

8.2
1 references
2 occur
3 revolutions
4 accommodate
5 structure
6 contracted

8.3
1 points
2 set
3 issue
4 channel
5 revolution

8.4

word	meaning in text	other meaning(s)
contain	keep something within limits	hold, include
maintain	say, claim	keep at a specific level; preserve; provide for
check	stop something from increasing or continuing	examine; find out about something; pattern of squares
monitor	watch, observe	screen
record	store information	store sound or pictures electronically; best or most extreme (noun)
allow	make possible	permit
measures	methods for dealing with a situation	sizes; amounts; ways of judging something
perform	operate	entertain by e.g. singing, dancing, acting

8.5 The joke is based on a couple of meanings of the word *charge*. The first meaning, familiar from general English, is that of cost as in 'There is a small charge for using the hotel car park.' However, in physics, *charge*, also known as electrical charge and symbolized as q, is a characteristic of a unit of matter that expresses the extent to which it has more or fewer electrons than protons. In atoms, the electron carries a negative elementary or unit charge, the proton carries a positive charge. A neutron is said to have no charge.

Unit 9

9.1

1 shone
2 remained, shed
3 light
4 illuminating
5 shadow
6 illuminate
7 highlighted
8 glaring

9.2

1 Scientists **opposed to** this theory have recently attacked its basic assumptions.
2 Governments need to **maintain a united front** on the issue of economic migrants.
3 Nowadays, we are **bombarded with** advertisements every time we watch TV or visit our favourite websites.
4 In the face of counter-arguments, several economists have recently **retreated** from the view that economic processes cannot be altered.
5 The **battle** against crime will fail without police and community cooperation.
6 Many traditional rural societies and cultures have been destroyed by the **onslaught** of urbanisation.
7 Following **a barrage** of hostile questions from reporters, the Minister suddenly ended the press conference and left the room.
8 Parents recently **scored a victory** by forcing the city council to reduce speed limits near schools.

9.3 *Suggested underlinings:*

The human brain is a remarkably complex organic computer, taking in a wide variety of sensory experiences, processing and storing this information, and recalling and integrating selected bits* at the right moments. The destruction caused by Alzheimer's disease has been likened to the erasure of a hard drive, beginning with the most recent files and working backward. As the illness progresses, old as well as new memories gradually disappear until even loved ones are no longer recognized. Unfortunately, the computer analogy breaks down: one cannot simply reboot the human brain and reload the files and programs. The problem is that Alzheimer's does not only erase information; it destroys the very hardware of the brain, which is composed of more than 100 billion nerve cells (neurons), with 100 trillion connections among them.

* bit here means a unit of information on a computer that must be either 0 or 1

Unit 10

10.1

1 from least to most frequent – **intermittent**, **frequent**, **constant**.
2 listening and writing
3 **excess energy** suggests more than enough whereas **sufficient energy** means simply enough energy
4 an **isolated phenomenon**
5 No, because they would not allow you to draw any conclusions.
6 **pivotal**
7 mother, father, teacher, friends, brothers, sisters ....
8 A **representative sample** = a sample chosen as typical of the population as a whole and a **random sample** = a sample chosen by chance.

10.2

1 came
2 consumes, generate
3 played / took on
4 investigated
5 invalidate
6 combines / combined

10.3 1 h 2 e 3 a 4 c 5 i 6 b 7 d 8 f 9 g

10.4

1 taking, random
2 define
3 acceptable, practical
4 maintaining
5 crucial
6 engaging, heated
7 publish, interim
8 discern, conflicting
9 natural, occurs

Unit 11

11.1

1 a considerable
2 particular
3 central
4 an enormous
5 A significant
6 minor
7 important
8 central

11.2

2 Destruction of the riverbank will cause **an inevitable decline** in the numbers of small mammals.
3 School standards are **a common / frequent concern** among parents nowadays.
4 Nowhere in the article does the author make **explicit mention** of the 20 cases which were never resolved.
5 There is very little **common ground** between the two ways of addressing the problem.
6 The paper is too general and lacks **specific / relevant examples.**
8 The work covers **a vast array** of themes from Asian political history.

11.3

adjective	noun	adjective	noun
significant	significance	important	importance
relevant	relevance	valuable	value
interesting	interest	useful	use
frequent	frequency	broad	breadth

11.4

2 The research will be **of great / considerable value** to anyone interested in economic planning.
3 It was an event **of huge / enormous importance** in the history of Latin American politics.
4 Partich's book is **a work of great / enormous breadth.**
5 Sorlan's book was **a work of great / huge / enormous / considerable significance** in the development of political theory.
6 This software will be **of considerable use** in the analysis of large amounts of numerical data.
7 The method outlined is **of great / considerable interest** to anyone investigating sleeplessness.
8 'You know' is an expression **of high frequency** in informal spoken English.
9 DNA evidence is **of huge / enormous / great importance.**

Unit 12

12.1

1 Paulson's research **convincingly demonstrated** the need for a new approach to the study of stress.
2 As **was observed earlier**, there is a strong correlation between house prices and inflation.
3 In the study of language, 'tense' **refers specifically** to the coding of time in form of the verb.
4 Classical liberal economics **is closely identified** with the theories of Milton Friedman.
5 Chapter 1 **briefly discusses** the main issues, but they are dealt with in detail in Chapter 2.
6 To date, no research exists that **firmly establishes** a connection between behaviour, personality traits, and leadership traits.
7 SENTA is a computer programming language **loosely based** on Logo.
8 Social research techniques were applied to **critically examine** the effects of the policy on the poor.

12.2

1 hypotheses
2 trends / changes
3 causes / origins / nature
4 issue / question
5 need

12.3

1 importance
2 factor
3 matters

12.4

The world is facing a looming water crisis. Disputes over allocation have steadily increased in the last decade, and demand has grown rapidly. Water is likely to generate the same degree of controversy in the 21st century as oil did in the 20th. If we take no action now, new conflicts are likely to occur periodically around the world. At the moment, instead of seeking solutions which directly address multiple needs, countries focus a little too narrowly on local issues and typically opt for expensive and inferior solutions. What is needed are decisions which can be quickly implemented and a debate which will seriously consider more than the short-term needs of individual states.

12.5

1 Various measures were introduced last year to **directly address** the issue of identity theft.
2 The justice system needs to **seriously consider** the impact of a prison sentence on offenders.
3 The number of university applications has been **steadily increasing** over the last 50 years.
4 The article **focuses narrowly** on one aspect of the problem rather than taking a broad view.
5 The suggested measures should be **quickly implemented** to avoid further problems.

Unit 13

13.1

1 Professor Soltero said that, **in line with** government guidelines, the team would consult the local community **as regards** the best solution to the siting of the drilling platform. She promised that the community would be fully involved **from the outset** and that her team, **in turn**, would inform the public at every stage.
2 A spokesperson for the company said that, **at this stage**, there is no proof of the side-effects of the drug, but **in view of / in the light of** the public concern, the company was withdrawing it. **In spite of** this necessary measure, she was sure that the drug would soon return to the market.
3 Dr Leiman said that while **on the one hand** the government wanted to encourage research, **on the other hand** they were reducing funding for universities; **in other words**, research would inevitably suffer.
4 **In addition to** a new building on the campus, the team will receive a very generous grant to conduct their research. **In relation to** the university's plan, this represents an exciting and much-awaited development. **In particular**, the new facility would attract outside investment.
5 **With the exception of** one study in 1986, no major research has been carried out into the problem, Dr Peters stated. The greatest need **by far** at the moment was a concerted effort to kick-start a research programme.
6 Professor Karpal said that, **on the basis of** her studies so far, she was optimistic that a cure for the disease would be found. **To some extent**, there was already cause for optimism, but, **for the most part**, hopes had to rest on the possibility of a breakthrough in the near future.
7 Lauren Charles said that, **on the whole**, social conditions had improved since the report, especially **in terms of** jobs and housing for the poorer sectors. If economic and social policy had failed **in any respect**, it was in child care for the less well-off.
8 The professor said that he was delighted to accept the award **on behalf of** the whole university. He said that, **in some ways**, he had been the lucky one, **so to speak**, in that he had been able to work **in conjunction with** such a wonderful team.

13.2

1 by chance
2 From then on
3 In accordance with
4 in the process
5 in turn
6 to a greater or lesser extent
7 By far
8 For the most part
9 In most respects
10 to some extent
11 On the other hand

Unit 14

14.1

1 on
2 to
3 on
4 of
5 on
6 from
7 on
8 on
9 on
10 of

14.2

1 for
2 for
3 to
4 with
5 to
6 from
7 for
8 to
9 of
10 of
11 with
12 from
13 with
14 to
15 to
16 for

14.3
1 referred us to
2 account for
3 associated with
4 dispose of
5 benefit enormously from
6 convince me of
7 searching for
8 provided us with
9 consented to
10 reacted positively to

14.4
1 The course leader divided her students **into** groups.
2 They had to trace everyone who had been exposed **to** the infection.
3 At the moment we have too few nurses attending **to** too many patients.
4 Excellent teaching coupled **with** first-class research have made this a successful college.
5 The country emerged **from** the crisis as a much stronger power.
6 Joe acquired an interest in politics from his uncle who often spoke **of** his days as a senator.
7 The government called **for** an investigation into the explosion at the nuclear reactor.
8 In your speech don't forget to emphasise the advantages of studying here.

Unit 15

15.1
1 with, for
2 on/about, of
3 of, into
4 on/about, into, for/behind
5 into/on, for (of is also possible)
6 into, to
7 about/on, at, between
8 of, to

15.2
1 Her dissertation produced some interesting insights **into** how young children develop a visual sense and the age **at** which development is most noticeable.
2 The reason **for** people being unwilling to be interviewed after the demonstration was that they were afraid of being arrested later.
3 As regards solar phenomena, Hierstat's approach **to** the analysis is different from that of Donewski. He questioned the assumptions **behind** much of the previous research.
4 Changes **in** the temperature of the soil were measured over time.
5 A lack **of** funding led to the project being cancelled, and social scientists blamed the government's negative attitude **to/towards** social science research.
6 Jawil's article puts great emphasis **on** the need **for** more research **into** the problem and argues the case **for** greater attention **to** the underlying causes.

15.3
attitude to/towards
difference between
effect on (or, more formally, upon)
emphasis on
insight into
preference for
principle behind
rationale for/behind
reason for
relationship between
tendency to/towards

15.4 The possible ecological <u>effects of</u> climate change are often in the news, as is the <u>matter of</u> whether the potential impact can be predicted. New <u>work on</u> a migratory bird, the pied flycatcher, takes things a stage further by showing how a climate-related population decline was actually caused. Timing is key. Over the past 17 years flycatchers declined strongly in areas where caterpillar numbers (<u>food for</u> the nestlings) peak early, but in <u>areas with</u> a late food peak there was no decline. The young birds arrive too late in places where the caterpillars have already responded to early warmth. Mistiming like this is probably a common <u>consequence of</u> climate change, and may be a major <u>factor in</u> the <u>decline of</u> many long-distance migratory bird species.

Unit 16

16.1
1 in a variety of ways
2 a great deal of
3 a wide range of
4 to some extent
5 in excess of

16.2
1 as a rule
2 at the same time
3 be that as it may
4 for the most part
5 for this reason
6 in general
7 in terms of
8 on the whole

16.3 My dissertation topic may be complicated but, **be that as it may**, I have absolutely no regrets about choosing it. I have always been interested in the Romantic movement in English literature and **for this reason** I decided to compare Romantic poetry in different European countries. I've focused **for the most part** on poets from Britain and Germany. Although **as a rule** essay-writing comes easily to me, I'm finding it difficult to get down to writing up my research because I'm supposed to be revising for a couple of exams **at the same time**. But I shan't have any problems **in terms of** finding enough to say on the subject.

16.4
1 by means of which – The others all mean *generally* or *for the most part* while *by means of which* means *using this method*.
2 with the exception of X – The others all focus on how X is affected by something whereas *with the exception of X* is focusing on other things rather than X.
3 in addition to – The others are all concerned with trying to be more specific in what they are talking about while *in addition to* is adding something extra to what is being said.

16.5 1 A 2 C 3 B 4 B 5 C

16.6 *Possible answers:*
1 I enjoy watching most sports with the exception of football.
2 A poor relationship between parents and children is often due to the fact that they do not spend enough time together.
3 I love reading novels as opposed to reading English textbooks / writing English essays / reading novels in my own language.
4 In your first year of graduate school you have to take an end-of-year exam in addition to writing a 4,000-word essay.
5 It was a very useful course in the sense that I learnt an enormous amount from it.

Unit 17

17.1
1 Timson **et al** (2008) discuss this issue extensively (however, **cf** Donato 2010, who takes a different view).
2 The article was published in a special issue of the *Journal of Sports Technology* in 2012 (**vol.** 10, **pp.** 256-279).
3 Some nouns in English have irregular plural forms, **e.g.** *mouse, sheep* and *woman.* For further examples, see Mitchelson and Friel (**eds.**) 1995.
4 **NB**: this and all further references to population statistics are taken from Aspenall (**op. cit.**).
5 Smart phones, tablets **etc.** have made mobile learning a reality for many students around the world (Dudeney **ibid.**).
6 Blended learning (**i.e.** integrating the use of technology into learning and teaching) is now the norm in many university programmes.

17.2
1 The war began in 1986 and ended in 1990. During the **pre**-war period (1980-86), the economy was stable, but in the **post**-war years (1991-1997) there were severe economic problems. **Hyper**-inflation meant that prices increased by 200% in just one year. Economic **co**operation with neighbouring countries had ceased during hostilities and only resumed in 1998. Attempts to un**ify** the different currencies of the region at that time proved unsuccessful.
2 The research symposium takes place **bi**-annually; we have one every six months in a different university. However, we need to public**ise**/**ize** it more on our website to increase the numbers attending. It is aimed at teacher train**ees**, especially those who will commence teaching in the following academic year.
3 There was a **mal**function and the circuit became **over**heated, so the equipment shut down. We need to mod**ify** the procedure so that it does not happen again. A new type of cool**ant** will be used to keep the temperature constant.
4 **Anti**-pollution measures brought in by the city authorities included reducing on-street parking spaces to discourage motorists from driving into the city centre and the closure of three **multi**-storey car parks with the same aim in mind. Better **inter**-connections between the various transport systems (buses, trains and ferries) were also planned.

5 In order to function in extreme conditions, the generator had to be both water**proof** and dust**proof**. An **eco**-friendly version of the generator, powered by wind, is also being developed. It is port**able**, so it can be easily carried to wherever it is needed.
6 Claims and **counter**-claims about the assassination of the president have been made in the media. What we need now is an objective investigation to clar**ify** the motives of the killers. There is a strong likeli**hood** that an extrem**ist** religious movement was been behind the attack.

17.3

noun(s)	verb	adjective
modernity	modernise/ize	modern
sadness	sadden	sad
fear		fearless
urgency		urgent
democrat, democracy	democratise/ize	democratic
beauty	beautify	beautiful
Marxism		Marxist
accuracy		accurate

Unit 18

18.1
1 No it isn't.
2 From other pages on the website or by asking the relevant department.
3 Yes, they need a transcript, translated, of your university courses and grades.
4 If you have spent at least one year in English-medium education.
5 At least 6.5.

18.2 1 g 2 f 3 h 4 i 5 a 6 c 7 e 8 d 9 b

18.3
1 To get a place on the course I need to get **a minimum score of 6.5 at IELTS**.
2 Most of the students on this master's course **have a first degree** in economics.
3 This college welcomes applications from **mature students**.
4 If you don't understand anything in our prospectus, the best place to **seek clarification** is our website.
5 Your **personal statement** must be no more than 300 words.
6 The university requires **financial guarantees**.

18.4 *Suggested order:*
1 decide on what **career** you would like to do after your studies
2 find an appropriate **course** at a university
3 check that you fulfil the necessary **entry requirements**
4 fill in the **application form**
5 wait for the application to be **processed**
6 be **called** for an interview
7 be **offered** a place

18.5
1 career
2 get
3 filled
4 profile
5 entry requirements
6 transcripts
7 grades
8 deadline
9 referee
10 call

Unit 19

19.1
1 the Arts Faculty Building
2 the Student Union
3 the halls of residence
4 the Arts Lecture Theatre
5 the Great Hall
6 the Administration Building
7 the University Health Centre
8 the library

19.2 1 a seminar; a tutorial is normally a smaller group
2 a supervisor
3 vacation
4 A personal tutor deals with academic matters. A student counsellor deals with personal problems.
5 A postgrad rep is a person, usually elected, who acts officially on behalf of postgraduate students. A research assistant is a person with a higher degree who is attached to a particular research project.

19.3
1 residence
2 lecture
3 lecturer
4 department
5 tutorial
6 semester
7 dissertation
8 supervisor
9 hours

19.4

people	places	events or institutions
counsellor sophomore lecturer librarian faculty (AmE) professor junior research assistant research student tutor	cafeteria library sports centre sports grounds lecture theatre	lecture seminar faculty (BrE) tutorial semester

19.5 1 American. In BrE, a *faculty* is a group of departments or schools in a university which specialise in a particular group of subjects.
2 British. AmE normally refers to *graduate students*.
3 American. *To go to school* in BrE means to attend a primary or secondary school (aged 5–18 years).
4 American. In BrE a junior would be a *third-year (student).*
5 American. BrE prefers *supervisor*.
6 American. BrE normally says *secondary school* instead of *high school*.

Unit 20

20.1 1 60
2 They are obligatory – all students must take them.
3 10
4 Assignment types include essays, projects, portfolios, or dissertations
5 15,000
6 Get an average mark of 70% for all modules

20.2
1 project
2 module
3 dissertation
4 Diploma
5 MA
6 sign
7 PhD
8 in-sessional

20.3
1 upgrade
2 pre-sesssional
3 enrolled
4 proceed
5 obligatory
6 supervisions
7 defer
8 Assessment

20.4

verb	noun	adjective
oblige	obligation	obligatory
opt	option	optional
supervise	supervision + supervisor	supervisory
assess	assessment + assessor	
	eligibility	eligible

20.5
1 supervisor
2 assess
3 options
4 eligibility
5 obliged
6 opt

Unit 21

21.1
1 asynchronous learning
2 learning environment
3 online community
4 synchronous learning
5 learning portal
6 distance education
7 LMS
8 e-learning

21.2
1 The LMS can **track** courses and see how the students are using them.
2 The online course provides **a virtual environment** which **facilitates learning** for students.
3 Students can access material from **multiple** sources via the learning portal. The portal gives them **consolidated access** to content, support and services.
4 In asynchronous learning, students only interact with their teachers **intermittently**. However, online learning encourages **collaboration**.

21.3
1 blogs
2 vlogs
3 wikis
4 forum/fora
5 pace
6 monitoring
7 conventional
8 peer
9 plagiarism
10 webinars

21.4
1 mobile learning
2 Adaptive learning
3 Computer-mediated
4 flipped classroom
5 virtual campus
6 Moocs

Unit 22

22.1
1 meet
2 to-do
3 mind map
4 request
5 curricular
6 rote
7 draft
8 management
9 term
10 taking
11 lecture
12 plan

22.2
1 meet deadlines, request an extension, study plan
2 first draft
3 lecture notes
4 draw mind maps
5 on long-term loan
6 time management
7 extra-curricular activities
8 to-do list
9 Rote learning
10 Note-taking

22.3
Author's answers:
1 I always remember the order of the colours of the rainbow by saying a mnemonic about English medieval history – '**R**ichard **Of** **Y**ork **G**ained **B**attles **I**n **V**ain' – **r**ed, **o**range, **y**ellow, **g**reen, **b**lue, **i**ndigo, **v**iolet.
2 I might write down such things as:
- revise regularly
- organise files systematically
- read round the subject
- ask if I don't understand.

3 Vocabulary in a foreign language, poetry, maths tables, formulae, etc.
4 It depends on the subject – a week before, perhaps.
5 Sometimes it wanders, of course. I probably think about holidays or of all the other things I'd like to be doing.
6 No, I don't think I have. Or if I have, I have successfully wiped the memory from my mind.
7 When I was a student I would always prioritise essays that had a deadline.
8 If you have rough notes in front of you, you can plan your answer better and there is less chance your mind will go blank.
9 Personal answers
10 Personal answers

22.4
1 which have been borrowed
2 brought back
3 not returned on time
4 pay in full
5 permission to take books out of the library
6 books borrowed from other libraries through a special arrangement with them

Unit 23

23.1
1 grants
2 accumulate
3 take out
4 tuition
5 meet
6 seek
7 scholarships
8 awards
9 cover
10 entitlement
11 maintenance

23.2
1 The bank gave me an interest-free loan.
2 Most people seem to be finding it harder to make ends meet.
3 Increasing numbers of students leave college having accumulated considerable debt.
4 My grant was paid as a lump sum.
5 The campus banks offer inducements to (persuade) students to open a bank account.
6 I find it difficult to calculate my annual expenditure (or: how much I spend annually).
7 The cost of living in big cities can be very high.

23.3
1 My **monthly** expenditure is rather high, so I had to get a **part-time** job.
2 Why are **hardback** books so expensive? I can only afford **second-hand** ones.
3 My **maintainance** grant is paid **in** instalments, so I get money every semester.
4 Our bills are very high so they're a big **drain** on our finances and I only have a low-**paid** (or low-**paying**) job.
5 When you're a student, there are always expenses that you just don't **anticipate**, like high **energy** bills, for instance.
6 Even though money is **tight** for me, I don't want to get a job and work unsocial **hours**.

23.4 *Possible answers:*
1 Pros: encourages students to work hard and to value their education more. Cons: Students often have to work part-time to pay the fees or else they accumulate debt.
2 Yes, because it makes it possible for students from poorer backgrounds to have the same opportunities as those from richer backgrounds. No, because students from richer backgrounds should be able to finance their own studies.
3 Some examples: government grants, grants from educational charities, competitive scholarships.
4 Such jobs often mean working unsocial hours and the work may be tiring, so students may be exhausted when they should be studying.

Unit 24

24.1
1 (a) meet or achieve an objective (b) to reach or achieve or attain a target
2 infrastructure
3 national debate
4 [academic] disciplines
5 standards [by which we judge something]; criterion
6 practice-led research

24.2
1 instigate
2 critical
3 challenges
4 meets
5 priority
6 motive

24.3
1 We must **give priority to** the privacy of our subjects.
2 We designed the questionnaire **with the intention of making** it straightforward to answer.
3 We had **as our goal the evaluation of** a new approach to urban planning.
4 I had **no intention of becoming** a scientist when I began my studies.
5 A **hypothesis-based** methodology does not work in some cases.
6 Our project is located **at the interface between** sociology and psychology.

24.4

verb	noun	verb	noun
intend	intention	hypothesise	hypothesis
define	definition	establish	establishment
achieve	achievement	base	base, basis
practise	practice	apply	application

24.5
1 base
2 define
3 apply
4 intention
5 establishment
6 hypotheses [the plural of hypothesis]
7 achieve

Unit 25

25.1 1 Krishnan 2 Lisa 3 Rana 4 Kevin 5 Joanna 6 Thomas

25.2
1 rush
2 relevant
3 clarify
4 pinpoint
5 encounter, note, key, summarise, page
6 bring, light

25.3
1 I'm hoping to **approach** some care workers to ask them to complete my questionnaire.
2 My plan is to **distribute** 40–50 questionnaires to carers in residential homes.
3 The **data** I **collect** from these **informants** will be very useful for my dissertation.
4 I intend also to **conduct** / **carry out** some interviews with social workers.
5 When I've done all that, I'll write my **review of literature**. I've already **mapped out** the various sections and made some notes. I use **bullet points** to help me list my ideas.
6 I will need to **formulate** some initial **hypotheses** about the psychological effects upon carers who work with terminally-ill patients.

Unit 26

26.1
1 It was a new **piece** of apparatus so we brought together all the things we needed and **assembled** it first. We then **checked** it before using it.
2 The team carried out a **pilot study** before conducting the main **experiment** to see if the **methodology** / **procedure** they were using was reliable.
3 The team needed to employ a different **technique** / **procedure** for measuring the pressure, so they used a new **device** which they manufactured in their own laboratory.
4 The researchers found the **traditional** method of collecting data that was usually used did not work well for their purposes and so they had to find a more **effective** / **reliable** method.

26.2
1 a longitudinal study
2 an exploratory study
3 a case study
4 a field study

26.3
1 experiment
2 conditions
3 manipulate
4 variables
5 controlled
6 replicate
7 determine
8 artificial
9 reflect
10 empirical
11 field
12 case
13 settings
14 in-depth
15 collected
16 interfering
17 time-consuming
18 representative
19 population

26.4
1 tentative
2 disprove
3 eliminate
4 over time
5 reflect
6 records
7 make inferences
8 misunderstanding
9 preliminary
10 replicate
11 observes
12 representative

26.5
1 It was very difficult to make clear **inferences** from the data as we had so little.
2 A correlational study is a good way of seeing if one **phenomenon** is related to another in a **systematic** way.
3 The experiment neither proved nor **disproved** Jessop's theory.
4 An **outside** / **external** observer can often unintentionally **disrupt** the behaviour the subjects they are observing.
5 The method they initially chose to use was not a very **reliable** one, so he had to find an **alternative**.

Unit 27

27.1 1 f 2 d 3 e 4 b 5 a 6 c

27.2
1 The article makes reference to the work of Hindler and Swartz (1988).
2 I consulted original government papers and Schunker's book was also a useful secondary source for understanding the pre-war period.
3 Tanaka's book draws on data from several Japanese articles on galaxy formation.
4 Elsewhere, Kallen reports on his research into cancer rates among farm workers.
5 Han consulted the archives in the Vienna Museum.
6 Deneuve accessed official websites during the period March to September 2015 and retrieved the relevant statistics to support his claim.

27.3
1 surveys, catalogues
2 laid
3 consulted
4 sets out
5 notes
6 cited

27.4

noun	verb	adjective	adverb
attribute /ˈætrɪbjuːt/	attribute /əˈtrɪbjʊt/		
document	document	documentary	
consultation	consult	consultative	
		primary	primarily
catalogue	catalogue		
foundation	found		
note	note	notable	notably
suggestion	suggest	suggestive	suggestively
extension	extend	extensive	extensively
citation	cite		

Unit 28

28.1
1 conclusion
2 side(s)
3 critical

28.2
1 critical review
2 come to/ draw/reach, conclusions
3 sides of the argument
4 critical comments

28.3
1 weighing
2 outweigh
3 disadvantages.
4 insights
5 take
6 rigorous
7 coming
8 robust
9 constitute
10 points
11 take into
12 relevant
13 course
14 deduce
15 basis
16 predict
17 scales

28.4
1 critically = seriously
2 a critical review = a review giving the writer's own opinion
3 criticism = condemnation
4 critical = essential
5 critical thinking = careful and unbiased thinking
6 critical = negative about

28.5
1 A recent survey has unearthed some interesting facts about commuting habits. [revealed – it is as if the researchers were digging into the ground like archaeologists]
2 In predicting trends in inflation, economists often look at which direction the political winds are blowing. [what the political mood seems to be; this makes a comparison between changes in the economy and changes in the weather]
3 Martin's controversial article on the causes of the crisis led to a storm of protest. [a large amount of angry protest; this makes a comparison between a protest and a storm]
4 By digging into the archives, Professor Robinson was able to shed important new light on the history of the period. [looking thoroughly at; give new information about – the first of the metaphors again relates to archaeology whereas the second makes a connection between knowledge and light]

Unit 29

29.1
1 Many educators believe that different learning styles are equally **valid**.
2 In the UK a university faculty is a unit where similar **disciplines** are grouped together.
3 The French impressionists were a key **movement** in European art.
4 The **essence** of international law is the application of a single standard for strong and weak nations alike.
5 Researchers spend much of their time trying to **interpret** their data.
6 Some 19th-century artistic styles were a **reaction** to the ugliness of industrialisation.
7 Harvey (2003) stresses that the findings of the study cannot be **generalised**, as only a small amount of data was used.
8 In the late 20th century, intellectual **thought** was greatly influenced by ideas of gender and race.
9 The article **asserts** that internet gaming can provide a useful educational experience.
10 **It can be argued that / Most would agree that** the theory of the big bang represented a **paradigm shift** in our way of thinking about the universe.

29.2
1 There are some interesting PhD theses on water resources in the library.
2 What was your main criterion in designing your survey?
3 She was interested in a strange phenomenon connected with comets.
4 The hypotheses were never proved, as the data were incomplete.

29.3 1 d 2 g 3 a 4 b 5 f 6 e 7 c

29.4
1 moral
2 profound
3 grounding
4 thinking
5 the humanities
6 autonomy
7 understanding

Unit 30

30.1
1 pinpoints – pinpoint would be used to focus on something much more unexpected and worthy of note, rather than on generally known background information
2 proves – if the theory is highly controversial it can't have been proved
3 claims – the structure would need to be *claims that Malwar's figures are inaccurate.*
4 asserts – the structure would need to be *asserts that ...* .
5 advances – the structure would need to be *advances the theory that ...* .
6 cast doubt – the structure would need to be *cast doubt on there being a causal link ....*

30.2

noun	verb	noun	verb
implication	imply	description	describe
observation	observe	statement	state
argument	argue	emphasis	emphasise
assertion	assert	explanation	explain
contention	contend	demonstration	demonstrate

30.3

2 'Global symmetry' is the statement that the laws of physics take the same form when expressed in terms of distinct variables.
3 The report makes the implication that no individual government will be able to control the internet.
4 Dudas provides a demonstration of / as to how dangerous genetic modification might be.
5 Groot puts an/the emphasis on the role of schools in preventing teenage drug abuse.
6 Lenard's observation that women use expressions such as 'you know' in English more than men was later proved to be inaccurate.
7 Plana's explanation of the possible origins of the pyramids has been disputed by Ruiz.
8 Wilson gives a description of the ancient alphabet of the Guelcoga people.
9 Wu puts forward the argument that daylight-saving time should be extended throughout the year.
10 The President makes the assertion that he cares about fighting poverty.

30.4

1 **In my opinion/view**, courses in academic writing should be compulsory for all new students.
2 It has not yet been **proved / There is not yet any proof** that the virus can jump from species to species.
3 Richardson **emphasises** a number of weaknesses in the theory.
4 Pratt **puts** a lot of emphasis on the relationship between geography and history.
5 Our latest results cast doubt **on** our original hypothesis.

Unit 31

31.1

1 define
2 terms
3 terminology
4 transparent
5 glossary
6 senses
7 distinguish
8 subtle distinctions
9 concise/coherent
10 coherent/concise
11 ambiguous
12 misinterpret
13 clarify

31.2

1 expressed
2 conveyed
3 nuances
4 denote
5 connotations
6 infer
7 discourse
8 evokes
9 perspective
10 comprehend

31.3

1 mistranslated
2 misunderstood
3 unambiguous
4 miscalculated
5 incoherent, misquotations
6 infrequently, inappropriately

Unit 32

32.1

1 The views she expressed were totally **irrational**.
2 The committee seemed to be **biased in favour of** applications from younger people.
3 The book is **a subjective** account of life in a small town in the 1920s.
4 The club rules were **prejudiced against** children.
5 The President's daughter was quite **immature** for her age.
6 He has rather **conservative/reactionary** views about marriage.
7 Her views on education are rather **reactionary/conservative**.
8 In my opinion that judge always acts in **an unbiased/impartial** way.

32.2
1 underlying, philosophies
2 to adopt
3 held
4 ethical
5 -rooted, encounter
6 shifted

32.3
1 philosophy (ideology would sound too negative to be the worthy focus of a whole degree)
2 objections (principles would not be followed by 'to')
3 changed
4 in
5 take
6 From

32.4
1 The people of the area hold some unusual views about nature.
2 Most young people seem to have objections to the proposals on student fees.
3 Examiners tend to be biased in favour of candidates with neat handwriting.
4 Girls look at their careers from a different standpoint than their mothers.
5 Let us now discuss the principles underlying this approach/the underlying principles of this approach.

32.5
Suggested meanings
taken the view – been of the opinion
intellectually independent – distinctive in its approach to learning
preconceptions – ideas formed before there was enough information to form accurate ideas
misplaced – inappropriate
liberal – open-minded
advocate – argue in favour of
fields of learning – disciplines
pushing the frontiers of knowledge – extending what we know
blending of ideas – combining of ideas
cross-fertilisation – mixing of ideas to produce something better
thought – ways of thinking

Unit 33

33.1
1 25
2 23
3 Each number is multiplied by 3 to produce the next number
4 41
5 7
6 $\frac{7}{9}$ is a fraction (a vulgar fraction – 0.5 is a decimal fraction) and 4 is a whole number.
7 In my country (the UK), in most salaried jobs tax is deducted automatically, but for other jobs (e.g. freelance or self-employed work), the worker has to declare their earnings and pay tax later on.
8 Pleased, because it suggests the figures are accurate. If they don't tally, there may be an error or omission somewhere.

33.2
1 calculate
2 approximate
3 precise
4 estimate
5 tally
6 constant
7 discrete
8 round
9 down

33.3
2 We estimated the final figure.
3 The graph shows the results in order of magnitude.
4 A computer program helped us calculate the significance of the different variables.
5 Subtracting x from y will help you arrive at the correct answer. (Do not include away)
6 The results from the first experiment did not tally with those we got from the repeat experiment.

33.4
1 workings
2 arrived
3 calculations
4 area
5 figures
6 values
7 variables

The deliberate mistake is *one and a half hour*. It should be *one and a half hours*.

Unit 34

34.1 1 mode, median, mean/average, mean/average 2 sum, halfway 3 range, extremes

34.2
1 probability
2 outcomes
3 variables
4 random
5 distribution
6 correlate
7 trends
8 significantly

34.3
1 Two to one. Two thirds.
2 Outliers.
3 Often.
4 No. To be reliable, results must be similar each time the same method is used.
5 Ten per cent.
6 18.
7 The total number of cases.
8 What the average difference from the norm is.
9 Probably not. To be valid, it must measure what it claims to measure. Breakfast and lunch alone will not tell us everything about eating habits.
10 It does show a normal distribution. A bell curve.

Unit 35

35.1
1 shows/indicates/plots
2 y/vertical
3 x/horizontal
4 key/legend
5 varied
6 reached
7 peak
8 decline/fall/drop
9 explained
10 fact

35.2
1 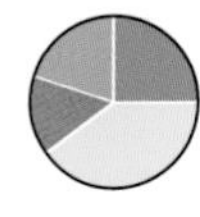 pie chart 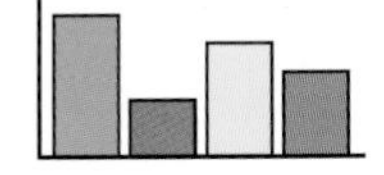 bar chart
2 A cross-section
3 Columns run vertically, rows run horizontally
4 A flowchart
5 Four
6 Next to each other
7 A key
8 A random sample
9 (a) they cross each other; (b) they run alongside each other with an equal interval between them
10 (b)

35.3
1 segments
2 plotting
3 peak
4 stages
5 intersect
6 adjacent (With 'adjacent' this sentence does not really need 'to each other' and would be best worded as 'Draw a line connecting the adjacent points'.)
7 decline
8 row

35.4
1 plummeted, risen
2 fell below
3 depreciates, more than halved
4 appreciate, soared
5 multiplied, fallen/decreased
6 exceeded
7 grew/rose, doubled
8 declining/falling

The mistake is in sentence 6. It should be *See figure 3*, NOT See the figure 3.

Unit 36

36.1

1 initial phase
2 temporary
3 permanent
4 final
5 ongoing
6 transitional
7 critical
8 current
9 forthcoming
10 annual
11 preceding [or previous]
12 century
13 decade
14 era
15 next few

36.2

1 At, near
2 at, intermediate
3 emergence
4 gone, last
5 distant
6 a problem nowadays
7 series, subsequent, concurrent
8 to, recent
9 with. contemporary, eventual
10 short, long

36.3

noun	verb	adjective	adverb
eventuality		eventual	eventually
succession	succeed	successive	successively
evolution	evolve	evolutionary	
emergence	emerge	emergent	
coincidence	coincide	coincidental	coincidentally
period		periodic	periodically

Unit 37

37.1

1 induces
2 generated
3 triggered
4 motivates
5 contributed to
6 provoked
7 determined
8 inhibits
9 accounted for
10 facilitate
11 stimulate
12 derived

37.2 1 d 2 e 3 f 4 a 5 c 6 b

37.3

1 no word is needed
2 effect
3 of
4 for
5 on
6 for

37.4

motivation
influence
trigger
contribution
inducement

37.5

1 influence
2 trigger
3 inducements
4 contribution
5 motivation

Unit 38

38.1

1 fall
2 categories
3 distinct
4 structure
5 belong
6 type
7 consist
8 components
9 feature
10 diversity
11 devise
12 gender
13 class
14 generations
15 senior citizens
16 occupational
17 blue collar
18 employment
19 homemakers
20 ethnic

38.2

noun	verb	adjective	adverb
similarity		similar	similarly
difference	differentiate/differ *	different	differently
allocation	allocate		
description	describe	descriptive	descriptively

* *Differentiate* is transitive(i.e. it takes an object) or it can be used with *between* (to *differrentiate between x and y*). *Differ* is intransitive (it does not take an object).

38.3
1 differentiate, similar, differ
2 allocate
3 descriptive
4 similarities, differences

38.4
1 devise, structure
2 allocated
3 includes
4 hierarchy

Unit 39

39.1
1 on
2 For
3 to
4 beyond
5 of
6 on
7 of
8 with
9 to
10 on
11 to
12 to

39.2
1 cons
2 time
3 forth
4 forward
5 but
6 which
7 to
8 as

39.3 There are a number of **advantages and disadvantages** to take into account when considering the purchase of a hybrid (gasoline-electric) car. Such cars are, **for instance**, undoubtedly better for the environment in the sense that they cause less air pollution. **Furthermore**, **the degree** to which they rely on oil, a natural resource which is rapidly becoming depleted, is much less than is the case with conventional cars, **Nevertheless**, hybrid cars are not without their problems. Cost may be an issue **as well as** the technical complexity of the engine. **Provided that** you take these factors into account, there is no reason not to buy a hybrid car.

39.4 1 B 2 C 3 A 4 B 5 C 6 B 7 B 8 B

Unit 40

40.1
1 aim/purpose
2 concerned
3 aim/purpose
4 consists
5 address/discuss/present/explore
6 devoted
7 divided
8 focus

40.2
1 War and Peace
2 After
3 No
4 Olaf
5 Before

40.3
1 Take
2 Firstly,
3 addresses
4 below
5 following
6 see
7 consider
8 later

40.4
1 **As can be seen in Table V**, there has been an increase in the numbers of students.
2 In Section 3 we take up again some of the arguments from **the preceding section**.
3 **At this point** let us turn our attention to developments in Constantinople.
4 The dissertation **is divided into** six chapters.
5 Let us now **turn to** the issue of the reunification of Germany.

Unit 41

41.1
1 verify
2 procedure
3 supplement
4 simulation
5 step
6 design
7 utilise
8 phase
9 select

41.2

1 It is hardly surprising that people **utilise** far more electricity than they did ten years ago.
2 The **advent** of mobile technology transformed the way people manage their social and professional lives.
3 A number of talented new designers have **emerged** this year.
4 You've missed out a letter in this word here – you need to **insert** a p between the a and the t.
5 He spent many years trying to **design** a machine that would automatically sort large numbers of coins.
6 The team had to **input** a huge amount of data to run the experiment.
7 We spent many months trying to **automate** the process of recording the temperature.
8 The **output from/of** the system was automatically **exported** to a spreadsheet.

41.3

verb	noun
apply to	application of
behave	behaviour of
simulate	simulation of
select from	selection of
design	design of
ratify	ratification of
insert into	insertion

verb	noun
verify	verification of
utilise	utilisation of
emerge from	emergence of
consume	consumption of
input into	input
display	display of

41.4

1 emergence
2 consumption
3 insert
4 ratification
5 application
6 input
7 behaviour
8 design

Unit 42

42.1

1 established
2 undeniable
3 offer
4 flimsy
5 convincing
6 collect
7 conflicting
8 hard
9 demonstrates
10 draws
11 distorting
12 little-known
13 growing
14 interpret

42.2

1 The data **indicate/demonstrate/suggest** that the drug education project has been successful.
2 The data in the latest study are more **comprehensive** than in the earlier one.
3 This is the most interesting **item** of data in the whole thesis.
4 What a **striking/an illuminating** example this is of the power of the human mind!
5 Unfortunately, the facts do not **support** the hypothesis.
6 We cannot **account for** the fact that attitudes are more negative now than five years ago.
7 The problem **stems** from the fact that the software was poorly designed.
8 The article **provides** examples of different methods which have been used over the years.
9 New evidence has **come to light** that the cabinet was not informed of the Minister's decision.
10 We need to **consider** the evidence before we can reach a conclusion.
11 The evidence suggesting that sanctions do not work is **abundant** and **irrefutable**.
12 A considerable **body** of evidence now exists, but we always try to get more.
13 We have a lot of **empirical** data which suggest the problem is on the increase.
14 This is a clear **instance** of how conservation can benefit local people.

42.3

1 bear out
2 emerges
3 reflected
4 growing
5 vivid
6 hard
7 considered
8 contradictory

Unit 43

43.1

1 f between
2 g by
3 h with
4 a of
5 b together
6 c together
7 d to
8 e to

43.2

1. There is usually a very strong **bond** between a mother and her child.
2. Salaries have fallen over the last few years, not in real terms but relative **to** inflation.
3. The report on care for the elderly revealed **evidence** of neglect by health professionals.
4. In the experiment, group A performed best on the manual dexterity test and least well on the memory test, whereas for group B the **reverse** was the case.
5. 'Malicious' is more or less **synonymous** with 'nasty'.
6. The problems discussed above are all closely **interrelated**.
7. **Taken** together, the studies by Kim and Li suggest earlier theories on the cause of the disease were flawed.
8. The research is original in **that** it approaches the topic from a completely fresh angle.
9. The painter loved to explore the **interplay** between light and shade.
10. In speech, verbal language is typically **accompanied** (two c's) by body language.

43.3

1. Interaction
2. relationships
3. reveals
4. reflects
5. mutual
6. evidence
7. corresponds
8. equivalent
9. associated

43.4 *Suggested explanations*

1. a chess competition between different universities
2. highways that connect one state to another
3. the fact that states depend on one another economically
4. marrying someone of the same social status
5. scholars can send each other information
6. the parts were all connected/linked to one another

Unit 44

44.1 1 f 2 g 3 h 4 a 5 b 6 d 7 c 8 e

44.2

1. It is no easy task mediating **between** unions and management.
2. In this lecture I plan to deal **with** the later novels of Charles Dickens.
3. The answer to most problems in agriculture lies **in** the soil.
4. He thought for a long time but was unable to come **up** with a solution.
5. Green tourism may initially feel like a contradiction **in** terms.
6. I wonder what the professor's reaction **to** the article will be.
7. The company has experienced a number of difficulties **with** the computer operating system.
8. Have you found a solution **to** the problem yet?

44.3

noun	verb	noun	verb
solution	solve	resolution	resolve
reaction	react	response	respond
content(s)	contain	contradiction	contradict
revelation	reveal	mediation	mediate

44.4

1. contradicted
2. revelation
3. solution
4. mediate
5. contains
6. response
7. resolved
8. reacted
9. contents
10. resolution

Unit 45

45.1

1. environment (check your spelling!)
2. status
3. presence
4. circumstances (check your spelling!)
5. absence
6. infrastructure
7. context
8. conditions

45.2
1 The economy has been **unstable** for several years.
2 **Instability** has been a feature of government in the country for the last decade.
3 The northern region possesses an apparently **infinite** supply of uranium.
4 The **absence** of cholera in the area was noted by scientists in 1978.
5 A **maximum** temperature of 20 degrees must be maintained at all times.

45.3
1 restrict
2 instrinsic
3 restrain
4 integral
5 minimum
6 imposed
7 circumstances
8 restraint

45.4
1 In the 1960s the government imposed a restriction / imposed restrictions on the amount of money people could take out of the country.
2 The problem is confined to the capital city.
3 Oil is a finite resource.
4 In the accident there was minimal damage to the car.
5 All research is subject to the constraints of funding decisions.
6 The fact that the country suffers from social instability deters investors. Or: The social instability of the country deters investors.
7 In normal circumstances we would not behave in this way.
8 Most small children believe in the existence of fairies.

Unit 46

46.1
1 as compared
2 difference/contrast/distinction
3 compared
4 comparison
5 from/to/than
6 comparison
7 analogy
8 In contrast. On the other hand would also be possible here but in contrast better expresses the sharp difference between the two scientists' views.

46.2
1 The two groups were **different from/to/than** each other.
2 The three liquids **were similar to** one another.
3 The data revealed **differences in the informants' responses**.
4 The title of her paper was **'Male attitudes towards prison sentencing compared to/with female attitudes'**.
5 The economy of the north is booming and, **similarly**, the south is also enjoying an economic upturn.
6 The Gaelic spoken in Ireland **is not the same as** the Gaelic spoken in Scotland.
7 Lecturers often explain a difficult concept by **drawing an analogy with** something familiar.
8 In the 1950s, public transportation enjoyed a boom but nowadays **the reverse is true**.

46.3 *Suggested answers*
2 In this case, face-to-face interviews, rather than a questionnaire, are better.
3 Asian languages such as Vietnamese are quite difficult for learners whose first language is a European one and, conversely, European languages are difficult for speakers whose first language is an Asian one.
4 On the one hand oil is plentiful at the present time but, on the other hand, it will run out one day.
5 Boys tend to prefer aggressive solutions to problems whereas girls, on the other hand, prefer more indirect approaches.

46.4
1 T
2 F – they could not both be used if they were incompatible. Compatible means that things can exist or work together.
3 T
4 F – if there are parallels between two things it means that there are some similarities between them.
5 T

Unit 47

47.1
1 misguided, inadequate
2 groundbreaking
3 important, significant
4 crucial
5 unique

47.2
1 credit, acknowledged, crucial
2 borne, mistaken, evidence, flaws
3 challenged, validity, flawed, limited
4 viewed, seminal, groundbreaking

47.3
1 highlights
2 solid
3 compatible
4 comprehensive, key
5 worth recalling, limited
6 underlines

47.4
1 By no means is it certain that all the students will pass their final exams.
2 He had rarely met such an outstanding student.
3 Seldom has the country witnessed such a display of public feeling.
4 We will in no way be able to halt the process of global warming.
5 Under no circumstances will students be allowed to defer the completion of their dissertation for longer than six months.
6 Only when we gather a lot more data will we know the answer

Unit 48

48.1
1 they go up and down
2 nothing at all
3 less
4 a big change
5 better
6 less strict

48.2
1 recovering
2 converting
3 refine
4 abandon
5 adjust
6 status quo
7 maintain
8 restore
9 sweeping
10 gradual

48.3
1 in
2 to/from/out of
3 (away) from
4 on
5 on
6 to
7 from
8 to
9 of
10 of; on

48.4
1 expansion
2 sustainable
3 perceptible
4 increasingly
5 development
6 elimination
7 modifications
8 adjustments
9 acquisition
10 relaxation

Unit 49

49.1
1 **In conclusion**, the tests suggest the drug has no dangerous side effects.
2 **To summarise**, losing the war was a humiliating defeat for the country on a number of different levels.
3 **In summary / In sum**, it is impossible to blame the disaster on one person alone.
4 From the survey we can **draw the conclusion / come to the conclusion** that advertising has a stronger effect on teenage girls than on other groups of the population.
5 **To recapitulate**, there were a number of different reasons why the experiment was less successful than had been hoped.

49.2
1 balance
2 abstract
3 put, eventually/ultimately
4 provide
5 analysis
6 words
7 main / key
8 a close / an end

49.3
1 at last
2 lastly
3 Lastly
4 at last

49.4 *In the end* means 'finally, after something has been thought about or discussed a lot'. *At the end* is usually followed by 'of (something)', and refers to the final point of a thing, time or place, e.g. *at the end of the film, at the end of the month, at the end of the street.*

49.5 The art of writing a **précis** is to remember, first and foremost, not to include anything that was not in the original text. Stated **briefly**, it is your job to **attempt** to capture the original writer's ideas **concisely**, to **provide** a summary and, in the final **analysis**, to give your reader a shortcut to the original text.

Unit 50

50.1
1 present
2 call, make/give
3 welcome
4 on, of
5 discuss/address

50.2
1 We need to consider family income too, but I'll **come back** to that later.
2 So, **moving on**, I'll **skip** item 4 on the handout and instead talk about number 5 in **more** detail.
3 I'll try to finish by 3.30, but **feel free to** leave if you have a class or other appointment to go to.
4 There is a handout **going round** and I have some **extra/spare** copies too if anyone wants them.
5 I'll finish there as my time has **run out**.
6 We didn't want to make people uncomfortable by having a camera in the room. **Having said that**, we did want to video as many of the sessions as possible.
7 I'd like to **go back to** a point I made earlier about river management.
8 So, I believe our experiments have been successful. **That's all I have to say**. Thank you.
9 **Going back to/To go back to/Getting back to** the problem of class sizes, I'd like to look at a study **done** in Australia in 2002.
10 I'll try not to **go over time**, so I'll speak for 30 minutes, to **leave** time for questions at the end.

50.3
1 on
2 with, to
3 to
4 to
5 by
6 for
7 in
8 on, out

50.4 *Possible answers*
Dr Fonseca will now take questions.
Our study draws heavily on earlier work done in this university.
I want to raise another issue at this point.
I'd just like to make a comment, if I may.
I will begin by giving an overview of the topic.
This is the first time I've given/made a presentation so I'm a bit nervous.
As the slide shows, more men than women support the policy.

Reading and vocabulary 1

1

1 optimal
2 moderate
3 yield
4 utilisation
5 converted
6 prolonged

2

1 mis = wrong, false – misspell, mistranslate, misinterpret
2 kilo = 1000 – kilogram, kilobyte, kilometre
3 half = half, partly – half-hearted, half-baked, half-understood
4 pre = before – prewar, preschool, precondition

3

1 spaghetti, potatoes, lasagna, cereals, fruits, milk, honey, sugar
2 (elite) athletes, long distance runners, cyclists, cross-country skiers, canoe racers, swimmers, soccer players

4

noun	verb	adjective
requirement	require	requisite, required
limit, limitation	limit	limiting
benefit	benefit	beneficial
intensity	intensify	intense
simplicity	simplify	simple
digestion	digest	digestive

Reading and vocabulary 2

1

1 held the view
2 there is thus little reason to suppose that
3 a large number of
4 known as
5 on the other hand
6 composed predominantly of

2

1 relatively
2 situation
3 considered
4 enabled
5 establish
6 puzzling
7 collection
8 extends
9 estimate
10 demoted

3

1 develop
2 thrive
3 consist of
4 circle, go round
5 turn [regularly round a fixed point]
6 give out

Reading and vocabulary 3

1

1 symbols
2 unit
3 capable
4 depending
5 known
6 signal

2

1 from
2 to
3 in
4 by; with
5 to
6 on
7 between
8 to

3

1 communication
2 distinction
3 reference
4 use
5 government
6 combination
7 application
8 development
9 introduction
10 representation
11 inclusion
12 adoption
13 appearance
14 knowledge
15 speech
16 pronunciation

Reading and vocabulary 4

1

1 For organising communal activities and public events, for scheduling the shipment of goods, for regulating planting and harvesting.
2 The solar day, the lunar month and the solar year.
3 Because there was less variation in the solar day or solar year than in areas further from the equator.
4 Normal hours are a fixed period of sixty equal minutes whereas temporal hours vary in length according to the length of day or night - ie there are always twelve of them and they will be longer on a long summer day and shorter on a short winter day.
5 In northern latitudes there are more likely to be clouds covering the sun (so sundials cannot function) and there is also more chance of the water in water clocks freezing thus stopping them from functioning.

2

1 to base calendars on natural cycles
2 periods of light and darkness
3 the waxing and waning of the moon
4 to divide something into equal parts
5 temporal hours varied according to the changing lengths of day and night
6 remained in use for a century

3

1 cycles (a) set of regular, repeated events (b) short form of bicycles (as noun or verb)
2 revolution (a) turning (b) political upheaval
3 waxing (a) growing in size (b) using wax e.g. to remove hair
4 civil (a) relating to society (b) polite
5 marked (a) characterised, indicated (b) corrected, graded
6 adopted (a) start using (b) legally take responsibility for a child

Reading and vocabulary 5

1

1 oral
2 generated
3 basis
4 mundane
5 impact
6 artefacts
7 perceptions
8 means
9 layers
10 insightful
11 discipline
12 adapted

2

1 clear and direct
2 behaviour considered a social mistake
3 customs
4 discover
5 packed with, full of
6 expected ways of behaving
7 building
8 getting rid of

3

routine activities
daily lives
written traditions
oral traditions
extraordinary events
unusual events
big events
written record
archaeological remains
unrecorded activities
mundane activities
significant impact
medical practices
Graeco-Roman world
past perceptions
textual sources
insightful discipline
critical discipline
scholarly discipline
vital questions
interesting questions
past lifestyles
social regulations
archaeological data
critical analyses
archaeological studies
complex interpretations

4

social – society
habitual – habit
explicit – explicitness
common – commonness, common
foreign – foreignness
unfamiliar – unfamiliarity
certain – certainty
familiar – familiarity
vague – vagueness
polite – politeness
replete – repletion
specific – specifics, specificity
silent – silence
medical – medicine
ill – illness

Reading and vocabulary 6

1

1 frequently seen
2 writing notes on
3 mainly
4 make use of
5 large number of
6 being found everywhere
7 simplify (dumb down has negative associations)
8 make to look more attractive (pretty up has negative associations)
9 claiming
10 intentionally choosing some things and not others
11 relating to the mind and learning
12 improve
13 closeness
14 implications, conclusions
15 come out in a clear way
16 painstakingly, painfully, with difficulty

2

1 representation
2 part
3 original
4 information
5 case
6 diagrams

3

Individual responses

Phonemic symbols

Vowel sounds

Symbol	*Examples*		
/iː/	sleep	me	
/i/	happy	recipe	
/ɪ/	pin	dinner	
/ʊ/	foot	could	pull
/uː/	do	shoe	through
/e/	red	head	said
/ə/	arrive	father	colour
/ɜː/	turn	bird	work
/ɔː/	sort	thought	walk
/æ/	cat	black	
/ʌ/	sun	enough	wonder
/ɒ/	got	watch	sock
/ɑː/	part	heart	laugh
/eɪ/	name	late	aim
/aɪ/	my	idea	time
/ɔɪ/	boy	noise	
/eə/	pair	where	bear
/ɪə/	hear	cheers	
/əʊ/	go	home	show
/aʊ/	out	cow	
/ʊə/	pure	fewer	

Consonant sounds

Symbol	*Examples*		
/p/	put		
/b/	book		
/t/	take		
/d/	dog		
/k/	car	kick	
/g/	go	guarantee	
/tʃ/	catch	church	
/dʒ/	age	lounge	
/f/	for	cough	photograph
/v/	love	vehicle	
/θ/	thick	path	
/ð/	this	mother	
/s/	since	rice	
/z/	zoo	surprise	
/ʃ/	shop	sugar	machine
/ʒ/	pleasure	usual	vision
/h/	hear	hotel	
/m/	make		
/n/	name	now	know
/ŋ/	bring		
/l/	look	while	
/r/	road		
/j/	young		
/w/	wear		

ˈ This shows that the next syllable is the one with the stress.

ˌ This is used when some longer words have a second stress, less strong than on the main stressed syllable.

Index

The numbers in the index are **Unit** numbers not page numbers. The pronunciation provided is for standard British English.

gather /'gæðər/ 26
gender /'dʒendə/ 38
general /'dʒenərəl/ 38
generalise /'dʒenrəlaɪz/ 29
generally /'dʒenrəli/ 5, 12
generate /'dʒenəreɪt/ 10, 37
generation /ˌdʒenə'reɪʃən/ 38
get in 18
getting back to 50
give a description of 3, 30
give an example 42
give an overview of 50
give a presentation 50
give a summary 49
give attention to 44
give credit to 47
give (top) priority to 24
give rise to 37
glaring /'gleərɪŋ/ 9
glossary /'glɒsəri/ 31
go against 6
go back over 6
go back to 50
go blank 22
go into 6
go on to 6
go over time 50
go round 50
go through 6, 36
goal /gəʊl/ 24
gradual /'grædʒuəl/ 48
graduate student 19
grant /grɑːnt/ 23
graph /grɑːf/ 35
(a) great deal of 7
Great Hall 19
ground /graʊnd/ 11
groundbreaking 47
grow /grəʊ/ 35
growing /'grəʊɪŋ/ 42
guarantee /ˌgærən'tiː/ 18
half /hɑːf/ 33
halfway point 34
halls of residence 19
halve /hɑːv/ 35
handful /'hændfʊl/ 7
happiness /'hæpinəs/ 17
hard evidence 42, 47
hardback /'hɑːdbæk/ 23
have an effect on 3
have an influence on 37
have a shot at 1
have (something) as a goal 24
have difficulty 44
have ethical objections to 32
have no intention of 24
have no time left 50
having said that 39, 50
head of department 19
heading /'hedɪŋ/ 25, 38
health centre 19
heated debate 10
heroism /'herəʊɪzəm/ 17
hierarchy /'haɪərɑːki/ 38
highlight /'haɪlaɪt/ 6, 9, 30, 47
histogram /'hɪstəgræm/ 35
hold a view 32
holiday /'hɒlɪdeɪ/ 19
homemaker /'həʊmˌmeɪkə/ 38
-hood /hʊd/ 17
horizontal axis 35
huge /hjuːdʒ/ 7
hyper- /'haɪpər/ 17
hyperactive /ˌhaɪpər'æktɪv/ 17
hyper-inflation /ˌhaɪpərɪn'fleɪʃən/ 17
hypothesis /haɪ'pɒθəsɪs/ plural
hypotheses /haɪ'pɒθəsiːz/ 12, 25, 29
hypothesis-based /haɪ'pɒθəsɪs beɪst/ 24
I'd like to begin by 50
i.e. /ˌaɪ'iː/ 17
I would argue that 30
ibid. /'ɪbɪd/ 17
idea /aɪ'dɪə/ 12, 15, 29
identifiable /aɪ'dentɪfaɪəbˌl/ 17
identification /aɪˌdentɪfɪ'keɪʃən/ 2
identify /aɪ'dentɪfaɪ/ 3, 12
ideology /ˌaɪdi'ɒlədʒi/ 32
-ify /ɪfaɪ/ 17
il- /ɪl/ 17
illogical /ɪ'lɒdʒɪkəl/ 17
illuminate /ɪ'luːmɪneɪt/ 9
illuminating /ɪ'luːmɪneɪtɪŋ/ 9, 42
illustrate /'ɪləstreɪt/ 3, 42
im- /ɪm/ 17
immature /ˌɪmə'tjʊə/ 32
impact /'ɪmpækt/ 11, 37, 48
impartial /ɪm'pɑːʃəl/ 32
implication /ˌɪmplɪ'keɪʃən/ 11
implicitly /ɪm'plɪsɪtli/ 5
imply /ɪm'plaɪ/ 30
importance /ɪm'pɔːtəns/ 11, 12
important /ɪm'pɔːtənt/ 11, 47
impose /ɪm'pəʊz/ 45
impossible /ɪm'pɒsɪbˌl/ 17
improvement /ɪm'pruːvmənt/ 11
in- /ɪn/ 17
in /ɪn/ 15
in a few words 49
in a systematic way 26
in a variety of ways 16
in absolute terms 10
in accordance with 13
in addition to 1, 13, 16, 39
in any respect 13
in any way 13
in broad terms 10
in comparison with 13, 46
in conclusion 49
in conjunction with 13
in contrast 13, 46
in-depth /ˌɪn'depθ/ 26, 50
in economic terms 10
in excess of 7, 16
in general 16
in general terms 10
in greater detail 16, 50
in light of 9, 25
in line with 13
in more detail 16, 50
in most respects 13
in my opinion 32
in no circumstances 47
in no way 47
in other words 13
in particular 13
in passing 12
in practical terms 10
in recent times/years 36
in relation to 13
in relative terms 10
in respect of 16
in-sessional /ɪn 'seʃənəl/ 20
in short 1
in some ways 13
in spite of 13
in sum 1, 49
in summary 49
in terms of 13, 16
in that 43
in the case of 16
in the distant future 36
in the final/last analysis 49
in the light of 9, 25
in the long term 36
in the near future 36
in the next section 40
in the preceding section 40

make ends meet 23
make inferences from 26
make reference to 27
make up 6
mal- /mæl/ 17
malfunction /ˌmælˈfʌŋkʃən/ 17
malpractice /ˌmælˈpræktɪs/ 17
manipulate /məˈnɪpjʊleɪt/ 26
mapped out 25
marital status 38
marked /mɑːkt/ 46, 48, 50
mathematical /ˌmæθəmˈætɪkəl/ 26
mature /məˈtjʊə/ 32
mature student 18
maximum /ˈmæksɪməm/ 33, 45
mean /miːn/ 34
meaningless /ˈmiːnɪŋləs/ 17
means of /miːnz/ 15
median /ˈmiːdiən/ 34
mediate between /ˈmiːdieɪt/ 44
mediation /ˌmiːdiˈeɪʃən/ 44
medical /ˈmedɪkəl/ 10
meet a deadline 22
meet an objective 24
memorise /ˈmeməraɪz/ 22
mention /ˈmenʃən/ 11, 30
merely /ˈmɪəli/ 5
message /ˈmesɪdʒ/ 31
method /ˈmeθəd/ 26
methodology /ˌmeθəˈdɒlədʒi/ 2, 26
(my) mind goes blank 22
mind map 22, 25
(my) mind starts to wander 22
minimal /ˈmɪnɪməl/ 45
minimum /ˈmɪnɪməm/ 18, 33, 45
minor /ˈmaɪnə/ 11
mis- /mɪs-/ 31
misguided /mɪsˈgaɪdɪd/ 47
misinterpret /ˌmɪsɪnˈtɜːprɪt/ 31
misinterpretation /ˌmɪsɪnˌtɜːprɪˈteɪʃən/ 31
misquote /ˌmɪsˈkwəʊt/ 31
misquotation /ˌmɪskwəʊˈteɪʃən/ 31
mission statement 24
mistaken /mɪˈsteɪkən/ 47
mistranslate /ˌmɪstrænˈsleɪt/ 31
mistranslation /ˌmɪstrænˈsleɪʃən/ 31
misunderstanding /ˌmɪsʌndəˈstændɪŋ/ 26
mnemonics /nɪˈmɒnɪks/ 22
mobile learning 21
mode /məʊd/ 34
model /ˈmɒdəl/ 2, 29
modernise /ˈmɒdənaɪz/ 17
modernism /ˈmɒdənɪzəm/ 17
modify /ˈmɒdɪfaɪ/ 48
module /ˈmɒdjuːl/ 20
monitor /ˈmɒnɪtə/ 21
monthly /ˈmʌnθli/ 23
MOOCs /muːks/ 21
more and more 7
more or less 1, 7
more than 7
moreover /mɔːˈrəʊvə/ 39
most (people) would agree that 29
mostly /ˈməʊstli/ 1, 5
motivate /ˈməʊtɪveɪt/ 24, 37
motivation /ˌməʊtɪˈveɪʃən/ 15, 24
motive for *-ing* /ˈməʊtɪv/ 24
move to/towards /muːv/ 15, 48
movement /ˈmuːvmənt/ 29
moving on 50
multi- /mʌlti-/ 17
multilingual /ˌmʌltiˈlɪŋgwəl/ 17
multiple /ˈmʌltɪpˌl/ 21
multiply /ˈmʌltɪplaɪ/ 35
multi-storey /ˌmʌltiˈstɔːri/ 17
mutual /ˈmjuːtʃuəl/ 43
national debate 24
natural /ˈnætʃərəl/ 10, 26
naturalistic /ˌnætʃərəlˈɪstɪk/ 26
nature /ˈneɪtʃə/ 2, 38
NB /ˌenˈbiː/ 17
need for 12, 15
nevertheless /ˌnevəðəˈles/ 39, 50
next /nekst/ 40, 41
no fewer than 7
none of 7
nonetheless /ˌnʌnðəˈles/ 39
normal distribution 34
notable /ˈnəʊtəbəl/ 47
note (v.) /nəʊt/ 25, 27, 30
note-taking /ˈnəʊt teɪkɪŋ/ 22
notes (n.) /nəʊts/ 22
noteworthy /ˈnəʊtˌwɜːði/ 47
notion /ˈnəʊʃən/ 29
nowadays /ˈnaʊədeɪz/ 36
nuances of meaning 31
nuclear energy 10
number /ˈnʌmbə/ 2, 7, 11, 33
objection /əbˈdʒekʃən/ 32
objective /əbˈdʒektɪv/ 24, 32
obligatory /əˈblɪgətri/ 20
observation /ˌɒbzəˈveɪʃən/ 26, 30
observe /əbˈzɜːv/ 6, 10, 12, 26, 30
observer /əbˈzɜːvə/ 26
obtain /əbˈteɪn/ 42
occupation /ˌɒkjʊˈpeɪʃən/ 38
occupational /ˌɒkjʊˈpeɪʃənəl/ 38
occur /əˈkɜː/ 8
-ocracy /ɒkrəsi/ 17
-ocrat /əkræt/ 17
odd number 33
of /ɒv/ 14, 15
of considerable importance 11
of great interest 11
of particular significance 11
offer /ˈɒfə/ 18, 42
offer a place 18
offer inducements 23
offer proof 3
office hours 19
omit /əˈmɪt/ /əʊˈmɪt/ 50
on /ɒn/ 14, 15
on balance 49
on behalf of 13
on no account 47
on purpose 24
on the basis of 13, 28
on the contrary 13
on the one hand 13, 46
on the other hand 13, 46
on the subject of 39, 50
on the whole 5, 13, 16
one of 7
ongoing /ˈɒnˌgəʊɪŋ/ 36
online community 21
only /ˈəʊnli/ 1, 47
onslaught /ˈɒnslɔːt/ 9
op. cit. 17
openness /ˈəʊpənnəs/ 17
opinion /əˈpɪnjən/ 29, 32
opposed to 9
opposition /ˌɒpəˈzɪʃən/ 11
opt for 20
optimist /ˈɒptɪmɪst/ 17
optional /ˈɒpʃənəl/ 20
order of magnitude 33
organise /ˈɔːgənaɪz/ 42
origin of /ˈɒrɪdʒɪn/ 12, 37
outcome /ˈaʊtkʌm/ 11, 34, 37
outliers /ˈaʊtˌlaɪərz / 34
output /ˈaʊtpʊt/ 41
outside observer 26
outweigh /ˌaʊtˈweɪ/ 28
over- /əʊvə/ 17
over the next few years 36
over time 26

overall /ˌəʊvər'ɔːl/ 49
overcome /ˌəʊvə'kʌm/ 44
overdraft /'əʊvədrɑːft/ 23
overload /ˌəʊvə'ləʊd/ 17
overview /'əʊvəvjuː/ 50
overworked /ˌəʊvə'wɜːkt/ 17
p. / pp. /piː/ 17
pace /peɪs/ 21
page nos. 25
paper /'peɪpər/ 15, 49
paradigm shift 29
part of 15
part-time /ˌpɑːt'taɪm/ 23
particular /pə'tɪkjʊlə/ 11
particularly /pə'tɪkjʊləli/ 5
partly /'pɑːtli/ 12
pathway through 25
pattern /'pætən/ 2
pay attention 10, 39
peak /piːk/ 35
peer assessment 21
per cent /pə'sent/ 34
percentage /pə'sentɪdʒ/ 34
perceptible /pə'septəbəl/ 48
perception /pə'sepʃən/ 29
period /'pɪəriəd/ 28, 36
permanent /'pɜːmənənt/ 36
personal /'pɜːsənəl/ 10, 23
personal statement 18
perspective /pə'spektɪv/ 2, 31
phase /feɪz/ 36, 41
PhD /ˌpiːeɪtʃ'diː/ 20
phenomenon /fə'nɒmɪnən/ *plural* phenomena /fə'nɒmɪnə/ 10, 11, 26, 29
philosophy /fɪ'lɒsəfi/ 32
pie chart 35
piece of apparatus 26
piece of evidence 42
piece of research 2
piece together 43
pilot study 26
pinpoint /'pɪnpɔɪnt/ 25, 30
pivotal /'pɪvətəl/ 10
place /pleɪs/ 18
plagiarism detection software /'pleɪdʒərɪzəm/ 21
play a role 10
plot /plɒt/ 35
plummet /'plʌmɪt/ 35
point (n.) /pɔɪnt/ 8, 11, 13, 28, 40, 49
point at 15
point of view 16, 32
point out 6, 30
point to 28, 42
point up 6
policy /'pɒləsi/ 18
population /ˌpɒpjʊ'leɪʃən/ 26
portfolio /ˌpɔːt'fəʊliəʊ/ 20
pose /pəʊz/ 12, 44
position /pə'zɪʃən/ 32
post- /pəʊst/ 17
post-colonial /pəʊstkə'ləʊniəl/ 17
postgrad rep 19
postgraduate representative 19
postgraduate student 19
post-war /'pəʊstwɔː/ 17, 36
potential /pə'tenʃəl/ 4
power /paʊər/ 11
practical /'præktɪkəl/ 10
practice /'præktɪs/ 11
practice-as-research /'præktɪs əz rɪ'sɜːtʃ/ 24
practice-led /'præktɪs led/ 24
pre- /priː/ 17
precedent /'presɪdənt/ 37
preceding /prɪ'siːdɪŋ/ 36, 40
précis /'preɪsiː/ 49
precise /prɪ'saɪs/ 4, 33
precisely /prɪ'saɪsli/ 5
predict /prɪ'dɪkt/ 28
predictable /prɪ'dɪktəbˌl/ 17
preference for 15
pre-industrial /priːɪn'dʌstriəl/ 17
prejudice /'predʒʊdɪs/ 32
prejudiced against 32
prejudiced in favour of 32
preliminary /prɪ'lɪmɪnəri/ 10, 26
presence /'prezəns/ 45
present (v.) /prɪ'zent/ 3, 6, 35, 40, 42, 44, 50
present (adj.) /'prezənt/ 27
present-day problems 36
presentation /ˌprezən'teɪʃən/ 15
pre-sessional /priː 'seʃənəl/ 20
pre-war /ˌpriː'wɔːr/ 17
primarily /praɪ'merəli/ 1, 5, 27
primary /'praɪməri/ 1
primary source 27
prime /praɪm/ 1
prime number 33
principal /'prɪnsɪpəl/ 4
principle /'prɪnsɪpəl/ 2, 15, 29, 32
prior to 36
prioritise /praɪ'ɒrɪtaɪz/ 22
priority /praɪ'ɒrəti/ 24
probability distribution 34
problem /'prɒbləm/ 11, 12, 15, 44
procedure /prə'siːdʒə/ 26, 41
proceed /prə'siːd/ 20
process /'prəʊses/ 18
produce /prə'djuːs/ 37
professor /prə'fesə/ 19
profile /'prəʊfaɪl/ 18
progress to/towards /'prəʊgres/ 15
project /'prɒdʒekt/ 15, 20
-proof /pruːf/ 17
proof /pruːf/ 3, 30
proper /'prɒpər/ 10
properties /'prɒpətiːz/ 12
proportion /prə'pɔːʃən/ 11, 34
propose /prə'pəʊz/ 30
pros and cons 39
prove /pruːv/ 3, 26, 30
provide /prə'vaɪd/ 3
provide a sample 10
provide a summary 49
provide an example 42
provide an explanation 3, 30
provide proof of 30
provide with 14
provided that 39
provoke /prə'vəʊk/ 37
public debate 10
publish /'pʌblɪʃ/ 10
purify /'pjʊərɪfaɪ/ 17
purpose /'pɜːpəs/ 11, 24, 40
put emphasis/stress on 3, 30
put forward 6, 30, 39
put (something) simply 5
qualification /ˌkwɒlɪfɪ'keɪʃən/ 18
qualitative /'kwɒlɪtətɪv/ 4
quantifiable /'kwɒntɪfaɪəbəl/ 1
quantifiably /'kwɒntɪfaɪəbli/ 1
quantification /ˌkwɒntɪfɪ'keɪʃən/ 1
quantify /'kwɒntɪfaɪ/ 1
quantitative /'kwɒntɪtətɪv/ 1, 4
quantitatively /'kwɒntɪtətɪvli/ 1
quantity /'kwɒntɪti/ 1, 11
quarterly /'kwɔːtəli/ 36
question (n.) /'kwestʃən/ 11, 12, 50
question (v.) /'kwestʃən/ 10, 30
questionnaire /ˌkwestʃə'neər/ 25
quite a lot 7
radical /'rædɪkəl/ 32
raise /reɪz/ 28, 44, 50
random /'rændəm/ 10, 33, 34, 35
range /reɪndʒ/ 11, 16, 34

solid /'sɒlɪd/ 1, 47
solution /sə'luːʃən/ 44
solve /sɒlv/ 44
somewhat /'sʌmwɒt/ 5
sophomore /'sɒfəmɔː/ 19
sought /sɔːt/ 18
soundly /'saʊndli/ 28
soundproof /'saʊndpruːf/ 17
source /sɔːs/ 37
sources 27
spare copies 50
speak of 14
speak to the topic of 50
specially /'speʃli/ 5
specific /spə'sɪfɪk/ 4, 11, 38
specifically /'spə'sɪfɪkəli/ 5, 12
spider diagram 25
sports ground 19
spring from 37
squared /skweəd/ 33
stability /stə'bɪlɪti/ 45
stable /'steɪbəl/ 45
staff /stɑːf/ 19
stage /steɪdʒ/ 13, 35, 36, 41
stance /stɑːns/ 29, 32
standard deviation 34
standpoint /'stænpɔɪnt/ 32
stark contrast 46
state /steɪt/ 30, 49
statement /'steɪtmənt/ 11, 30
status /'steɪtəs/ 38, 45
status quo /ˌsteɪtəs'kwəʊ/ 48
stem from 37, 42
step in /step/ 41
stimulate /'stɪmjʊleɪt/ 37
story /'stɔːri/ 12
strategy /'strætədʒi/ 24
strengthened /'streŋθənd/ 10
stress /stres/ 3, 14, 30
striking /'straɪkɪŋ/ 42
strongly suggest 12
structure /'strʌktʃə/ 8, 38
student counsellor 19
student loan 18, 23
Student Union 19
study /'stʌdi/ 15, 26, 27, 50
study plan 22
subject /'sʌbdʒekt/ 2, 26
subject to 45
subjectively /səb'dʒektɪvli/ 32
submit /səb'mɪt/ 18
subscription /səb'skrɪpʃən/ 23
subsequent /'sʌbsɪkwənt/ 36
substantial /səb'stænʃəl/ 7
subsume /səb'sjuːm/ 38
subtle /'sʌtəl/ 31
successive /sək'sesɪv/ 36
sudden /'sʌdən/ 48
sufficient /sə'fɪʃənt/ 10
suggest /sə'dʒest/ 12, 27, 30, 42
suggestion /sə'dʒestʃən/ 30
sum /sʌm/ 11, 34
sum up 1
summarise /'sʌməraɪz/ 25, 49
summary /'sʌməri/ 49
supervision /ˌsuːpə'vɪʒən/ 20
supervisor /'suːpəvaɪzə/ 19
supplement /'sʌplɪmənt/ 41
support /sə'pɔːt/ 3, 11, 30, 42
surprising /sə'praɪzɪŋ/ 7, 47
surrounding /sə'raʊndɪŋ/ 10, 45
survey /'sɜːveɪ/ 26
survey the literature 27
sustainable development 48
sweeping (changes) 48
synchronous learning 21
synonymous with /sɪ'nɒnɪməs/ 43
systematic /ˌsɪstə'mætɪk/ 26
table /'teɪbəl/ 35
tackle /'tækəl/ 44
take a sample 10
take a stance 32
take, for example 40
take into account 28
take issue with 8
take on a role 10
take out a student loan 23
take priority over 24
take questions 50
taken together 43
talk /tɔːk/ 15, 29, 50
tally /'tæli/ 33
target /'tɑːgɪt/ 24
technique /tek'niːk/ 26
telling /'telɪŋ/ 42
temporary /'tempərəri/ 36
tendency to/towards /'tendənsi/ 15, 34
tentative /'tentətɪv/ 26
term /tɜːm/ 10, 12, 19, 31
terminology /ˌtɜːmɪ'nɒlədʒi/ 31
thank you for listening 50
that's all I have to say 50
theme /θiːm/ 2, 11, 12
theory /'θɪəri/ 2, 12
there's no way 1
therefore /'ðeəfɔːr/ 37
thesis /'θiːsɪs/ *plural* theses /'θiːsiːz/ 15, 29
third(ly) /θɜːd/ 40
third-year /'θɜːdjɪər/ 19
thoroughly /'θʌrəli/ 12
thought /θɔːt/ 25, 29
threat /θret/ 12
tight /taɪt/ 23
time is running short 50
time-consuming /'taɪmkənˌsjuːmɪŋ/ 26
time management 22
tip the scales in favour of 28
to /tuː/ 14, 15
to a certain extent 13
to a greater extent 13
to a lesser extent 13
to conclude /kən'kluːd/ 49
to put it briefly 49
to recap 49
to recapitulate /ˌriːkə'pɪtjʊleɪt/ 49
to return to 50
to some extent 13, 16
to sum up 1, 49, 50
to summarise /'sʌməraɪz/ 49
to what extent 16, 39
together /tə'geðər/ 43
too many 7
too much 7
top priority 24
topic /'tɒpɪk/ 2, 12, 50
total /'təʊtəl/ 7, 33
towards /tə'wɔːdz/ 15
trace 14
traditional /trə'dɪʃənəl/ 26
trainee /ˌtreɪ'niː/ 17
transcript /'trænskrɪpt/ 18
transfer /træns'fɜː/ 48
transform /træns'fɔːm/ 48
transition /træn'zɪʃən/ 48
transitional /træn'zɪʃənəl/ 36
transparent /træn'spærənt/ 31
treat /triːt/ 27
trend /trend/ 12, 34
trigger /'trɪgə/ 37
try /traɪ/ 1
tuition fees 23
turn to /tɜːn/ 14, 40, 50
tutor /'tjuːtə/ 19
tutorial /tjuː'tɔːriəl/ 19, 20
type /taɪp/ 11, 38
typical of /'tɪpɪkəl/ 1, 4

ultimately /ˈʌltɪmətli/ 5, 49
undeniable /ˌʌndɪˈnaɪəbəl/ 42
under no circumstances 47
underline /ˈʌndəˈlaɪn/ 1, 47
underlying /ˌʌndəˈlaɪɪŋ/ 32
understanding /ˌʌndəˈstændɪŋ/ 24
undertake /ˌʌndəˈteɪk/ 3
undivided attention 10
unforeseen /ˌʌnfɔːˈsiːn/ 10
unify /ˈjuːnɪfaɪ/ 41
unique /juːˈniːk/ 47
united /jʊˈnaɪtɪd/ 9
united front 9
universal /ˌjuːnɪˈvɜːsəl/ 10
university /ˌjuːnɪˈvɜːsəti/ 19
unlike /ʌnˈlaɪk/ 46
unsocial hours 23
unstable /ʌnˈsteɪbəl/ 45
upgrade /ʌpˈgreɪd/ 20
urban-rural dimension 38
urgency /ˈɜːdʒənsi/ 17
use /juːz/ 11, 26
useful /ˈjuːsfəl/ 10
utilise /ˈjuːtɪlaɪz/ 41
vacation /vəˈkeɪʃən/ 19
valid /ˈvælɪd/ 29, 34
validity /vəˈlɪdəti/ 47
valuable 10, 27
values /ˈvæljuːz/ 33
variable /ˈveəriəbəl/ 26, 33, 34
variation /ˌveəriˈeɪʃən/ 11
variety /vəˈraɪəti/ 38
vary /ˈveəri/ 35
vast /vɑːst/ 7, 11
verify /ˈverɪfaɪ/ 41
vertical axis 35
victory /ˈvɪktəri/ 9
view /vjuː/ 2, 11, 32, 47
viewpoint /ˈvjuːpɔɪnt/ 29
virtual /ˈvɜːtjuəl/ 21
virtually /ˈvɜːtjuəli/ 1
visualise /ˈvɪʒuəlaɪz/ 22
vivid /ˈvɪvɪd/ 42
vlog /vlɒg/ 21
vol. 17
volume /ˈvɒljuːm/ 34
wander /ˈwɒndər/ 22
waste /weɪst/ 10
waterproof /ˈwɔːtəpruːf/ 17
way /weɪ/ 1, 10
webinar /ˈwebɪnɑːr/ 21
weigh up 28
welcome /ˈwelkəm/ 50
whereas /weəˈræz/ 46
while /waɪl/ 46
white collar 38
whole number 33
wide range 16
widespread /ˈwaɪdspred/ 11
wiki /ˈwɪki/ 21
with /wɪð/ 14, 15
with a focus on 40
with reference to 39
with regard to 16, 50
with respect to 16
with the exception of 13, 16
with the intention of *-ing* 24
word /wɜːd/ 12
word limit 20
work /wɜːk/ 15, 50
work on 6
work out 6, 10
workings /ˈwɜːkɪŋz/ 33
workshop /ˈwɜːkʃɒp/ 20
write about 29
write of 14
write up 6
x axis 35
y axis 35